The Spiritual Vision of Frank Buchman

The Spiritual Vision of Frank Buchman

PHILIP BOOBBYER

The Pennsylvania State University Press
University Park, Pennsylvania

Library of Congress Cataloging-in-Publication Data

Boobbyer, Philip.
    The spiritual vision of Frank Buchman / Philip Boobbyer.
       p.   cm.
    Summary: "Explores the main ideas of Pennsylvania-born religious leader Frank Buchman (1878–1961), his work in the movement known as the Oxford Group and Moral Re-Armament, and his enduring legacy in the areas of peace-building and interfaith understanding"—Provided by publisher.
    Includes bibliographical references and index.
    ISBN 978-0-271-05979-2 (cloth : alk. paper)
    ISBN 978-0-271-05980-8 (pbk. : alk. paper)
    1. Buchman, Frank Nathan Daniel, 1878–1961.
    2. Moral re-armament.
    3. Moral Re-armament (Organization).
    4. Holy Spirit.
    5. Social change—Religious aspects.
    6. Religious awakening.
    7. Religion and politics.
    I. Title.

BJ10.M6B66 2013
267'.16092—dc23
2012051008

Copyright © 2013 The Pennsylvania State University
All rights reserved
Printed in the United States of America
Published by The Pennsylvania State University Press,
University Park, PA 16802-1003

The Pennsylvania State University Press is a member of the Association of American University Presses.

It is the policy of The Pennsylvania State University Press to use acid-free paper. Publications on uncoated stock satisfy the minimum requirements of American National Standard for Information Sciences—Permanence of Paper for Printed Library Material, ANSI Z39.48–1992.

Frontispiece: Frank Buchman, Sarasota, Florida, 1944.
Photo: Arthur Strong, Oxford Group Archives.

That's what I want.
To be in touch with the Holy Spirit—
for a world in a very serious situation.

—FRANK BUCHMAN, *late 1950s*

CONTENTS

List of Illustrations / ix

Preface and Acknowledgments / xi

Introduction / 1

1 Origins / 9

2 Guidance / 33

3 Personal Work / 56

4 Theological Questions / 83

5 Strategy and Organization / 106

6 Politics and Ideology / 132

Conclusion / 159

Notes / 167

Bibliography / 199

Index / 211

ILLUSTRATIONS

1   Buchman with a group
    from Penn State, 1914 / *16*

2   Buchman, guidance book in hand, 1935 / *35*

3   Buchman with Robert Schuman, Caux, 1953 / *53*

4   Buchman speaking at the Mackinac
    conference center, 1952 / *69*

5   Buchman with Max Bladeck
    and Paul Kurowski, 1953 / *73*

6   Buchman meeting Mahatma Gandhi, 1924 / *88*

7   Buchman with B. H. Streeter, mid-1930s / *99*

8   J. A. E. Patijn, with Buchman and
    Carl Hambro in background, 1938 / *113*

9   Buchman being decorated by
    the Japanese government, 1956 / *121*

10 Buchman with Mary McLeod Bethune
    and the Tolon Na, 1954 / *149*

PREFACE AND ACKNOWLEDGMENTS

I have long been interested in Frank Buchman and the movement he founded, known successively as the Oxford Group, Moral Re-Armament, and more recently Initiatives of Change. The reasons for this are partly academic. Buchman's outreach into ecclesiastical, political, and industrial circles was remarkable, and he merits attention from anyone who wishes to understand how religious leaders and movements responded to the ideological battles of the mid-twentieth century. Yet there is no book that offers a scholarly synthesis and exploration of his main ideas, which seemed to me an important gap to try to fill. At one level Buchman and Russian intellectual history— the focus of much of my work hitherto—have little in common. Yet writing this book has meant more an expansion of perspective than a new departure. Much of my research on Russia has centered on how religious thinkers responded to the challenge of Marxism and the Soviet experiment. Looking at Buchman has allowed me to gain an American perspective on some of the same questions—although Buchman's thinking was in a larger sense a spiritual response to the emergence of a global society and not just a response to communism.

Yet the interest is also personal: my parents knew and worked with Buchman, and I myself am a trustee of the Oxford Group, a charitable trust originally set up in the United Kingdom in 1938 that supports the work he started. Initiatives of Change—a registered NGO with special consultative status with the Economic and Social Council of the United Nations—grew from Christian origins but is now made up of people from different religious traditions and sometimes without a defined faith. This has led to much internal debate about Buchman's religious ideas and how he managed to hold together people from very different cultures. In this sense the nature of Buchman's thinking is still a live issue for some. In addition, I sense that the connection Buchman made between spirituality and social change remains relevant to our own world, half a century after his death, and I wanted to examine more deeply the thinking that underpinned it.

I am indebted to a number of people for the research and writing of the book. My university department gave me time to write it and financial support for some of the expenses arising from the research. Colleagues and friends have helped me in a variety of ways, for example by sending helpful references, passing on ideas, or commenting on drafts of the manuscript. In this connection, I would particularly like to thank Colin Armstrong, Mike Brown, Anthony Craig, Grayson Ditchfield, Peter Everington, Tyler Flynn, Stefan Goebel, Eva Gundersen, Fleur Houston, Brian Kelly, Stanley Kiaer, Mary Lean, Justin Lewis-Anthony, Kenneth Noble, Bhavesh Patel, Ian Randall, Richard Ruffin, Daniel Sack, Don da Silva, Margaret Smith, Andrew Stallybrass, Peter Thwaites, David Turley, and Peter Vickers. Among those who knew Buchman personally, Jim Baynard-Smith, Ailsa Hamilton, Michael Henderson, Archie Mackenzie, Geoffrey Pugh, Michel Sentis, Pierre Spoerri, Gordon Wise, John Wood, and David Young passed on suggestions or commented on drafts. The Penn State University Press's peer review process gave me valuable insights. I am grateful, too, to Anne Evans, the archivist for the Oxford Group in the United Kingdom, for helping me locate relevant material. I would also like to thank my wife, Laura, for her constant support during the writing process.

Introduction

"The world is slow to realise that the spiritual is more powerful than the material," declared the American religious leader Frank Buchman in November 1938. He was talking on the BBC, with the growing polarization of Europe on his mind, and wanted to alert his listeners to the power of what he called "valid religious experience" to generate personal and social change. There was a missing ingredient in contemporary attempts to avert war, he thought: an awareness of how an encounter with God could change people's lives and give them the resources to live peacefully and unselfishly.[1] In other words, the answer to the crisis in the world lay at the spiritual level. This view was typical of Buchman. Throughout his life he stressed the importance of faith and moral standards for resolving conflict and bringing about social change. The Holy Spirit, he believed, had plans for humanity that could bring unity out of division and which people could work toward in practical ways.

Buchman first came to prominence through his work as secretary of the Young Men's Christian Association (YMCA) at State College, Pennsylvania (henceforth Penn State) in 1909–15. The mixture of well-coordinated campaigns and focused work with individuals that he adopted led to a resurgence of Christian commitment on the campus and gained him a reputation as a gifted evangelist. Further appointments resulted—as a YMCA missionary in Asia in 1915–19 and a visiting lecturer at Hartford Theological Seminary in 1916–22—before he branched out to work in an independent capacity. The beginnings of the international movement that subsequently grew out of his work were often traced to a visit he made to Oxford University in May 1921, when his presence at a meeting of a college debate society sparked the emergence of a network of students dedicated to working with him.[2] Although he had been ordained as a Lutheran minister in 1902, Buchman's approach was nondenominational. He also placed little emphasis on platform speeches, at that time spreading his message mainly through one-to-one conversations, small fellowship groups, and house parties. This was the basis for his work in Oxford and elsewhere, which grew steadily in the 1920s, and rapidly in the 1930s, to the point that house parties were often attended by thousands of people and the movement attracted much attention from the press.

In the 1920s Buchman and his supporters called themselves the First Century Christian Fellowship (FCCF). That name gave way from 1928 onward to the Oxford Group (OG), particularly because of the strength of the work at Oxford University—although the OG was in fact an increasingly international endeavor that made appeals to people of all ages and classes. Much of the group's work was concerned with helping people at an individual level. It was also practical rather than theological in orientation, placing emphasis, for example, on confession of sin, listening to God, and absolute moral standards. In the 1930s, however, the OG increasingly tried to relate its message to wider national and international issues and to stress the link between spirituality and politics.

The OG became one of the more influential movements of Christian revival in the interwar era in a number of northern European states and also in dominions of the British Empire such as South Africa and Canada. Its influence in parts of the United States was also considerable. Yet in the late 1930s Buchman was looking for a new way to articulate his message and in that context launched "Moral Re-Armament" (MRA), a program of moral and spiritual renewal running through national and international life that was conceived as an answer to bitterness and militarism; the OG soon came to be known by that name. His desire to express this in the context of the ideological battles of the time led him in 1943 to describe MRA as an ideology, and in subsequent decades it was presented as offering an alternative to materialist thinking in both the East and West. As MRA tried to apply this philosophy to urgent political issues—like postwar reconciliation and reconstruction, industrial conflict, and decolonization—its identity began to change. Its adherents increasingly came from all continents and religious traditions, and this turned it from what had initially been a kind of evangelistic enterprise into something increasingly multireligious in character. The expansion of the work meant that at its peak in the 1960s an estimated three thousand people were working with MRA across the world, although this is on the high side and exact numbers are hard to gauge.[3]

The growth of Buchman's work, along with the fact that he was involved in varying degrees with many of the big events of his time, meant that he became a well-known personality in many countries. His influence—if not always easy to measure—was sufficient for one British commentator, writing in 1954, to call him "the most successful evangelist of his age."[4] Some thought him a groundbreaking figure. An influential cardinal, talking in 1984, even declared that his ideas were a "turning-point" in the history of the modern world—for the way they linked Christ's teachings to the transformation of society.[5] He was particularly praised for his work as a bridge builder and reconciler. After World War II he was decorated by a number of governments, including France, Germany, Japan, and the Philippines, for his contribution to postwar reconciliation.[6] This bridge-building work seems sometimes to have had a significant political outcome. If analyst Edward Luttwak is right, for example, MRA helped to facilitate the realization in Europe of the postwar Schuman Plan—through establishing a dialogue between the French and the German elites at its conferences.[7] Buchman's work also had spin-offs. Movements inspired by OG spirituality included Alcoholics Anonymous (AA) and Faith at Work, and Buchman's influence could also be found in the origins of the National Prayer Breakfast in the United States.[8]

Yet Buchman's outreach was often accompanied by controversy. In his early years as an evangelist he was often outspoken about what he saw as the failure of Christian workers and institutions to be effective, and this was not always well received. Then in the mid-1920s his work was investigated by the university authorities at Princeton University after reports in *Time* magazine and elsewhere that suggested it was having an unhealthy effect on students. Throughout his life his spirituality elicited support across the churches, but there were always some who questioned whether it really fitted into the mainstream Christian tradition. In regard to his politics, there was a variety of accusations. In particular, his judgment was questioned when he tried to spread his message to Nazi leaders in the 1930s; indeed, some claimed he was a Nazi sympathizer. In addition, his work during the Cold War was considered overly anticommunist by some—although, conversely, there were also suggestions that MRA was pro-communist. Even today, he is often the target of criticism. While his legacy is increasingly being taken seriously by historians, accounts of his life and opinions often contain an element of sarcasm or caricature.[9]

Although Buchman was famous in his lifetime, observers sometimes found it hard to connect the influence he had with a personality that at first seemed unremarkable. To people meeting him for the first time, he did not generally seem striking or imposing. Peter Howard, the English journalist who was Buchman's successor as leader of MRA and who wrote two books about him, even said in 1946 that his personality was "not always pleasing." He was, Howard suggested, an example of how the Holy Spirit transcended human personality. It was thus not charisma in an ordinary sense that drew people to him. In a well-known, if somewhat unflattering, portrayal of him that came out in *Life Changers* (1923)—the first popular account of his work with students—the English religious author Harold Begbie described him as "a young-looking man of middle life, tall, upright, stoutish, clean-shaven, spectacled, with that mien of scrupulous, shampooed, and almost medical cleanness, or freshness, which is characteristic of the hygienic American." On the other hand, Begbie noted, there was also an "invariable alertness," a "quickness of eye," and an "athletic erectness of body" about him, and he exuded a spirit of "contagious well-being."[10]

It would be wrong, then, to attribute Buchman's influence to some form of personal charisma. This is not to say that his character was not important. There was a single-minded quality about him, for example, which was certainly vital for the development of the OG and MRA. But his personal qualities are not sufficient to explain his effect on people. Another possible source of his impact—which is the focus of this book—was the sphere of his spirituality and ideas. Buchman was suspicious of abstract intellectualism; indeed, the fact that his faith was not expressed in particularly sophisticated or scholarly language was probably one reason why the "Christian intelligentsia" sometimes found it hard to embrace him.[11] Yet the relative simplicity and, at times, folksiness of his talks and speeches concealed a lively mind that was very responsive to the world around him. He was a thinker of sorts, if not a theorist. According to one of his supporters at Oxford University, the educationalist and churchman, Julian P. Thornton-Duesbery, he had a mind of "extraordinary speed and range."[12]

In this context, the wider intellectual and spiritual influences on Buchman need explanation. Buchman was not a voracious reader—although he regularly read newspapers and some biographies—and in this sense his thinking was not primarily constructed from books. But there were writers and people, especially from the early twentieth-century Anglo-American evangelical tradition, whose ideas affected his outlook. Understanding these influences is essential for building a picture of the underlying elements in his thought and for understanding the spirituality of the OG and MRA more generally. If, as one scholar has argued, the OG and MRA had no specific creed or dogmas of their own, they nevertheless promoted a cluster of spiritual practices that formed an identifiable tradition.[13] The spiritual heritage that Buchman drew on gave shape to that tradition.

Unlike the main works on Buchman, which are broadly chronological or biographical, this study is organized thematically. There are dangers to this approach. In structuring the book according to theme rather than chronology, there is a risk of missing the evolution of Buchman's thought and implying that it was static. But attempts have been made to address this by showing the development of Buchman's thought or life experience in relation to particular topics. Moreover, the early chapters are weighted toward Buchman's early life, and the later ones toward his later ideas and activities.

While offering an overview of Buchman's spiritual vision, this study places particular emphasis on his thinking about the Holy Spirit. The central thesis of the book is that the Holy Spirit was the unifying element in his philosophy and that it is possible by focusing on this theme to see the range and interconnectedness of his ideas and the continuities in his outlook over time. Buchman's concerns in this area were not theological. He never sought to address the science of pneumatology or to modify Christian doctrines about the Holy Spirit. Swiss literary scholar Theophil Spoerri—an admirer of the OG and MRA—rightly argued in an important portrait of Buchman that if his theological outlook were to be defined, it should be described in relation to his "practical down-to-earthness." Whereas his Swiss contemporary Karl Barth sought to forge a "theology of the Holy Spirit," Buchman's emphasis was on the "practice of the Holy Spirit."[14]

On the other hand, the way Buchman used and adapted certain religious practices was itself interesting. For example, Buchman's thinking had a lot in common with the traditions of German evangelical pietism. Indeed, the theologian Henry Van Dusen—who worked with Buchman in the 1920s before later becoming president of Union Theological Seminary—observed that Buchman's spirituality had roots in "conservative Lutheran pietism," and David Belden, in an Oxford University dissertation, took a similar view.[15] Buchman's attempt to bring practices associated with pietistic communities, like silent prayer and small-group fellowship, into the more secular, political arena was an implicit statement that the capacity of the Holy Spirit to resolve human problems had not yet been fully understood.

The Holy Spirit is also a good lens through which to explore Buchman's thought in relation to some of the areas where his approach was controversial. For example, his understanding of the Holy Spirit was evident in his attitude to God's "guidance." Buchman believed that in a kind of prayerful reflection that he called the "quiet time," God could give people wisdom or guidance as to what to do. It was an idea that was given a central place in the OG and MRA. One scholar, J. Calvin Keene, writing in a dissertation of 1937, even suggested that the level of emphasis given to it in the OG was unique in Christian history.[16] There were plenty of defenders of the practice, including some distinguished theologians, yet some thought that Buchman exaggerated the possibility that God could speak to people. Buchman's attitude to the Holy Spirit also informed his approach to the relationship between Christianity and other faiths. This was another area of debate, with some people—particularly from some conservative evangelical or Catholic positions—worrying that MRA promoted a theologically ambiguous mixture of Christian and syncretist teachings.

Buchman's ideas about the Holy Spirit also shaped his approach to politics, including his response to the European dictatorships and the Cold War. In general, he approached political questions by focusing on people rather than policies. Indeed, one of his American colleagues, T. Willard Hunter, argued in a recent study that what he called the "Buchman doctrine" was an approach to public affairs that involved encouraging the finest instincts in individuals rather than campaigning on particular policy issues. But the emphasis on people was always combined with a larger vision of how the world could change and be brought under God's direction. Here Buchman was very ambitious—he talked in terms of "remaking the world." As Buchman's biographer, Garth Lean—one of MRA's most influential writers—noted, this wider agenda informed all of Buchman's main initiatives.[17] Buchman believed that the Holy Spirit could teach people how to think and live and through that transform the character of national and international life.[18] His approach to public life was thus personalist in the sense that it combined the personal with the political. The historian Anders Jarlert called it "social personalism on a national and supranational level."[19] While some people were enthusiastic about this approach, others thought it was naive. For example, the idea that the world could be transformed through the agency of changed individuals was rejected as simplistic by the American theologian, Reinhold Niebuhr, and MRA was dismissed as utopian by Buchman's most long-standing British opponent, the Labour member of Parliament, Tom Driberg.[20]

If Buchman emphasized the possibility of changing the world, his optimism was tempered by a strong dose of realism in dealing with people and a readiness to adapt the OG and MRA to changing circumstances. As historian Daniel Sack has suggested, MRA was constantly reinventing its message to accommodate new situations. In other words, Buchman was both idealistic and pragmatic. Here, perhaps, can be found another key dimension to his outlook: there were paradoxes, or at least different tendencies, at work in the message that he forged. This was evident, for example, in the fact that in the interwar period the OG promoted both a nondogmatic spirituality and traditional evangelicalism. The historian Ian Randall noted that the tension was resolved through the deployment of a vocabulary that centered on the Holy Spirit.[21] This offers a clue to understanding more generally how Buchman tried to give a spiritual unity to the OG and MRA. It was through the inspiration of the Holy Spirit, rather than some kind of intellectual system, that he thought the different strands of his work could be reconciled.

This study is largely based on a reading of Buchman in his own words. That in itself is not original, for Lean's book in particular was very well researched. Yet there is a greater emphasis here than in Lean's book on the primary sources, on the assumption that Buchman's written and recorded words, taken as a whole, form a discrete body of thought that deserves analysis. Important sources include Buchman's speeches, many of which remain unpublished. Buchman was not a natural orator—although he did have a gift for coming up with memorable phrases. The talks that he gave at the Lily Valley missionary conference in Kuling, China, in August 1918 are a particularly good pointer to his early thinking.[22] His later speeches, published in the collection *Remaking the World*, are a good guide to his understanding of the world situation before and after World War II—although Buchman's colleagues increasingly had input into the speeches in later years.[23] The transcripts of Buchman's talks at MRA assemblies from the 1940s onward, particularly at the movement's conference centers on Mackinac Island, Michigan, and in Caux-sur-Montreux, Switzerland, are also full of useful material and give a less polished and more "live" picture of him as he engaged with audiences. Buchman's voluminous correspondence, mainly found in the Library of Congress and the OG archive in the United Kingdom, is of course important too, although Buchman's earlier letters generally revealed more about his spirituality than the later ones. In the last decades of his life most of his letters were drafted by Morris Martin, his secretary from the late 1930s onward, and were increasingly just summaries of what MRA was then doing, with a few personal remarks added in.[24]

Other useful sources include the transcript of an OG house party in Putney, London, in 1922, in which Buchman was extensively quoted, and the verbatim notes of comments made by Buchman to colleagues in 1937, taken by a Scottish aide, Lawson Wood. A short collection of statements by Buchman in the 1950s, edited by MRA full-time worker William Conner, was published at the end of the 1950s, and a couple of other unpublished collections of statements by Buchman from the 1940s and 1950s were also put together by aides. Martin left a number of notebooks containing statements by Buchman, an unpublished biography of him, and a memoir.[25] The English tennis star H. W. "Bunny" Austin, who worked with MRA full-time from the late 1930s onward, and Ray Purdy, a Princeton graduate who helped to run MRA in the United States for a number of decades, also left important memoirs. Among the many unpublished portraits of Buchman, the recollections of Signe Strong, a Norwegian artist who worked with MRA beginning in 1938, are notable for their details and insights.[26]

Sifting through all this material to highlight what was most important in Buchman's evolving vision remains a challenge. Many of the things he said were meant for specific individuals or were responses to particular situations, rather than being intended to reflect some overarching theological or spiritual system. For all that, his outlook did contain a set of underlying principles and insights, and these are discernible through his speeches, letters, and writings, as well as the memoir literature written about him.

1
Origins

Frank Nathaniel Daniel Buchman was born on June 4, 1878, in Pennsburg, Pennsylvania, to a Pennsylvania Dutch family that had roots in eastern Switzerland. His father, Franklin, owned a general store on Main Street, Pennsburg, before buying a small hotel by the railway, the Buchman House Hotel. It is likely that Buchman got some of his later sociability from growing up in the environment of a hotel. His mother, Sarah Greenwalt, came from a farming family, and she exercised a strong spiritual influence on him. He had an older brother, John, who died of diphtheria when he was two, and later an adopted brother, Dan, who was eighteen years younger than he. The family spoke a dialect of German that was a mixture of Swabian and Swiss German, and the language and culture of the town and surrounding area were German. As there was no high school in Pennsburg, the family moved in 1894 to Allentown, a town nearby that was expanding with the growth of the railways. Buchman's father opened a restaurant and saloon there.[1]

A possible early influence on Buchman's spiritual outlook came when at the age of eight he started to attend Perkiomen Seminary, a local private school run by the Schwenkfelders, a German sect similar to the Quakers that stressed the importance of the "inner light."[2] In particular, he was influenced by a young Schwenkfelder pastor, Oscar Kriebel, who was principal of the school, and the two of them kept up a correspondence into later life.[3] After high school he attended Muhlenberg College, which had been set up in 1867 to prepare young men for the Lutheran ministry. Then in 1899 he went on to the Lutheran Theological Seminary at Mount Airy, Philadelphia, before being ordained on September 10, 1902.[4] His years of training gave him a typically Lutheran mixture of pessimism about unregenerated human nature and optimism about the possibility of redemption.[5] The theological schooling was very traditional. He himself was subsequently critical of it, declaring that he had come out of it without any real understanding of people. He had been product of a "mould" and a "stereotyped education," he said in 1918.[6] He also said later that his local Lutheran clergyman had "missed the bus" with him.[7]

At the same time, Buchman seems to have drawn a lot on the German pietist tradition. Significantly, he once said that he got his emphasis on the Holy Spirit from the Lutheran pietism of the Halle School, particularly from the educationist August Hermann Francke (1663–1727).[8] Another possible source of inspiration was the so-called father of pietism, Philipp Jakob Spener (1635–1705)—who was himself a key influence on Francke. There were some notable similarities between Spener's ideas and Buchman's methods. For example, the house-party culture associated with the OG had much in common with Spener's practice of arranging small weekday meetings for serious-minded believers and his tendency to emphasize the religion of the heart as opposed to doctrine.[9] The Lutheran influence on Buchman was probably also evident in the late 1930s, when he commended a devotional manual, *True Christianity*, to his colleagues, suggesting that it was superior to Thomas à Kempis's fifteenth-century classic *The Imitation of Christ* on the grounds that it was less "legal." He was likely referring to the book of that name by another well-known German pietist, Johann Arndt (1555–1621).[10] In a general sense, Luther himself was probably an influence too; Henry Van Dusen thought that the voice of Luther himself was present in some of Buchman's teaching.[11]

Buchman was also influenced in these early years by contact with the American YMCA. He was particularly impressed in 1901 and 1902 by visits to the Northfield student conferences in Massachusetts, which were designed for students who had come into contact with the YMCA. These encouraged him to emphasize the importance of personal evangelistic work. The first of them, Buchman reported enthusiastically to his parents, "completely changed" his life.[12] The Northfield conferences, first initiated by the preacher Dwight L. Moody, were then run by John R. Mott, who was associate general secretary of the Foreign Department of the American YMCA, 1901–15, and then general secretary, 1915–28; he was to play an important role in Buchman's career.

Already at this early stage, Buchman was exhibiting signs of the kind of fixedness of purpose that would mark him out in later years—a factor evident in his attitude to marriage. During his years at Muhlenberg College, Buchman had thought about getting married and seems to have had a number of women in mind as possible wives. But he was fascinated to be told by a cousin that, according to the English philosopher Francis Bacon, a man could do better work if single than married. He was never to marry, and the kind of peripatetic life that he came to lead would not have been conducive to marriage.[13]

Following ordination, Buchman became pastor of a church in Kensington, Philadelphia, and a year later of the Church of the Good Shepherd in Overbrook, Philadelphia.[14] Then, during a visit to Europe in summer 1903, he stayed in Christian hospices run by the Lutheran Inner Mission in Switzerland and Germany and also visited Friedrich von Bodelschwingh, the founder of a community for helping epileptics and the mentally disabled near Bielefeld, Germany. "I made a thorough study of Bodelschwingh's principles," he said.[15] Buchman's encounter with Bodelschwingh, with whose family he remained in contact over subsequent decades, encouraged him to start, in May 1904, a *hospiz* for underprivileged boys in Overbrook. It was a successful initiative and led on to the founding of the larger Luther Hospice for Young Men in June 1905. That too flourished and inspired the establishment of an outreach center in one of the poorest areas of Philadelphia, modeled on Toynbee Hall in London's East End, a kind of residents' social club founded by the social reformer Samuel Barnett. Buchman's venture was particularly attractive to the city's immigrant communities.

But Buchman found it difficult to keep the costs of the hospiz down, and this led in October 1907 to a clash with the hospiz trustees over what he saw as their lack of generosity with money. Exhausted, Buchman resigned, believing that his life's work was somehow over and harboring a strong feeling of bitterness toward the trustees. Tired by the years of hard work in Philadelphia and in turmoil over the way he had been treated, Buchman became ill. A Philadelphia doctor suggested that he needed a long holiday, and in January 1908 he left by ship for Europe to convalesce on a tour that included travels around the Mediterranean.[16] In terms of recuperation, the trip was not a great success. Buchman remained burdened by what had happened. On the other hand, it was during a visit to Greece at this time that he first met Crown Princess Sophie of Greece, the mother of Helen, crown princess and later queen of Romania, and he was to have a lifelong connection with the Greek and Romanian royal families.[17]

It was during that summer that Buchman had a life-changing experience that particularly shaped his thinking about Christ and the Holy Spirit. In July 1908 he went to Keswick, in the north of England, at the time of the Christian Convention there. This was a yearly gathering of British evangelicals that had become well known worldwide for its emphasis on purity, holiness, and obedience, following what was called a "second blessing."[18] During the visit Buchman heard a sermon by a renowned preacher, Jessie Penn-Lewis, which affected him deeply. There are various, slightly different accounts of what happened on this occasion, most of them indicating that the doctrine of the atonement, hitherto something of a theory for him, became a personal reality.[19] According to one of his own most vivid descriptions, he "saw suddenly as in a vision a cross some distance away shining before [him]" and a "wide, deep gulf" lying between him and the "Crucified." He continued, "In the same moment I was conscious of the fact that this gulf could only be bridged by the Crucified himself, and as I recognized this, the chaos in my mind disappeared. . . . [At the foot of the cross] I completed the surrender to the Divine Will."[20] In another description of the experience, Buchman recalled, "I felt that [Christ] hung on that Cross for my sin."[21]

Buchman also said about this episode that some kind of powerful spiritual energy had come into his life. He said that it was as if a "strong current of life" had suddenly been poured into him and that afterward he had a "dazed sense of a great spiritual shaking up," and the feeling of having had a "divided will" disappeared. Significantly, he seems to have had this experience at the same moment as he surrendered his life to God: "I remember only one feeling very plainly. It was to me as if a strong stream of life suddenly passed through me, at the same time as my surrender."[22] Toward the end of his life, in 1959, he used the metaphor of the "wind" of the Spirit to describe the experience: "[The] speaker that day had the wind of the Spirit. . . . [The wind of heaven] passed over me and through me, and I walked out of that place a different man."[23]

Penn-Lewis's sermon apparently personalized the Crucifixion in a particularly real way, for Buchman also talked of having had a "poignant vision of the Crucified."[24] There is certainly evidence to suggest that Buchman hitherto approached the Crucifixion in a more impersonal way. In a surviving sermon, probably from his days at college or just after, he tried to conjure up in his listeners some of the feelings of sadness that he might have thought appropriate at Easter: "How dejected & sad we would feel if one of our dear ones should suffer as he suffered, and then finally die, and if you had expected some great thing from that dear one, as those faithful ones did."[25] After 1908 he talked about the cross in more vivid, experiential terms.

Prior to the visit to Keswick, Buchman had considered writing to the hospiz trustees to confess his ill will toward them, but he decided against it and remained adamant that he could never forgive them. But the experience in Keswick immediately brought this idea back to him. He wrote contrite letters to all six of the trustees, asking forgiveness for the unkind feelings he had toward them and stating that with God's grace he would never again speak disparagingly of them. He also cited the opening verse of Isaac Watts's famous hymn, "When I Survey the Wondrous Cross." This act of apology was, as Buchman saw it, an important outcome of his religious experience and appears to have contributed to the sense of inner liberation that he felt. His bitterness had deprived him of spiritual power, he recalled, but writing the letters meant that his life became "different." The spiritual power that had been absent from his life for a year or so, returned.[26]

An immediate upshot of these events—as Buchman often recounted—was a revitalization of his evangelistic contact with others. Specifically, he had a conversation with a Cambridge undergraduate about what he had just experienced that led the student himself into making a Christian commitment.[27] More generally, the experience at Keswick led him to have a much stronger sense of the Holy Spirit's presence in his life. Some years later, apparently referring to the Keswick episode, he said, "I had a Ministry without the Holy Spirit, and I know how futile it was, and how unhappy I was; I know the Ministry with the power of the Holy Spirit, and I know it is sheer joy and fun and romance all the time."[28]

If at one level Buchman's experience at Keswick was very personal, there was also a sense in which it reflected currents in wider Anglo-American evangelical culture. The Keswick Convention itself emphasized the possibility of transformative experiences of the kind that Buchman had. The history of American evangelicalism was also marked by stories of sudden conversion experiences, often featuring God's intervention in the life of a soul. Like Buchman, for example, the preacher Charles Finney (1792–1875), who played a central role in the Second Great Awakening, used to recount his conversion experience in such a way as to emphasize that it was not his own achievement, but God's free gift of grace; Finney was also immediately able to pass on something of his experience to someone else. More generally, such stories were typical of the evangelical revival of the eighteenth century. Buchman's experience at Keswick, then, although it was very personal, also reflected features of a wider transatlantic pattern.[29]

The tradition associated with the Keswick Convention helped to shape Buchman's spiritual outlook in subsequent years. Buchman had connections with people associated with it right into the 1920s. For example, he took two Cambridge undergraduates with links to Keswick, Godfrey Buxton and Murray Webb-Peploe, on a trip to the United States in early 1921.[30] In addition, Keswick's emphasis on practical religion and personal change bore some similarity to what was to follow in the OG. The common ground was reflected in the fact that Buchman often recommended reading the Quaker writer Hannah Pearsall Smith's *The Christian's Secret of a Happy Life* (1885), one of the most influential guides to the spiritual life in the Keswick tradition.[31] On the other hand, OG methods of evangelism differed from the more conservative Keswick approach in their emphasis on testimony rather than teaching. The two were not easily compatible.[32]

In January 1909, following his trip to Europe, Buchman was appointed as YMCA secretary at Penn State, a post he took on Mott's recommendation. It was there that Buchman's skills as an evangelist first became evident. Outwardly, it was not the most promising field for evangelism, for, according to Mott, it was the most "godless" university in the country. Buchman himself recalled that there were seventeen "liquor parties" taking place on the first evening after his arrival.[33] When Buchman was first introduced to the students at chapel, he seems to have cut a somewhat pompous and eccentric figure, for his opening statement, "Men of Penn State, I greet you," was met with laughter and stamping of feet. Yet his huge energy and capacity to befriend people quickly began to influence the campus. Personal work, in combination with intense campaigns, led to large numbers of students being drawn into Christian activities and commitment. Three years before he arrived, the number of students who were members of the YMCA was 166, out of a total student body of 809. Two years after he had arrived, it had jumped to 1,200, out of a total of 1,620.[34] Many students came to formal Christian commitment. For example, after a campaign there in 1911 one campus evangelist reported enthusiastically that more than one hundred decisions for Christ had taken place.[35] The work was integrated with student evangelism going on elsewhere. Buchman took or sent groups of students to the Northfield conferences, and evangelists from outside were often brought in. Buchman's methods became widely known and replicated on campuses such as Yale, Illinois State, Williams, and Cornell.[36]

Buchman's discovery of "guidance" took place while he was working at Penn State. He was already at that time making space for morning meditation. This was a practice that was given much emphasis in YMCA circles. Mott, for example, wrote a pamphlet called *The Morning Watch* and himself spent the first half hour or hour of each day alone with God.[37] But it was through the British Baptist minister, F. B. Meyer, the author of a well-known book on the subject, *The Secret of Guidance* (1896), that Buchman gained fresh insight into the importance of listening to God. Meyer was one of Keswick's leading international figures and had been the principal guest speaker from abroad at the Northfield conference in 1902—where Buchman probably first heard him.[38] Visiting Penn

State in 1912, in the course of an American lecture tour, Meyer found Buchman frustrated that, in spite of a lot of activity, there seemed to be few people changing at a deeper level. He asked him whether he allowed the Holy Spirit to guide him in all that he was doing. When Buchman said that he read the Bible and prayed in the morning, he questioned him as to whether he really gave God enough uninterrupted time to tell him what to do. He also challenged him to place an emphasis on personal interviews rather than the organization of meetings. The upshot of the conversation was that Buchman decided to spend at least an hour every morning listening to God, initially from five to six o'clock.[39] It was a turning point in his life. Regular "quiet times" to seek God's guidance became a permanent feature of his schedule.

Buchman's meeting with Meyer in 1912 did not result in a sudden abandonment of large-scale methods of evangelism. In fact, already at Penn State Buchman showed signs of the instinct for publicity that characterized his later work. This was evident when the YMCA evangelist Sherwood Eddy visited the campus for a five-day campaign in 1914. Banners with Eddy's name on them were hung from every fraternity house on campus, and heralds announced campaign events at student eating clubs. Trees had cardboard clocks on them to show at what time Eddy's first sermon would take place. The auditorium was packed each night, with people turned away, and on the final evening—"decision night"—five hundred people stood up.[40]

Yet Buchman's work as a YMCA secretary increasingly involved trying to help specific individuals. This included spending time with three people whose change or conversion he thought could affect the whole Penn State campus: Blair Buck, a graduate student from Virginia; the local bootlegger, Bill Pickle; and the dean, Alva Agee. In later years Buchman sometimes recounted the stories of his encounters with these men, emphasizing the diverse ways in which he interacted with them. He challenged Buck, a Confucianist, to deploy his Confucianism to try to change a local chicken thief. When Buck then failed in this endeavor, he started to become interested in religion in a more traditional sense. Throughout this process, Buchman adopted a policy of what he called "intelligent restraint and nonchalant reserve," spending time with the young man and waiting for him to raise the subject of faith himself. Buchman approached Pickle, who had an unsavory reputation, differently, getting to know him through their common love of horses and then inviting him to a student conference in Toronto, where they prayed together and Pickle became a practicing Christian. Agee, who was an agnostic, was then much influenced by the change that he saw in Pickle.[41]

Fig. 1   Buchman (*front center*) with a group from Penn State at a camp, 1914. *Seated on right*: Bill Pickle with his wife, Maria. Photo: Oxford Group Archives.

If it was with Mott's endorsement that Buchman acquired the post at Penn State, it was also with his blessing that he left the college in April 1915 to go to support YMCA missionary outreach in Asia. The invitation came from Eddy—who was obviously impressed by his visit to Penn State in 1914 and who had again worked with Buchman during a campaign at Yale the following year.[42] Buchman's time at Penn State had not been without difficulties. The directness and enthusiasm with which he had approached the task of evangelism had aroused some opposition. Furthermore, he did not always feel adequately supported financially by the YMCA. His departure also reflected the fact that he was ready for a new challenge.

Buchman arrived in Ceylon (Sri Lanka) in August 1915, before moving on to India and then visiting Japan and China the following year. He was in the United States for the academic year 1916–17, but then went back to Asia for a stint that lasted nearly two years, visiting China, Korea, the Philippines, and Japan, before returning home in the spring of 1919. His work with Eddy involved laying the groundwork for large evangelistic meetings at which Eddy and sometimes he would speak. For example, in India in late 1915, the two men addressed huge audiences in the Princely State of Travancore. By Eddy's estimate the numbers totaled four hundred thousand. Buchman himself spoke to sixty thousand there on Christmas day.[43] The two men also worked closely together again during Buchman's second Asian visit, in China in 1918. Their strategy then involved Buchman organizing personal work groups, containing ten to fifteen people each, in different places, which prepared the ground for visits and speeches by Eddy. Sometimes these were divided by profession so that, for example, there were separate groups for businessmen, professionals, missionaries, local pastors, and women.[44]

Buchman was enthusiastic about the work with Eddy. For example, he wrote to his parents in November 1915 of the "happy and satisfactory" time he was having.[45] Moreover, the organized approach to evangelism that he supported in these years often produced striking results. During a visit by Buchman to Korea in May 1918, this time without Eddy, it was reported that at one boys' school 180 decisions for Christ were made out of a total of 400 boys at the school. Furthermore, in one church forty personal work groups were operating in the months following Buchman's visit.[46] At the same time, Buchman was sometimes uneasy with the large-scale methods being used. The roots of this lay in the lessons he had learned at Penn State, but they were reinforced by his work with Eddy. He once likened some of the meetings that he and Eddy had organized in India in late 1915 to "hunting rabbits with a brass band."[47] He thought a more informal way of operating, based on the activity of small teams, would lead to deeper changes in people.[48] It was a theme that he increasingly stressed in his interactions with the missionary community in Asia. In China he helped with the regular summer conferences for missionaries at Kuling and Petaiho, first as an observer in 1916, then as the organizer of the section on "personal work" in 1917, and then, along with two other missionaries, as the general conference organizer in 1918. It was at this latter conference that he gave the "Kuling" talks, in which he outlined his thinking about the nature of personal work in greatest detail.[49]

While working in China, Buchman also established a base at the nondenominational Hartford Theological Seminary in Connecticut. Buchman's reputation as an evangelist, already strong from his activities at Penn State, had been reinforced by his early work in Asia. The president of Hartford, Douglas Mackenzie, was looking for someone to teach courses on personal evangelism, and Buchman was recommended by the YMCA missionary in India, Howard Walter, who was himself a Hartford graduate and who had worked with Buchman in Lahore and also in the United States.[50] Buchman took up the post in September 1916 and remained there until February 1922. The courses he taught were practical in their emphasis. For example, his classes for the academic year 1921–22 included a beginner's course on personal evangelism, an advanced course covering themes such as "Diagnosis, Personalization, [and] Illustration," and a course on how to use the Bible with individuals.[51]

One of the distinctive features of Buchman's work as an evangelist was his self-confidence. He had no doubts about the importance of the work he was doing. For example, in his report of activities for 1912–13, he suggested that the Penn State YMCA had a "unique place" in association history and that it was receiving "international attention." He also cited the opinion of one wealthy YMCA supporter that the work at Penn State was the "most outstanding piece of student work" being done in the country. He added that he was not saying these things to claim credit for himself but simply to emphasize the reputation of the work on the campus and to note that his promises about how the work would develop had not been idle dreams but "realities."[52] Later Buchman attributed his success at Penn State to God. "I hadn't any part in it other than I let God use me," he insisted, in a typical formulation.[53] The same confidence was evident in Asia. He said in 1917 that the meetings he was organizing in China were "history making in Evangelism." "God has been working with us in wonder-making power these days," he reported in the same year.[54]

Buchman's self-confidence was an important factor in his success as an evangelist. Yet his self-assured and sometimes blunt manner also meant that not everyone found him an easy person to work with. At Kuling in 1918 he broke with convention by organizing the conference around a loose, informal structure and then suggested that many of the missionaries were handicapped by private sins and lacked a real knowledge of China. Logan Roots, the Episcopal bishop of Hankow, thought he had shown a "censorious and dictatorial frame of mind"—although he later regretted his criticism and became a supporter of the OG and MRA. At Hartford—where he was never a full-time member of the faculty—Buchman's approach was also controversial. He was always an unconventional teacher in the sense that he tried to train people to be evangelists themselves rather than emphasize the academic side of the subject. He also spent a lot of time trying to help students pastorally. Furthermore, he was often away from the seminary, working on other campuses or in Europe. Not everyone was comfortable with these ways of working, although Mackenzie remained supportive of him throughout his time there.[55]

After leaving Hartford Buchman never again had a formal salary. Indeed, he was rarely based in any one place for an extended period of time and tried to move around as he thought the Holy Spirit was prompting him.

Among the many people who helped to shape Buchman's spiritual vision, two academics with evangelistic interests stand out as particularly significant. These were the Yale University classicist and professor of Christian methods,

Henry Wright (1877–1925), who was influential in YMCA student evangelism, and Henry Drummond (1851–1897), the Scottish devotional writer and speaker who had also been professor of natural science at the Free Church College in Glasgow. In a letter to Wright in 1918, Buchman told the Yale scholar that he came closer than any man he knew to incarnating the principles of Christ and that the best of his message derived from his teaching.[56] Many of Buchman's ideas can be traced to Wright; indeed, Keene and another specialist on Buchman's early work, Walter Houston Clark, called Wright the "father" of the OG.[57] Drummond, whom Buchman once called the "prince of personal workers," had been well known in missionary circles for his stress on personal work in evangelism.[58] In his attempts to reconcile science and religion, *Natural Law in the Spiritual World* (1883) and *The Ascent of Man* (1894), and addresses on the social dimension of Christianity such as *The City Without a Church* (1892), he had also been able to strike a chord with people looking for fresh expressions of the Christian message. There is a good case for saying—as David Belden does—that Buchman's vision had much in common with the evangelical pietism of the Drummond school, even if he was less concerned with trying to formulate an intellectually coherent picture of faith than the Scotsman.[59]

One of Wright's enduring concerns was to try to help students find a sense of purpose for their lives and careers. In a series of Bible studies, *The Will of God and a Man's Lifework* (1909), he argued that God had a plan for the development of the world that touched all departments of human life and activity. In this context, he suggested that each person had a particular part to perform in the plan, which was carefully tailored to fit his or her character—although the details of how that plan would unfold depended on the person's response to the divine call. He also stressed that the role of the church in this was to train Christian laymen for the task of Christianizing their particular professions or spheres of life.[60] Wright often visited Buchman at Penn State to help him with his work there, and Buchman used his book as a training resource.[61] Buchman's sense that each person had a unique calling under God, an enduring tenet of his philosophy, was doubtless reinforced by this element of Wright's thinking. More generally, the Yale scholar also stressed the importance of small groups meeting for sharing and fellowship, and this probably influenced Buchman too.[62]

Wright was also responsible for a more specific development in Buchman's spiritual commitment. While based at Hartford in early 1917, Buchman regularly attended some of Wright's lectures at Yale. These lectures were often prefaced with silent meditation on a sentence originating with Moody: "The world has yet to see what God can do in, for, by and through a man whose will is wholly given to him."[63] Buchman subsequently declared that it took him six weeks to accept the challenge inherent in these words, and he later used the phrase to challenge audiences himself.[64]

Buchman's lifelong respect for Drummond was shown by the fact that he told Peter Howard in 1945 that he would be the "Henry Drummond of this generation for the nations."[65] The Scotsman's influence on Buchman probably came partly through Wright's *Will of God and a Man's Lifework*, where he was generously quoted. He was also impressed by reading an influential essay on evangelism, "Spiritual Diagnosis," which Drummond had written when he was a student. During a visit to Westminster College, Cambridge, an English Presbyterian foundation where he was occasionally based in the years 1920–22, Buchman specifically said that he was trying to follow the ideas of "Spiritual Diagnosis."[66] Another text by Drummond that Buchman admired and used to recommend was his well-known address on 1 Corinthians 13, *The Greatest Thing in the World* (1889).[67]

In terms of Buchman's understanding of the Holy Spirit and guidance, there were, of course, other spiritual influences too. For example, Buchman may have been affected by the Quaker influences that were felt everywhere in the state of Pennsylvania. He was certainly impressed by some Quaker writers—in addition to Smith. He cited the diary of the eighteenth-century preacher John Woolman in one of his speeches in China, and referred to Quaker biblical scholar James Rendel Harris's *The Guiding Hand of God* (1905) in some of his courses at Hartford.[68] There were indeed some overlaps between Quaker spirituality and OG culture. For example, the custom in Quaker meetings of people sitting in silence to await inspiration from the "inner light" was similar to the OG practice of listening to God. Both traditions were also nondogmatic. Buchman's approach to individuals may also have had something in common with that of the founder of the Quakers, George Fox, for—if Keene is right—Buchman was similar to the Quaker leader in his ability to see into other people's lives.[69] But direct connections between Quakerism and the OG are in fact hard to find. Moreover, Buchman specifically stated that it was from Lutheran pietism and not Quaker spirituality that he acquired his emphasis on listening to the Spirit.[70]

Other writings that Buchman drew on included *The Secret of Inspiration* (1916) by South African evangelist Andrew Murray. This was an anthology of extracts from the writings of the eighteenth-century English clergyman William Law that focused on the leading of the Holy Spirit.[71] Buchman also made use of Saint Augustine and the Christian mystics in his courses at Hartford and knew of the spirituality of Brother Lawrence, the seventeenth-century author of *The Practice of the Presence of God*.[72] Another contemporary who impressed him was the English Congregationalist minister, John Henry Jowett (1864–1923), the pastor of Fifth Avenue Presbyterian Church, New York, 1911–18. At Kuling Buchman recommended Jowett's *In the School of Calvary* (1910), stating that reading it during the conference had been one of his richest recent experiences. He highlighted in particular a chapter titled "The Neglected Cup," which stressed Jesus's pain over sin and the importance of Christians sympathizing with the sufferings of others.[73] Buchman was also taken with *A Book of Prayers* (1912) by Samuel McComb, a well-known Episcopalian priest with an interest in the psychological dimension of religious healing. Buchman said in 1918, "If you want to know how to pray so as to reach the hearts of men read Samuel McComb's prayers."[74]

Another writer whose works impressed Buchman when he discovered them a few years later was the Scottish Baptist minister, Oswald Chambers—also a man who had been influenced by Meyer in his youth. Buchman read many of Chambers's books in the 1920s. He was struck, he said in a letter of 1923, by Chambers's view that the voice of God was not being heard because people were "full of noisy, introspective thoughts." He was also impressed by *My Utmost for His Highest* (1927), a collection of daily readings by Chambers, which became widely used in the OG.[75] It is revealing that Chambers had been inspired by the Wesleyan spiritual tradition.[76] Buchman, too, was an admirer of the legacy of John Wesley, and the hymns of his brother Charles—as were a number of his supporters.[77] It reinforces the sense that Buchman's work had roots in the transatlantic religious culture that grew out of eighteenth-century evangelicalism.[78]

Buchman was also impressed by the Princeton Conference, a regular evangelistic gathering that first met in 1913 in Oxford, Pennsylvania, before moving the following year to use the buildings of the Princeton Theological Seminary. A leading figure in this was C. G. Trumbull, editor of the *Sunday School Times* and son of a well-known specialist on personal evangelism, H. Clay Trumbull. Speaking in China in 1918, Buchman referred very positively to the 1916 report of the Princeton Conference, titled *Victory in Christ*, suggesting that the outcomes he was seeing in Kuling were similar to those that had been evident at the Princeton Conference. The report included a series of addresses by C. G. Trumbull on the "victorious life," and the idea of "victory in Christ" was central to Buchman's vision at Kuling.[79] Letters Buchman wrote to Trumbull in 1918 also contained positive references to the work of the Princeton Conference.[80]

Another element of Buchman's thinking inspired by the wider movement of college evangelism was his emphasis on moral discipline. Buchman seems to have had an interest in the moral dimensions of religion from early on, for in 1899 he received the Butler Analogy Prize from Muhlenberg College for an essay on Joseph Butler's *Analogy of Religion* (1736), a well-known defense of Christian morality and teaching from the perspective of natural theology.[81] While it is possible that Buchman was influenced by Butler, his thinking was always more practical than theological, and for dealing with moral issues at a pastoral level he turned to some of his American contemporaries. One of the contributors to *Victory in Christ* was the author Robert E. Speer, secretary of the Presbyterian Board of Foreign Missions. Buchman had a high opinion of Speer, and at Kuling recommended one of his books, *The Marks of a Man*—on the importance of character.[82] Speer's influence on him, however, was most strongly felt in the formulation of what became the "absolute moral standards" of the OG and MRA. In *The Principles of Jesus* (1902), Speer had distilled Jesus's moral teachings into four "absolute standards" for behavior—truth, unselfishness, purity, and love—stating that Jesus, unlike the scribes of his time, was a teacher of "absolute principles."[83]

Although Speer formulated the absolute moral standards, it was probably through Wright that Buchman discovered the concept, for Speer had only sketched out the idea of the standards briefly, while Wright gave them a central place in *The Will of God and a Man's Lifework*. Wright modified the standards slightly by replacing the word "truth" with "honesty." He called them "touchstones" as well as standards and outlined in some detail the spiritual principles that lay behind them. One of his points was that there was a link between adherence to absolute standards and the discernment of God's will. By always doing what pleased God, he suggested, Jesus "cleansed and strengthened his will to receive the compelling conviction from God" and was thereby able to be sure of God's presence and guidance.[84]

Buchman's conviction about the importance of morality had been reinforced by what he saw as the immorality of much of student life at Penn State. It had also been strengthened in 1912 by an experience he had on a train in Canada, when there came to him a special conviction that Christianity had a moral backbone.[85] Morality and self-discipline forged character, he thought. "Salted with the fire of the discipline," a variation on the Moffat translation of Mark 9:49, was a favorite phrase of his in later years, reflecting the same idea.[86] It was in this context that the absolute moral standards became a central tool in Buchman's work. Throughout his life Buchman used them as a shorthand summary of Christian morality. They were partly intended to be a tool for helping people to discern where there was sin in their lives, and he understood sin to mean anything that interfered with the vitality of a person's spiritual life.[87] "Sin blinds, binds, multiplies, deafens, deadens," he once said.[88] But the standards were also intended to offer people positive ideals to live by.

Some have argued that Buchman's emphasis on the four standards pointed to a rule-based religion at odds with the message of Saint Paul, or at least that it could be interpreted in that way. One of the founders of AA, Bill Wilson, for example, took that view, and although AA was much influenced by OG ideas, it dropped the emphasis on the standards, with the exception of the standard of absolute honesty.[89] But neither Wright nor Buchman intended the standards to be interpreted in a legalistic way. Wright observed that where scripture did not offer clear guidelines as to what was right and wrong, people could make up their own minds. For example, in what he described as "doubtful pleasures" (smoking, drinking, theater, dancing, etc.), it was a matter of personal conviction whether a person's actions matched up to the four touchstones or not.[90] Buchman was likewise wary of seeing the standards in terms of rules. Indeed, for all his emphasis on morality, he was never primarily a moralist. In explaining the standards at Kuling, he suggested that people should use them as a way of testing their motives, an approach that differed from seeing them as a tool for distinguishing in an abstract way which actions were right and wrong.[91] Garth Lean relates that in later years Buchman was inclined to say, "Do anything God lets you," and that he once observed, "The Cross is an alternative to living by the book."[92] Speaking in 1937 to his team—he often called OG and MRA groups the "team"—he cited approvingly a German woman who had stated, "I had rules. But if I had the principles of the Oxford Group, I might have avoided that."[93]

The rather general nature of the absolute moral standards is one reason why it can be argued—as Daniel Sack does—that Buchman's definition of sin was subjective and that it focused less on a prescriptive code of behavior than on what people personally felt to be sinful.[94] A newcomer to the OG who once asked whether drinking was right or wrong was met with the question, "What do you think?"[95] It was a typical response. The moral framework adopted by the OG and MRA was one that gave people space to come to their own conclusions. Yet the subjective element should not be overemphasized. Buchman was also prepared to challenge people directly about what he saw as immoral behavior, sometimes mentioning very specific sins. It would be more accurate to see this as an approach to morality where the distinction between the subjective and objective was kept deliberately vague, or perhaps as an example of Buchman's readiness to live with paradoxes.

Buchman seems to have thought that in addressing pastoral issues it was by referring to the Holy Spirit that Christian workers would know whether to stress the individual conscience, or morality in a more objective sense, in any particular situation. Indeed, it is not possible to understand Buchman's approach to morality in general without seeing it in conjunction with his thinking about the Holy Spirit. He thought that the Holy Spirit played a central role in convicting people of their sins. In 1927, for example, he wrote to Queen Marie of Romania that although "marvellous on a human basis," she lacked the "maximum power." He suggested that the Holy Spirit had to convict her of her sins, rather than he.[96] If the Holy Spirit brought conviction of sin, it also brought a cure. In a speech in Riverside, California, in 1948, he declared that there was a cure for any sin, no matter how enticing it was; "God's Holy Spirit" had the answer.[97] People responsive to the Spirit could stop being governed by unhealthy feelings, he said in the 1950s: "If you cut the nerve of your instinctive actions and reactions by obeying the Spirit, then you are on track."[98]

Buchman's emphasis on morality was combined with an interest in the nature of character and psychological development. This was evident in some of the books that he recommended at Kuling. For example, he was impressed by *Adolescence* (1904) by psychologist and educator G. Stanley Hall, an admirer of Darwin and Freud who sought to explain religion in scientific terms and who was the first president of the American Psychological Association. Buchman did not give any detail on what he saw in Hall's work, but he would certainly have endorsed Hall's view that conversion was a normal, natural, universal, and necessary process in adolescence.[99] Buchman also recommended Mary Eliza Moxcey's *Girlhood and Character* (1916), a popular study of female adolescence, and Francis L. Wellman's famous study of the psychology of courtroom trials, *The Art of Cross-Examination* (1903).[100]

It is clear from these book references that Buchman's thinking about morality and character was shaped by influences that went beyond Christian culture narrowly conceived. Another factor that reflected this same wider influence was mediated through Wright. In a book on the dangers of even moderate drinking, *Drink and Be Sober* (1915)—appearing just four years before Prohibition—the American literary critic Vance Thompson used the phrase "drunk at the top" to refer to people who had let drink interfere with their higher moral faculties.[101] Wright was so taken with the idea that he expanded on it and used it to refer not only to people with a drinking problem but also to those who had let the abuse of tobacco, food, sex, or conceit paralyze their moral judgment. For example, he used the phrase "narcotized on top" to describe the harmful moral influence on people of alcohol and drugs and "satiated on top" to refer to the effects of too much food. Buchman found the "on top" idea appealing and made considerable use of it in China in 1918.[102]

Drinking was in fact an area where Buchman regularly stressed the need for discipline. He had given up alcohol while at Overbrook to try to help his then housekeeper, Mary Hemphill, get free of a drinking problem. At Penn State, the "change" in Bill Pickle had required a complete break with alcohol, and this had reinforced Buchman's commitment to temperance. He seems to have concluded that there was a link between a refusal to touch alcohol and effective personal work. At Kuling he commented that in the first years of his ministry he had occasionally taken a glass of wine when he visited his parishioners, while noting that he did not then have what he called a "converting ministry" in his life. He went on to cite a Chinese home where the decision not to serve alcohol had led to a "new atmosphere" in the home. It was not a question, he stressed, of whether a person could be a Christian and drink but whether he could drink and be a "miracle worker" at the same time. He clearly doubted it. Drinking was what he called a "debateable" sin, and that in itself was something to be concerned about, for, in his view, "doubtful linen was dirty linen."[103] This wariness of alcohol remained with Buchman throughout his life and permeated the OG and MRA too. On the other hand, Buchman occasionally had a glass of wine in cultures where it was an ordinary part of the meal.[104]

Buchman's association of nondrinking with spiritual effectiveness reflected an issue that was always in his mind when addressing moral questions: the importance of living in "spiritual power." In this he was again influenced by Wright. In *The Will of God and a Man's Lifework*, Wright had suggested that little sins could undermine a person's relationship with God, listing a number of examples of dishonesty that people should be wary of.[105] Impressed by this, Buchman put together a list of dishonesties at Kuling that bore a marked similarity to Wright's examples. Little sins, he explained, were spiritually unhelpful because they robbed people of "power." In an allusion to a verse in the Song of Songs (2.15), he used the phrase "sly foxes" to illustrate his thinking. A lie is a "sly fox," he said, and "these sly foxes keep us from power."[106] How to live in "spiritual power" was in fact a central concern of contemporary American evangelicalism. Books such as Moody's *Secret Power* (1881) and S. D. Gordon's

Quiet Talks on Power (1901), both of which were referred to in the bibliography of Wright's *The Will of God and a Man's Lifework*, addressed the subject directly.[107] Buchman's thinking was certainly shaped by this. It was also reinforced by what Buchman saw as the deadness in much of the religious work around him. There were plenty of churchmen living fruitless lives, he thought. He said in China that when he first arrived at Penn State, the Christians there had the "form of godliness but no power" and were like "squirrels in a cage."[108]

Buchman thought that honesty—one of the absolute moral standards—was a condition of spiritual power. Certain episodes in his life had strengthened this conviction. At one point in Pennsylvania, he had owned up to the habit of using passes on the railway to which he was not entitled. Restitution of the money that he had gained from the deception had led to restoration of contact with God; he said later, "It was not until I decided to send a cheque that was adequate that peace came."[109] Similarly, during one of his trips to China he had told a lie to someone, and the following day found that he had a barren quiet time with no distinctive thoughts. He associated the two events and decided to go to the person whom he had lied to and confess what he had done. The result, he said afterward, was the "return of power."[110] Buchman came to the slightly different conclusion that talking about people behind their backs was also a hindrance to power. He said in China that one of the main causes of spiritual ineffectiveness in evangelism was what he called the "withering hand of criticism": constructive criticism meant going directly to people to pass on thoughts or criticisms, whereas the destructive form of it, which involved talking about people behind their backs, deprived the average Christian worker of power.[111] He also stressed the importance of discretion. He thought that God's guidance would not come to people who did not keep confidences.[112]

It was on the basis of these kinds of experiences that Buchman came to place such an emphasis on honesty and transparency. The stress on honesty was to become a central element in the cluster of practices that made up OG and MRA spirituality. Lying and stealing—even in small things—and dishonest relationships were regarded as a hindrance to spiritual growth, and restitution for wrongdoing was encouraged. Wright normally listed the standards as purity, honesty, unselfishness, and love.[113] By contrast, Buchman placed "honesty" at the head of the list, thereby indicating the importance he placed on it.

If, according to Buchman, honesty was a condition of spiritual power, so too was "purity," a word that in his mind was associated with sexual discipline but that also covered purity of motive in relationships. At least from his time at

Penn State onward he took the view that there was a connection between purity in sexual behavior and the extent to which people were available to be used by the Holy Spirit. He once talked of people who had become "sterile in spiritual experience" through a "lack of carefulness on the second standard"—by which he meant purity—and this reflected an enduring pattern of thought.[114] Sexual sin, he thought, left a damaging imprint on the soul. It always left a person with a "heavy thud" he said in the early 1950s, suggesting that freedom could be found through honesty and the cross of Christ.[115]

Yet if, in Buchman's mind, sexual sin deadened a person's spiritual sensitivities, so, correspondingly, he saw a direct connection between purity and constructive moral energy. The section on purity in Wright's *The Will of God and a Man's Lifework* included extracts from an essay by the American Congregationalist Horace Bushnell, "The Lost Purity Restored," which associated purity with a series of positive images: "Purity is, in character, what transparency is in the crystal. It is water flowing, unmixed and clear, from the mountain spring. Or it is the white of snow."[116] The implication was that purity should be seen as a positive virtue rather than a principle associated with a set of prohibitions. Buchman certainly saw it that way. "No heart is pure that is not passionate," he would say in later years—using a phrase that came from the nineteenth-century portrayal of Christ by John Seeley, *Ecce Homo* (1866).[117] It was also widely believed in OG and MRA circles that there was a link between personal purity and creativity.[118] It was probably for such perceived links that Buchman once said—citing a line from one of Charles Wesley's hymns—that "make and keep me pure within" were the greatest six words in the English language.[119]

Buchman believed that many students were anxious for advice or a listening ear regarding sexual morality. Indeed, he thought that sexual temptation in a variety of forms was particularly common to young people. Talking about his work at Princeton, for example, he once said that 85 percent of students there were troubled by the subject of sex.[120] His readiness to discuss sexual temptation and morality openly with students—rare for his time—was almost certainly one of the reasons why so many of them came to talk with him.[121] One of his concerns was to try to help people deal with impure thoughts. He said in China that 97 percent of the men he saw in interviews had a problem with impure thoughts. "Emasculated on top" was the phrase he used to describe the problem, echoing Thompson. He warned strongly that a person's thoughts needed to be guarded carefully: "[A person] must learn to say, 'No, Evil Thought, you can't come in.'"[122] His questions to people were often very direct. "What about the women you were with last night," he once asked a couple of students who visited him to discuss their difficulties with Christianity. The pair later apparently admitted some wrongdoing had taken place.[123]

Drummond thought that young men were often prevented from becoming Christians by "one particular sin," and that this was different for each person.[124] Buchman had a similar view, and for this reason often encouraged students to be specific about the issues they were facing. Many evidently confessed that they had problems with masturbation, a practice that Buchman believed was self-indulgent in a way that was harmful to people's moral and spiritual growth. Here his thinking was probably shaped by contemporary opinion as well as traditional Christian teaching. In *Adolescence*, for example, Hall had warned that the practice caused unbalanced development, mental weakness, and moral decay.[125] Another subject that sometimes came up was homosexuality. Here again Buchman's ideas reflected wider Christian and social attitudes. Personal change was possible in this area, he insisted. Already at Penn State he was saying that people could find an answer to what he saw as homosexual sin, and he continued to make the same point in later life.[126] Saint Paul's thinking was, or at least became, a particular inspiration for him. He thought certain verses from Paul's First Letter to the Corinthians about breaking with sexual immorality were evidence that people could alter their sexual habits. "1 Corinthians 6, 9–11 can be a reality and people can not only forgive but forget," he said in 1937, talking privately about people with homosexual tendencies.[127]

T. Willard Hunter emphasizes Buchman's lightness of touch in discussing such matters, citing an occasion when a young man came to his room at the Shoreham Hotel in Washington, D.C., and confessed to having a problem with masturbation. Asked how old he was, the fellow said that he was twenty-five. Buchman replied, "I stopped doing that when I was twenty-six. So you have a year to go."[128] The challenge was to avoid overintensity and make people feel relaxed discussing such questions. This was probably the reason why, while discussing purity with some of his team some years later, Buchman referred to a line from the English poet, Alfred, Lord Tennyson, "In the spring a young man's fancy lightly turns to thoughts of love."[129] Excessive seriousness when discussing sexual morality or relationships could be punctured by poetic references of this kind.[130]

Buchman's remarks at the Shoreham Hotel about masturbation in his own life may indicate that his thinking about purity arose from personal experience. He also once said that he could not listen to the "slightest suggestive," apparently referring to sexual temptation in a general sense, and this would seem to reinforce the idea.[131] He was clearly keen to avoid any impropriety with women because he once emphasized that his relations with women were of what he called a "clean-cut" character.[132]

In his memoirs Morris Martin suggested that Buchman might privately have wrestled with a homosexual tendency. In support of this, he cited an occasion when he thought Buchman himself hinted that this was the case. Buchman was listening to some negative news reports about MRA that featured Tom Driberg—who was an active homosexual—when he said a prayer for the British politician: "Help that man. There but for the grace of God go I."[133] Yet it is hard to be certain what Buchman meant by this. Others were skeptical that homosexuality was an issue in his life. Lean, for example, could not find any concrete evidence to support the idea.[134]

Central to Buchman's approach here was the idea that temptations of all kinds would lose their appeal or persistence when people had the courage to acknowledge their existence.[135] In short, victory over sin and the recovery of spiritual power depended on confession. At Kuling Buchman said of one Christian worker that he would "never have power" until he had confessed the deepest sin in his life.[136] Accountability to others, and confession where necessary, were thus much encouraged in the OG and MRA. This mainly took place at a one-to-one level. People were encouraged to open up to peers or mentors—which were informally chosen—when the need arose. Confession was one aspect of what Buchman and his team called "sharing." Julian P. Thornton-Duesbery, who later explained the idea in an OG pamphlet, noted that such sharing had to be in strict confidence and that it would find its completion in "personal confession to God." He added that as part of true repentance it was often necessary for a person to make confession and restitution to any other person who had been wronged.[137]

The confession or acknowledgement of sin also sometimes took place in small fellowship groups—although when it did so it was generally not as detailed as it was at the one-to-one level. This kind of confessional practice was not unique to Buchman's work. Wesley, for example, had stressed the importance of people making confession in small groups.[138] On the other hand, confession of sin in a more public way was not encouraged. Public confession, Buchman said at Kuling, was appropriate only if a person's sin was a public one—like that of a leader in a church quarrel. Moreover, he insisted that there were certain sins that should never be confessed in public. If there were sins of impurity in a person's life, for example, it was wrong to mention them specifically. "Just say, 'impurity,'" he said. A public confession needed to be "brief, honest, simple, contrite"; where a sin did not concern the public, it should be confessed only to the person concerned.[139]

In encouraging open sharing in the way he did, Buchman created a movement in which people were very open about their inner lives. In this he was arguably reflecting an American cultural tradition running from the Puritans to modern-day confessional television.[140] Not everyone was happy with it, and it aroused considerable opposition in some quarters. Some people, in particular, thought that the FCCF did in practice encourage a form of public confession or that it countenanced an overly introspective culture. Such concerns were central to the controversy surrounding Buchman's work at Princeton in the mid-1920s. In October 1926 *Time* magazine sensationally described the influence of what it called the "Buchman cult" at the university, highlighting the way in which Buchman's supporters encouraged the confession of sin and noting in particular the group's "pre-occupation with 'washing out' from its members . . . the strain of auto-eroticism."[141] The article implied that there was an overemphasis on the confession of sexual sin in the FCCF that made the work unhealthy and dangerous. This, along with other accusations, led to an inquiry into Buchman's ways of operating that, although it largely exonerated him, meant that it became difficult for him and his supporters to continue working there.[142]

If confession or the sharing of personal needs in the small group context was controversial, it was also one of the areas where Buchman's influence was most strongly felt—through AA. In the group meetings that later became central to AA's twelve-step program, it was through acknowledging sin or wrongdoing that the atonement process worked and guilt and shame were washed away.[143] There was in fact a growing emphasis on groups and group therapy in religious and intellectual circles in the 1930s, which Buchman's work reflected and, to a degree, helped to shape. Indeed, Paul Tournier, the Swiss doctor and religious writer who was influenced by Buchman in his early life, thought Buchman's work contributed to the growing appeal of group therapy techniques at that time.[144] The reason for the effectiveness of sharing certainly seems partly to have been psychological. When the Oxford New Testament scholar B. H. Streeter became involved with Buchman's work in the mid-1930s, he found the idea of sharing appealing for this reason. It worked, he thought, not as a preliminary to absolution, but more as a therapeutic act in which the expression of moral conflicts, resentments, or phobias helped to bring about psychological relief.[145] At the same time, Streeter's Oxford contemporary William Brown, a reader in mental philosophy, warned that the practice needed to be handled wisely if it was not to fetter people to one another rather than free them and that OG leaders would benefit from a deeper understanding of analytic psychology.[146]

Another central theme in Buchman's spirituality, which had roots in pietism, college evangelism, and the Keswick movement, was "surrender." People looking for the sources of Buchman's influence sometimes suggested that his own surrender was a key element of it. Van Dusen, for example, thought that the secret of Buchman's spiritual power lay in the "absolutely unqualified gift of himself to his God."[147] Buchman himself clearly believed that he had surrendered his will to God at Keswick in 1908—although it is unlikely that he thought that surrender was a one-off decision that never needed to be repeated. He certainly challenged others to surrender their lives to God. To one student at Hartford who had told Buchman about his personal difficulties in detail, he simply said, "What you need is to surrender your life completely to Jesus Christ."[148] Similarly, he wrote in 1918 to David Yui, general secretary of the Chinese YMCA, suggesting that there were areas of his life that were not fully possessed by God: "I feel you have not surrendered *all* to Christ. There is much of self that will have to go. You are not willing to go all the way."[149] "Shed every secondary allegiance forever," he said elsewhere.[150] Buchman believed that adolescence, in particular the age of sixteen, was a critical time in a person's life and thus a good moment for making a decision.[151] Surrender of self to God, involving a definite decision of the will, came to be greatly stressed in OG and MRA spirituality. Such surrender, it was believed, led not to the deadening of a person's faculties but to an awakening of them—"with the infinite power of God behind them."[152]

In emphasizing the importance of the will, Buchman was echoing points that had often been made by Drummond. Inspired by the English preacher F. W. Robertson, the Scottish writer had suggested that God's purposes were best discerned by means of a form of spiritual apprehension conditional on a fully surrendered will. He also used to say that an entire satisfaction of the intellect in matters of faith was unattainable and therefore that commitment should precede a fuller understanding.[153] Buchman's views were similar. His approach to evangelism involved appealing to people's minds through presenting them with evidence of changed lives and then suggesting a decision of the will. The emphasis was on demonstrating rather than proving the reality of the spiritual life. Buchman also thought that there was a danger in trying to arouse the emotions rather than the will. "Emotion is a fruit and not a root. The thing you want is to reach the will," he said at Kuling. He commended the conversion of

Horace Bushnell in 1831 for Bushnell's refusal to allow himself to be swayed by emotion.[154]

Buchman thought that people who had "changed" needed to embark on trying to change others if they were to consolidate changes in their own lives and remain free from sin. Spiritual victory depended on them channeling their energy in a new and constructive direction. In dealing with sexual sin, for example, Buchman once said that what was most needed was the "expulsive power of a new affection."[155] He told one young man who he thought lacked a sense of focus that avoiding sin was not the goal of life and that he needed to embrace a wider purpose: "What's the fastest you have ever driven a car? If you are moving fast enough, the dirt does not stick. . . . Same with sin. Your heart's got to come alive."[156]

It was at Penn State, then, and in the years soon after, that Buchman developed a sense of the spiritual growth patterns that he thought were typical of people who had found or rediscovered the presence of God in their lives. A journey to spiritual wholeness contained a number of key features or practices: listening to God, the acknowledgement or confession of wrongs, restitution where appropriate, release from oppression, and the rediscovery of spiritual power. In addition, surrender of the will was a condition for getting guidance, as was obedience to God's leading, whenever it came. People who put their faith into action were most likely to retain a vital contact with God. Absolute moral standards and accountability to other believers were also emphasized.[157]

If much of Buchman's spirituality in these earlier years was focused on personal change, mention should also be made of his interest in social issues. Buchman's work in the hospiz in Philadelphia reflected the social dimension of his work, as did the fact that while he was at Penn State some evangelistic outreach was organized in jails and reformatories. He did not always attribute human problems to specifically moral issues. He once said, in relation to his work with the hospiz in Philadelphia, "You're more prone to sin if your stomach isn't full," and some years later he complained to the dean of Hartford that the students there were "insufficiently nourished."[158] In other words, feeding people was important, as well as giving them faith. The ambition of Buchman's thinking was also evident early on. Already in 1915 he was encouraging people to "think in continents."[159] A few years later, in 1921, he defined his aim as "a programme of life issuing in personal, social, racial, national and supernational change."[160] This larger desire to influence national and international life would become increasingly important over time.

2
Guidance

Henry Wright frequently compared prayer to a "triangle," involving God, the Christian worker, and the person being prayed for, and Buchman often used this analogy during his missionary journeys in Asia.[1] The idea seems partly to have been that instead of people praying that God would help their neighbors, they should pray that God would use them to help their neighbors.[2] Buchman also thought that in doing Christian work an evangelist should begin with the God point of the triangle. He was critical of those who, in his mind, started on the horizontal line of the triangle—humans.[3] Post-1945 Buchman also used the triangle metaphor: "Here is a triangle—God, you and the other person. God is at the top. You and the other person are there. If you want to win the other person, God must be at the helm."[4]

This kind of prayer certainly involved intercession, and there is no doubt that Buchman believed in the importance of intercessory prayer. At the same time, he placed greater emphasis on listening to God in silence. For example, he said in Korea in 1918 that people who had set aside an hour for prayer should talk to God for about fifteen minutes and then listen silently to God for the other forty-five minutes.[5] "Listen twice as much as you talk when you pray," he said some decades later.[6] Buchman also once noted the advice of Saint Francis de Sales that half an hour a day of listening to God was a basic minimum, except if a person was very busy, in which case a full hour was necessary.[7] He was obviously not being scientific about the amount of time that ought to have been given to listening; it was simply that it needed to be the priority. The "premier sin," Buchman once said, was "being out of touch with God, not taking time to be holy, not taking time to be good."[8] The kind of prayer that involved attentive listening to God was his preferred way of addressing that problem.

In the OG and MRA people were encouraged, even expected, to have regular morning quiet times, and the thoughts that arose in these quiet times were usually given the shorthand name of "guidance." Frequently people sat in bed or in a chair for their quiet times, often with a cup of tea or coffee. Sometimes in his early years, Buchman himself seems to have remained lying down during these times of silence—possibly because he wanted to avoid waking roommates who might then interrupt his quiet time.[9] Buchman also advised people to write down their thoughts, on the grounds that if they did not they would soon forget the ideas that had come up. "The strongest memory is weaker than the palest ink" was a Chinese proverb that he later used to emphasize the point.[10] The notebooks in which people jotted down their thoughts came to be called "guidance books" in the OG and MRA.

Buchman once attributed the power that informed his work to his quiet times.[11] For this reason it is important to try to piece together how they functioned and how he believed the Holy Spirit manifested himself to him. From some comments he made in 1918, it seems that he usually started a quiet time by concentrating his thoughts on God. He would then ask God whether there was anything in his life that prevented him from experiencing God's presence and search his mind on what he would have him do that day. He would then wait for inspiration.[12] There was an element of spiritual planning here. Reading the Bible played an important part in this. Buchman thought that God could lead him to the specific Bible verses that would be helpful for each day. "The Holy Spirit brings to your mind the Bible verse that is to be your guide for that day," he said at Kuling, adding that it might be a "series of verses."[13] Buchman seems to have read the Bible daily, for he once said that to leave the house in the morning without having read the Bible was like not being properly dressed or shaved.[14]

In the first quiet time Buchman had after his conversation with F. B. Meyer in 1912, the thought that came to him was "Tutz, Tutz, Tutz." Tutz was the name of a student on the Penn State campus who was supposedly keen on saying his prayers while at the same time regularly getting drunk. Buchman felt what he called an "insistent urge" that it was the right time to talk to him about his faith. He approached him and then recommended a third person whom, he thought, he could helpfully consult about his spiritual life. This was a regular occurrence with Buchman. He often tried to connect people with those who he thought were in the best position to help them. Indeed, he had a considerable reputation for his gifts in doing this.[15] The upshot with Tutz, according to Buchman, was that he gave his life to Christ.[16]

The nature of Buchman's guidance about Tutz was to be replicated elsewhere. Buchman's notebooks indicate that he often sensed a phrase or name

Fig. 2 Buchman, guidance book in hand, 1935. Photo: Arthur Strong, Oxford Group Archives.

coming repeatedly into his mind. The words often appeared in threes. His diary of 1921–22, for example, contained phrases like "beware, beware, beware" or "stop, stop, stop."[17] His guidance for Paul Campbell, a Canadian doctor who attended an MRA conference in Richmond, Virginia, in 1942, was "stay, stay, stay." Buchman meant by this that Campbell should stay and work with him. Campbell's own guidance, which was initially different, came round to coinciding with Buchman's, and he set aside his medical career for MRA work.[18]

Buchman sometimes described specific thoughts of this kind as "luminous thoughts"—a phrase that may have originated with Wright.[19] For example, he talked of luminous thoughts in the first preparatory session for the Kuling conference in 1918: "What does it mean to listen to God? It means an unhurried time when God really can have a chance to implant His thoughts in your mind. For me personally at five o-clock or an earlier hour, I am awake and conscious of the presence of God. Some days it is simply a series of luminous thoughts of things God wants me to do that day. Some days it is just a sense of peace and rest and one or two outstanding things. Other days it is a sense of need for intercession on behalf of certain people. . . . It takes all the fret, strain and worry out of life. . . . [God] implants and rivets with luminous thoughts that which [H]e would bring to you."[20] Buchman used a variety of images to try to capture the nature of these luminous thoughts over the years. He referred, for example, to the "arresting tick" of God's guidance and to people being "prompted" by the Spirit; he also used the term "hunches."[21] Likewise, he once talked of how the Holy Spirit "prints" thoughts in the mind.[22] In the 1950s he talked about guidance as "something that descends," referred to the "quiet, modulated voice" of God, and spoke of the Holy Spirit "just dropping his truth."[23]

There was no sense that Buchman's luminous thoughts came in the form of audible voices. It seems that there was a real, but somewhat elusive, quality to them. At Kuling Buchman cited some lines from New England Romantic poet James Russell Lowell's poem "The Cathedral" to try to capture this: "A grace of being . . . / That beckons and is gone."[24] Perhaps at times his guidance was little more than becoming aware of something. For example, again at Kuling, he referred to an occasion when he "became conscious" that a certain person was in need.[25] He also believed that the thoughts that came in guidance often looked ordinary. In a radio broadcast of 1936, he said, "God can put thoughts into your mind. Have you ever listened for them? They may look like ordinary thoughts. But be honest about them. You might get a new picture of yourself."[26] Sometimes the thoughts seem to have involved a kind of illumination. This was illustrated by the way in which Buchman understood conviction of sin. "If there has been some sin, the Holy Spirit just flashes a light on it, making it loom up in all its blackness," was how one of his listeners reported his message in 1918.[27]

Buchman's suggestion that the Holy Spirit could "flash" a light on a problem was replicated in one of his descriptions of his encounter with Bill Pickle at Penn State. "The thought flashed into my mind: 'Give him your deepest message,'" Buchman recalled about his first meeting with the bootlegger. "Bill, we've been praying for you," he then said to him.[28] Such flashes could be one way of explaining the many stories concerning Buchman, which both he and others recounted, that involved him appearing to see into situations in an almost telepathic way. For example, recounting the way in which he had helped a young soldier get out of some moral difficulty in the early 1920s, Buchman said, "I knew I had to see this man. I knew, too, directly I saw him what his trouble was. . . . I helped him by telling him what his trouble was."[29] The directness was characteristic. Buchman evidently thought that it was sometimes necessary to state very specifically what he believed a person's problem was. A meeting he had in 1957 with an American actor, Anne Buckles, contained a similar combination of insight and directness. Buckles, who was then on the point of divorce but had told no one about it, came to see Buchman and was met with the unprompted comment, "Divorce is old-fashioned."[30] Buchman perhaps thought that the actor was more likely to be troubled by a suggestion that her thinking was unfashionable than that divorce was morally wrong.

The use of the adjective "luminous" to describe the Holy Spirit's promptings indicates that Buchman sometimes associated the leading of the Holy Spirit with light. The idea that the Holy Spirit flashed a light onto a person's sins reflected the same idea. This association of God's wisdom with light was also evident in Buchman's description of another of his experiences. When his mother died in May 1925, Buchman was traveling on a night train in India. He claimed that God had forewarned him of her passing at the exact time of death, and a day before he in fact heard the news. "At the moment of death, the carriage suddenly seemed lit up, as bright as day," he said.[31] Buchman continued to use metaphors associating God's guidance with light in subsequent years. For example, he used to liken God's wisdom to electric light. He met Thomas Edison, inventor of the lightbulb, in 1924, after Edison's nephew had become involved in the OG at Princeton; references to Edison, and the way in which God's guidance was comparable to electric light, appeared in some of his later speeches.[32]

Buchman's experience in the train at the time of his mother's death seems to have been unexpected, and certainly many of Buchman's thoughts were unpredicted. Ray Purdy was struck by one such incident in 1919 when Buchman suddenly left a student camp meeting, stating that somebody nearby was unwell. It turned out that there was a student with acute appendicitis who needed to be taken to hospital. But even when these promptings were unexpected they often made sense to Buchman in the context of what he was doing. According to another story recounted by Purdy, Buchman was once traveling on a train from New York to Boston when he had a compelling thought to return to New York to talk with an anxious student with whom he had been talking about moral problems. He arrived just in time to prevent the young man from committing suicide. The thought to return to New York evidently did not come out of nowhere but arose in the context of his concern for the young man.[33]

Buchman's thoughts sometimes made sense to him in the context of the international situation, and in this sense his guidance can be interpreted as a kind of response to the issues and culture of his time. Riding a bicycle in Cambridge in May 1921, he had the dramatic thought that God would use him to play a part in changing the world. "You will be used to remake the world" was the phrase that came to him, according to traditional MRA accounts. The idea kept returning to him, and he concluded that it came from God. Yet what at first glance might have seemed like an unexpected thought, when examined more closely was perhaps less out of the ordinary. First, the rebuilding of broken societies was a major public concern after World War I. Second, Buchman was himself preoccupied by the world's needs at that time. Third, this kind of phraseology was being widely used in Christian circles. For example, the evangelist Billy Sunday—with whom Buchman had worked in New York in 1917—had talked a couple of years before of the task of "rebuilding the world" according to Christian ideas.[34] Finally, the sense that God had a major task for Buchman to do was in keeping with thoughts he had previously. For example, he wrote on the flyleaves of his Bible in May 1918 that God was commissioning him for "special" and "mighty and far-reaching" work.[35]

Later, in 1938, Buchman's decision to use the term "moral re-armament" to describe his work came after a somewhat similar process. In the late 1930s Buchman was trying to express the idea that Europe's greatest need was for moral and spiritual renewal. In this he was like other religious leaders. For example, in his encyclical *Atheistic Communism* (1937) Pope Pius XI talked of the "anxious appeal to moral and spiritual forces" that was taking place in the world, suggesting that the world's evils were primarily spiritual in origin.[36] According to Garth Lean, Buchman got the "re-armament" image itself from a Swedish socialist author with links to the OG, Harry Blomberg. Blomberg, reflecting on the Europe-wide arms buildup, had come up with a theme for a Group publication that included the phrase "We must re-arm morally."[37] The phrase resonated with Buchman and kept returning to him in a vivid way, particularly during a walk in the Black Forest outside the German town of Freudenstadt in May 1938. "Moral and spiritual re-armament. The next great movement in the world will be a movement of moral re-armament for all nations" was the guidance he dictated to a friend who was with him at the time.[38] Here, as in other episodes, it was the clear and recurring nature of the thought, and its apparent relevance to the world's needs, that seems to have persuaded Buchman that he was receiving a message from God.

Buchman's experiences clearly led him to believe that guidance could be very accurate. One metaphor that illustrated this was that of picking up radio signals. He said in the late 1920s that the word "pray" (P-R-A-Y) could be turned into the acrostic "Powerful Radiograms Always Yours"—although some questioned whether this was in good taste.[39] Likewise, in a speech in Kronborg Castle, Denmark, in 1935, he suggested that anybody could pick up divine messages if his or her "receiving set" was in order. "Definite, accurate, adequate information" could come from the mind of God to the minds of humans, he told the crowd.[40] Buchman expected people to seek guidance in planning for occasions, often in regard to very specific issues. The Holy Spirit was "intelligent enough" to tell people how many they should cater for, he said to a group of people preparing a conference in the Netherlands in 1937.[41] He also thought that guidance could bring untapped resources into play. In a speech in 1955 he talked of listening to God in terms of electricity: "Take the Electronics of the Spirit. It works with Infinite Mind. It circles the globe instantly. It taps resources hitherto unexplored and forces hitherto unknown. . . . The thought that slips in any time, day or night, can be the thought of the Author of mind."[42]

Buchman was clearly eager to try to explain guidance with images that resonated with contemporary culture. In general, he wanted to try to normalize guidance in people's minds. He once said of it, "It needs to be taken out of the unusual and to be practically applied as a constant."[43] Getting guidance from God, he said in 1935, was "normal prayer."[44] Buchman's linkage of the word "normal" with the leading of the Holy Spirit was reflected elsewhere. He said in the 1950s that faith kept people "normal and guided" and that the "still, small voice" would give people the "normalcy" they needed.[45] He also sometimes used the phrase "normal living" to describe life under God.[46] Although he did not express this in theoretical terms, there were anthropological implications here. Buchman seems to have taken the view that only the God-oriented person was human in the fullest sense. If the idea of living by God's guidance was "normal" in Buchman's mind, it was also natural and unstrained, even when involving grander schemes. "You'll change the world by a plan I'll show you. It will be simple, complete, natural," he wrote in his guidance book in Geneva, in late 1938.[47] Asked in 1960 what advice he would give to a young politician at the start of his career, he replied, "Live the life, listen to God, and be natural."[48]

Not only was listening to God normal, it was also open to all, Buchman stressed. Writing in 1920 to Sam Shoemaker, a Princeton graduate and later Episcopalian priest who worked with him in the interwar period—and who played a central role in passing OG ideas into AA—Buchman said that there was a biblical sanction for this in the books of Ezekiel and Acts and that even very new Christians—"babes in Christ"—could have the experience of being led by God. "Someone once compared the Bible to a lake, in which lambs could walk and an elephant could swim. The same analogy holds in hunches," he suggested. He also emphasized that it was not a matter of temperament but more one of coming to God with the right attitude: "It is a matter of simple faith. It is much more willingness to become as little children. It is given to all alike if they will accept it in a childlike spirit."[49]

Buchman's concept of normality clearly incorporated openness to the supernatural side of religion. He believed in a "supernatural God" who could communicate with people directly.[50] He sometimes even referred to the practice of guidance in terms that suggested that a person listening to God was simply a scribe who just had to record what God was saying. Speaking at an MRA assembly at Riverside, California, in 1948, Buchman said that the conference had been planned in guidance and that a phrase he had used in a world broadcast at the conference had come to him during a quiet time: "Take the broadcast. Simple waiting for guidance. God gave me that sentence 'unity is the grace of rebirth.' All I did was to write it down." The meaning of the phrase, it seems, was that unity between people was an outcome of them going through a process of change at a more personal level.[51]

The linkage of guidance with the fostering of unity was reflected elsewhere. Buchman thought that the Holy Spirit could give different people the same direction and thus help to overcome their divisions. At a Mackinac conference in 1944, he asked a person who was resisting a certain course of action, "Suppose [God would] tell us all the same thing?" The other man apparently doubted that Buchman's guidance would tally with his own, but in fact it did—the two of them had the same thoughts on the matter in question. It was, according to Buchman, a testimony to the unifying power of guidance. "God works at both ends of the line," he declared.[52] This was of course a key element in Buchman's whole philosophy: God's purposes for people would unite rather than divide them, if they unconditionally surrendered themselves to his will.

Buchman also believed that guidance was often morally challenging. He told this same Mackinac audience that God often did not speak to people in prayerful language because their minds were not "keyed" to that sort of response. His wisdom, instead, was often conveyed in the form of "pretty blunt truth." "[God] sometimes tells me I am a fool in no uncertain terms," he said. In addition, he tried to emphasize what he saw as the dynamism of the Holy Spirit. He had, he reported, an "overmastering passion" to spend an hour with those attending the conference, stating that this thought had been "so compelling, so real [and] so dynamic." He also suggested that such a passion could become the dominant life and thought of everyone at the gathering and then come to dominate the life of America and Canada.[53]

A few years later, again trying to give expression to the strength of the Holy Spirit, Buchman declared that the Holy Spirit was the "most powerful force" in the world, stronger even than the destructive forces associated with the atomic bomb: "Man can split the atom. The Holy Spirit is uniting humanity through men who listen to him and obey."[54] It was with the power of the Holy Spirit in mind that Buchman regularly said that the thoughts people had in their quiet times could have great significance. He said in Caux in 1946 that anyone might be given a sentence from God that could change the thinking of the world. "The average Christian has to turn the tide of the thinking of the world—that is our privilege," he said.[55] It was an idea that was regularly stressed in MRA culture.

Some observers thought that guidance was given an exaggerated and overly supernatural emphasis in the OG and MRA. In Britain in the 1930s the most vociferous of the critics was the bishop of Durham, Herbert Hensley Henson. In his attack on the OG, *The Group Movement* (1933), Henson argued that although the leading of the Holy Spirit was a central feature of Christianity, the OG placed too much emphasis on it, overstressing the importance of intuition and luminous thoughts at the expense of reason.[56] Similarly, writing a year later in the *Atlantic Monthly*, Henry Van Dusen warned that the way guidance was practiced in the OG could undermine people's capability of making their own decisions. God did not intend people to be "robots," he said, but to develop what he called "self-achieved discretion" in "divine undertakings." Buchman's approach to the subject, he suggested, was a departure from the prevailing "catholic Protestant conservatism" of the time.[57]

Some thought that a more careful presentation of the subject was needed. The prominent Scottish theologian, D. S. Cairns, an admirer of Buchman's work—he had been particularly impressed with his outreach at Penn State—thought that the business culture of the United States had influenced the OG too much. He wrote to Buchman in 1929 suggesting that the quiet time was too often presented on American business lines; God was being depicted as a man who rang up to pass on his instructions to his colleagues, whereas Christ wanted his followers to be friends, not servants.[58]

The way Buchman himself talked about quiet times may at times have helped to create the sort of image of guidance that Cairns so disliked. After all, Buchman thought that people really could get instructions from God about practical issues. In reality, however, his conception of how God communicated with people was not as mechanistic as it might first have appeared. For one thing, luminous thoughts were only one element in what he understood as guidance. He told Shoemaker, "I do not for one moment limit God's direction simply to these luminous thoughts."[59] He certainly did not dismiss the importance of reason. The Oxford college chaplain Geoffrey Allen, who was involved in the OG in the early 1930s, observed in his OG-influenced *He That Cometh* (1932) that in the fully surrendered life what was right and what was reasonable coincided. That was Buchman's view, for he himself once said that although faith transcended reason, it was not "unreasonable."[60] He insisted that people used their minds. "Let us have a hundred suggestions before we have a quiet time," he said in the Netherlands in 1937.[61] Buchman also thought that it was sometimes necessary to have a broad vision of the world prior to receiving guidance. Guidance, he wrote to one colleague in 1939, came from having "an adequate conception and vision of a world need."[62]

If Buchman thought that an adequate level of thinking was necessary before people could get guidance, he also saw the process working in reverse; contact with God could help people to use their minds in a deeper or more effective way. In the late 1940s, when MRA was trying to foster good industrial relations in the British coalfields, he suggested that contact with God would help people appreciate more the importance of coal: "How many people depend on coal from England? Well, now think. Some of you don't think. The Holy Spirit will teach you to think."[63] Buchman also once said that during a time of guidance God used a person's "higher thought life."[64] Buchman would have concurred with the view of one of his supporters that guidance was a form of "consecrated common sense."[65] Indeed, he once called MRA a "hurricane of common sense" sweeping through the world, suggesting that the "still small Voice of the living God" could be found in the midst of the hurricane.[66]

Buchman also linked guidance to a certain kind of creativity of thought. This view was particularly evident in some of his speeches of 1938, when he was anxious to try to find solutions to the deteriorating international situation. At the launch of MRA he declared, "We have not yet tapped the great creative sources in the Mind of God."[67] A few months later, he suggested guidance could become the "daily source of all our creative thinking and living."[68] In fact Buchman's quiet times, and the sharing sessions that followed them, often seem to have functioned as forums for creative thinking and brain storming. When people approached Buchman for advice, Buchman would often suggest a joint quiet time and then ask them to share their thoughts. "What thoughts did you have?" he asked some young men from Finland who were exploring with him how to make use of an MRA play at the time of the Finnish Olympics in 1952. The quiet time they then had produced the idea that the play could be put on outside Finland, and it led to the use of the play in Eindhoven and collaboration with Frederik ("Frits") Philips, the Dutch businessman who was involved with MRA.[69] The thought that he had in a quiet time with the Norwegian businessman Abram Vereide, whom he met in a hotel in Ottawa in 1934 and who went on to start the Prayer Breakfast in the United States, was simply, "Christianize what you have. You have something to share." It was obviously not a dramatic thought, but it apparently helped to focus the young Norwegian's sense of calling.[70]

An obvious danger in the idea of guidance was that, wrongly applied, the practice could lead to an unhealthy form of passivity, in which listeners subconsciously substituted their own desires for what God wanted them to do. It was a point raised by Charles Raven, the Cambridge Regius professor of divinity, in an essay on the OG in 1934.[71] It was in addressing this kind of problem that Buchman once said that guidance came best in "activity, not passivity," noting that in the latter case the mind had a "childlike deceptiveness."[72] He also once said, in a speech of 1938, that he gave his mind to "disciplined direction."[73] This reinforces the sense that Buchman's own mind was at work in his quiet times and that he did not wait passively for the Holy Spirit to speak. There was almost certainly an element of intercession or supplication here: Buchman brought his concerns to God and then left space within a prayerful atmosphere for creative thinking to emerge.

Listening to God for Buchman also sometimes involved a quest for guided thinking, rather than the production of clearly definable "thoughts." Reflecting in December 1936 on the abdication crisis in Britain, Buchman wrote to Lean, expressing a regret that the prime minister, Stanley Baldwin, had failed to help Edward VIII in his spiritual life. He evidently believed that with greater wisdom he could have helped the young king at some deeper level. He concluded his remarks to Lean by saying, "I am just writing to you as the spirit moves without, in any sense, feeling that it is a finished product, but sharing my mind with you."[74] Buchman's guidance also sometimes prompted him to seek out the opinions of others about common tasks. For example, he once wrote to John Roots, a son of Logan Roots who became a full-time worker with the OG and MRA: "It came to me in my early guidance, 'Get these letters off for John's perusal and reflection.'"[75]

Buchman also did not attribute everything he did to guidance. Dining with the journalist A. J. Russell, author of *For Sinners Only* (1932)—the most popular book on the OG in the 1930s—Buchman observed that the second helping of food that he had just taken was not specifically guided: "I don't pretend that every detail of my life is guided. For instance, I did not have guidance to take that asparagus. I was hungry, and I like asparagus. But if I am alert for guidance, it comes whenever I need it. And so it does to anybody."[76] It also seems that Buchman had lots of thoughts that never had a significant outcome. Van Dusen reported that he had heard Buchman claim twenty to twenty-five instances of guidance during a day, only a fourth or a fifth of which came to pass.[77] Buchman himself acknowledged that sometimes his guidance did not exactly work out, even while insisting that it often did.[78]

Many of Buchman's thoughts reflected a need he evidently felt for spiritual reassurance. For example, his guidance books often contained observations or commands of a general nature, such as "All is well!" or "Have no fear."[79] "A very great day" was sometimes his guidance in the evening.[80] At times, he was unsure about what he should be doing. "I wish I knew what I ought to do," he wrote during a quiet time in the late 1930s.[81] In early 1940 he was depressed about the future of MRA and where God wanted him to go. "I feel as if I were in a thick forest," he said.[82] Some years later he said that he could not get guidance as to how to reply to a letter from the French foreign minister, Robert Schuman. "What do I say to [S]chuman[?]. . . . Have you any thoughts?" he asked his friends.[83] Sometimes Buchman's quiet times did not produce any thoughts at all. "I didn't get a thing," he said following a quiet time at one conference.[84] "Buchman's reality was that he wasn't always orientated," recalled Oliver Corderoy, an aide to Buchman in the late 1940s. Yet these occasions seem to have been rare. Lean recalled that he met Buchman in an anxious state only once in thirty years.[85]

The fact that Buchman did not think that quiet times could take place in an intellectual vacuum, or that guidance was always unexpected or dramatic, is confirmed by the wider OG and MRA culture. A contributor to a group newsletter of 1938, for example, stressed that guidance did not relieve people of the responsibility of thinking things through; it was not "mechanical" but came through "Reason, Evidence, Luminous Thinking." Interestingly, the author of the article also observed that "very clear leadings [came] seldom to most people." He also said that guidance was not so much a search for "information" as "illumination."[86] It was a point made by a number of thinkers influential in the OG. For example, Henry Drummond once wrote that God's light did not supersede, but illuminated, men's thoughts.[87] Likewise, in his Warburton lectures, *The God Who Speaks* (1936), B. H. Streeter observed that God's wisdom came as an "enhancement" of a person's natural insights and intelligence. In his view the right functioning of reason depended on the attainment of a higher wisdom, and without the aid of religion, as expressed in quiet times, reason easily became shackled to unhealthy, subconscious desires.[88]

All this suggests that Buchman may have understood guidance partly to mean a heightened form of thinking in which the Spirit of God was present. If that is true, his approach was not unique in the history of spirituality. For example, it had something in common with the Jesuit approach to the discernment of God's will. Significantly, the Jesuit chaplain at Basel University in the 1950s, Father Trösch, suggested that MRA and Ignatian traditions of guidance were similar—although he also expressed a concern that "less advanced" members of MRA might interpret guidance in an unreasonable way.[89]

Buchman did not confine his quest for God's leading to those moments in which he was having quiet times. The evidence suggests that from early on in his life he was constantly seeking God's wisdom. He told Shoemaker in 1920 that he had gone away on a retreat to have "a fresh Holy Ghost power and to live more constantly under His influence." He also suggested that the gift in diagnosing people's problems that Shoemaker saw in him came from the Spirit's guidance—which he also called "God consciousness."[90] It is likely that God consciousness meant for him just that: being conscious of God and that he tried to be conscious of God all the time.[91] Almost certainly Buchman carried this quest to align himself with the Holy Spirit into much of his public activity. A Swedish reporter, observing him in 1938, suggested that he often appeared to be "questing, at a loss, not to say helpless."[92] In later years, when he attended receptions and public occasions, it seems he would wait for guidance as to what to do, sometimes giving the impression of being a little lost before moving forward to meet people.[93]

The same sense of continuous questing was present in Buchman's approach to meetings. He said at Kuling, for example, that it was necessary to be listening to God's leading in a spirit of abandonment: "I go into an hour like this with an utter sense of abandon. I am not disturbed if one speaks, or no one, or if there are pauses. Shall we be here under the Spirit's guidance, with a sense of abandon that comes when you feel under the control of the Holy Spirit?"[94] This desire to create a quiet atmosphere, where people would share only as led by the Holy Spirit, was replicated on a larger scale at the conferences at Caux and Mackinac. Buchman declared at a meeting in Caux in 1946, "This is an opportunity to share everything that you are moved by God's Holy Spirit to share." Conversely, at a meeting a year later, he told those assembled, "Don't you speak until you are led [by] the Holy Spirit."[95]

The idea that Buchman was constantly trying to listen to God is reinforced by Signe Strong's recollections. Strong—who described Buchman's contact with God as "communing with the Spirit"—recalled that Buchman was often awake during the night, apparently praying or listening to God in some way. "You have no idea what goes on during those hours," Buchman once said, after one such night.[96] He also said, in a speech in 1955, that he regularly had guidance "most of the night."[97] "Watching and waiting for the living God to break through the shadows of the night" was how he once described the process.[98] Sometimes during the night he asked his aides to take down the guidance he thought that he had received.

It seems, then, that Buchman's actual experience of quiet times did not reflect the somewhat mechanistic picture of guidance that he sometimes conveyed. Some interwar-era observers thought that OG theology was dualistic in the sense that it seemed to imply a God who was external to the natural order and who sent thoughts into people's minds from outside. Noting this, Keene argued that although there was a dualism of this kind in some early OG texts, OG spirituality also contained a current of thinking in which both the transcendence and immanence of God were implied and that this became more strongly emphasized during the middle of the 1930s.[99] Buchman's actual experience of guidance, and the fact that he received "luminous thoughts" in the context of a larger background of regular prayer, suggests that for him God was both transcendent and immanent. His underlying message was perhaps similar to that of such American contemporaries as the Quaker writer Thomas Kelly and the missionary Frank Laubach, whose writings emphasized the possibility of a more permanent communion with God.[100] In this context, his more dramatic explanations of guidance, and use of metaphors like the radio to describe it, should be read as sound bites designed to draw people into experimenting with guidance, rather than as reflecting the full range of his thinking or experience.

In some ways Buchman's concept of what the quiet time should entail evolved. If the guidance of his early years was generally focused on the needs of individuals, his later quiet times were taken up with social and political issues. Yet the change of focus should not be overemphasized. His ambition to bring the guidance of God to bear on national questions was in fact already evident in China in 1918. Early that year he and some Hartford colleagues formulated a plan to bring together the fifteen most influential Christians in Peking and train them in the practicalities of Christian work. Among these Chinese leaders Buchman made particular friends with the vice-minister of justice and later acting prime minister, Hsu Ch'ien. Hsu subsequently became chief secretary to the nationalist leader, Sun Yat-sen, and through his connection with Hsu, Buchman was himself able to meet Sun, twice, in February 1918.

In preparation for one of his meetings with these men, Buchman wrote down some thoughts that were indicative of his belief that God could give him specific guidance about what to say to people and the wider political relevance of what he was doing. The thoughts related to both Hsu's possible future in Chinese life, as well as to Sun's recent divorce and remarriage to his concubine, Ching-ling Soong: "Mr Hsu will be like Lincoln. He will occupy high position, but always do the right. . . . Dr. Sun will be an ally. I will save him from the sin of self-sufficiency. I will make him a great liberator of China. He will do away with his wives. Tell him." In the same note Buchman also wrote down a Bible verse on the saving power of the cross, John 12:32, in relation to the power of Christ to help China: "You are learning the secret of saving China. 'I, if I be lifted up, will draw all men to me.' Yes, even China."[101]

Buchman's optimism about the future of China was, of course, not borne out. But the kind of guidance he had here was replicated in his quiet times in later years. It was, for example, visible in some of his thinking about Europe after World War II. In June 1951, just before the summer conferences at Caux, he had guidance that God would use him "mightily" and envisaged a "mighty movement of God's Holy Spirit." He also sensed God saying to him, "The statesmen will come to you. Adenauer, Schuman, Kraft, the President of Switzerland, Marazza, de Gasperi. You will have a gathering [at Caux] where they can guidedly find the answer to Europe."[102] It did not exactly work out that way: for example, the German chancellor, Konrad Adenauer, came to Caux in 1948 but did not come again; French foreign minister Robert Schuman came only in 1953; and Alcide de Gasperi, Italian prime minister 1945–53, never came to Caux.[103] Nevertheless, it reflected Buchman's sense of expectation about how God might use the MRA work, and Buchman's touches with the leadership of Europe were indeed impressive.

The same kind of thinking was evident eighteen months later, during an MRA campaign in India in 1952–53. Buchman thought God had a specific role for MRA in India at this time and also that he had received guidance on what strategy to adopt and how to reach the prime minister Pandit Nehru—whom he had first met on a visit to India in 1924: "I will lead you forth in Delhi as I led you years ago, and I will work through you mightily. . . . [Nehru] will commit to you his strong right arm. . . . Build up constructive personalities who can handle the situation everywhere."[104] Here, as Lean notes, there was little direct correlation between Buchman's guidance about Nehru and what actually happened to him, although Nehru did come to see Buchman at Jaipur House in early January 1953.[105]

Buchman's thoughts about China, Europe, and India, and more specifically about the leadership of these countries, suggest that his guidance was sometimes more about developing a vision for what he thought could happen under God than an exact science. He was clearly not worried if his thoughts were not exactly borne out in reality. His quiet times here seem to have functioned as a forum for his own creative thinking. They also seem to have given him encouragement in his endeavors. Buchman's main wartime aide, the Scotsman Michael Barrett, suggested that the underlying role of Buchman's guidance in these situations was to provide a sense of God's "assurance" and that his thoughts also reflected a sense of optimism about what God could do.[106]

The presence in Buchman's guidance of thoughts that were both ordinary and far-reaching in their implications, as well as words of spiritual reassurance, was replicated in the guidance of some of Buchman's supporters. For example, the guidance books of H. Alexander Smith, a supporter of Buchman who was a Republican senator from 1944 to 1959 and earlier a lecturer in the Department of Politics at Princeton, contained similar characteristics. The historian William Inboden relates that Smith's guidance was often made up of to-do lists of forthcoming activities or phrases such as, "I need the guidance and inspiration of God in the coming days." But in September 1949, while preparing for a trip to the Far East at a time when the independence of Formosa (Taiwan) from China was becoming an option, Smith wrote, "It comes to me to . . . find out about Formosa and perhaps go there. This will be a thrilling guided trip. God grant that we may save Asia for Christianity. It is a wonderful challenge—the Western tradition and our spiritual heritage. . . . Have no fear or hesitation that God will guide this trip step by step."[107] As with Buchman's quiet times, Smith's guidance involved a sense of being led into particular national or regional situation and finding reassurance that God would be with him. It points to the fact that Buchman's linkage of spirituality and politics, by means of the quiet time, had become a wider feature of MRA practice.

The concept of guidance was clearly a kind of umbrella term. It was used to refer to a number of different practices. This was reflected in one widely used FCCF pamphlet that suggested that guidance came through the Holy Spirit by a variety of means: the scriptures, conscience, luminous thoughts, cultivating the mind of Christ, Bible reading and prayer, circumstances, reason, and church groups, or fellowship.[108] Even the term "luminous thoughts" was an umbrella term for different kinds of experience. Keene, in particular, tried to express this. He grouped the thoughts that people had in their quiet times under four headings: the "moral type" of guidance, which involved a person having a conviction of sin and then making restitution for it; the "telepathic type," which occurred when people had "thoughts" that came unexpectedly; the "right thing type," which involved a person finding the right thing to say or do to help another person; and the "personal type," which occurred when someone had a personalized sense of direction about their lives that involved something that was not itself ethically right or wrong.[109] Buchman clearly had guidance that fitted all these categories. But a fifth category should be added. Increasingly, Buchman's quiet times, and indeed those of his supporters, were taken up with attempts to get guidance or creative thinking for nations or national situations as well as individuals.

The reference to "conscience" in the FCCF pamphlet was indicative of another side to OG and MRA teaching on the discernment of God's will. The metaphors that Buchman used to explain guidance were an indication of the way he was always trying to reexpress the practice in terms that people could relate to. In this context, the term "conscience" had merit not only because it was widely used in religious circles but also because it could be used to appeal to nonbelievers or agnostics who were nervous about the idea of listening to God. If having a quiet time meant listening to one's conscience, then anybody could try it, even if they were not sure that God was there at all. There were some theological challenges here. Streeter, for example, thought that although guidance and conscience were different, they were still related and shaded off into each other.[110] This was almost certainly Buchman's view too. Using the term conscience as a substitute for guidance, however, could allow people with a more secular mindset to explain the movement in a nonreligious way, which often happened in the decades after Buchman's death. This meant that the distinction between the religious and secular aspects of the OG and MRA message was sometimes blurred. Indeed, as with AA, it was not always easy to determine exactly whether MRA was a religious or a secular organization.[111]

If OG and MRA literature was full of stories of how people, in following what they saw as guidance, came to make creative and apparently positive decisions in their lives, there were others who, after trying out the practice, concluded that they had misinterpreted God's leading in this area.[112] Popular guidance manuals, such as Meyer's *Secret of Guidance*, mentioned the pitfalls as well as the possibilities. Buchman knew that there were dangers. For example, he told Shoemaker that there were six tests of whether a person's guidance was genuinely from God or not: whether or not a person was unconditionally willing to obey God; the indication of circumstances; whether guidance was in keeping with absolute moral standards; the teachings of scripture; the advice of friends who were also seeking guidance; and the teachings of the church.[113] He often referred, in different ways, to the point about the need for people to be willing to obey God. In 1936 he said that one of the rules of listening to God was that people should listen honestly to whatever thoughts arose.[114] A couple of years later he contrasted the idea of listening to God with what he called the "egocentric way" in which people talked without listening.[115]

Conscious of the fact that thoughts from God could easily be misinterpreted, Buchman sometimes questioned people's guidance in very direct ways. For example, responding to a woman who approached him to say that she had guidance to get married, he said abruptly, "Stop having guidance."[116] Sometimes it was necessary to wait before following God's leading, he also thought. Using a maritime analogy, he once said that just as a ship, on leaving harbor, had to wait for the removal not just of one but of two warning signals before embarkation, so it was also necessary to wait for a second prompting before taking action.[117]

On significant matters, guidance needed to be "checked" with others before decisions were made. Writing to Shoemaker in 1924, proposing that he join him on a round-the-world trip rather than go on a high-profile speaking tour with Sherwood Eddy and the peace activist Kirby Page, Buchman said, "You need the drab, not the dramatic. . . . I can only say this—that if you are led to go [with Eddy] and your convictions differ with mine after you have checked with everyone . . . go, and God abundantly bless you." But he was convinced that Shoemaker should not join Eddy's venture, and he also shared this in a forceful way: "My guidance lately has been, 'Be firm with Sam.' NO! NO! NO! with Eddy and Page."[118] Shoemaker decided to go with Buchman and remained closely associated with him until 1941. The episode was an indication of Buchman's confidence in his own judgment about what was genuine spiritual inspiration or not, as well as his stress on the practice of checking guidance.

The need to check guidance would become greater as the work expanded, Buchman thought. "More and more as the Fellowship grows and the diverse people coming in with variant backgrounds we need to check all the more carefully [sic]," he wrote to Purdy in 1930.[119] He was suspicious of people who believed they could discern God's guidance outside of accountability to others. Individualism needed to be countered. This was probably what he meant when he said, in July 1939, that people should get what he called a "group mind" in their communities, states, and nations—adding that MRA itself was a "group mind."[120] This stance was sometimes a cause for tension. As Jarlert notes, there was a difference between people simply applying OG principles in their personal lives and living in full fellowship with Buchman's international team. Buchman could clash with people who he felt were just doing the former, without submitting to OG discipline.[121]

For Buchman, then, accountability to the team was an essential check on the kind of guidance that was little more than wishful thinking. If the lines of accountability were too strong, however, this could also raise problems.[122] The Oxford professor of the philosophy of the Christian religion, L. W. Grensted, who was involved with OG in the early 1930s, wrote to Buchman in 1936 expressing concern about the "dangers of team pressure" in the movement, with particular reference to the way in which guidance could be misused.[123] One full-time worker, Ailsa Hamilton, looking back on MRA in the 1950s, noted that the culture of transparency and openness sometimes led to pressure on young people from elders who were keen to control the movement and that this forced on them a choice between "conformity or rebellion."[124] As with all religious movements, it was not always easy for people to distinguish what might be thought of as genuine spiritual inspiration from the ideas of the wider team.

Buchman himself was seeking after a kind of leadership that was rooted in the authority of the Holy Spirit. Wright believed that "consecrated leadership" was not the same thing as command. In his view, leadership that was commissioned by the Holy Spirit was different in character from that of ordinary human diktat.[125] Buchman also took that view. Although clearly the main source of authority in the OG and MRA, he was uncomfortable with the idea that he was the leader in any formal sense. As he understood it, authority came not from him but from God. "It is God who leads, not I," he used to say.[126] This obviously did not mean that he was not ready to be assertive. Indeed, although his style of leadership was often surprisingly unobtrusive—for example, he often remained in the background while other people led meetings—there is no doubt that he was ready to give and exercise leadership when he thought that the Holy Spirit was behind his actions. For example, he took charge of leading one meeting in Caux in 1947, setting aside someone else's suggestions as to who should speak on the grounds that they did not come from the Holy Spirit.[127] He was clearly ready to back his own judgment in this kind of situation.

Critics thought that only an exaggerated respect for Buchman in the OG and MRA gave him this kind of authority. Some suggested, for example, that the phrase "Frank's guidance is always right" was commonly used.[128] There is no evidence that this was so. Yet it is true that Buchman's judgment was decisive. The reasons for this are obvious: he was the initiator of the movement, and he had gained a reputation as someone who was close to God.[129]

Yet Buchman was often wary of giving direct advice. There were many occasions when he insisted that people should get their own sense of God's leading. When in October 1949 Schuman asked him whether he ought to retire from politics and enter a monastery, Buchman responded with the question: "What in your heart, Mr. Schuman, do you think you should do?" Whether or not Buchman's response was decisive is not clear, but Schuman decided to remain in politics.[130] Furthermore, although Buchman was sometimes assertive in his leadership style, he often let other people take the initiative. William Jaeger, who was central to the development of MRA's industrial work in Europe and North America, recalled, "He never told me what to do, but he always wanted to know what I was doing."[131]

Buchman frequently declared that people should depend on God rather than on him. "Don't follow me—follow Him," he told his supporters in the late 1950s.[132] He wrote to Purdy in 1930, "I want you to feel that your movements are to be checked by your guidance as well as mine," perhaps concerned that the young American was becoming too dependent on him.[133] He insisted that people should depend on God rather than on their friends.[134] For example, according to Jim Baynard-Smith, a young British assistant to Buchman in the 1950s, Buchman thought that the British were overkeen on pleasing people and needed to acquire an "independent touch with God's Holy Spirit" that would free them from deferring to any group. Such a touch with God, he thought, would release "latent powers" hidden under the cover of a false reserve and attributed to national character.[135] Buchman also often said that others might see situations more clearly than he and that members of his team should question him if their guidance differed from his.[136] "I must have people's correction," he

Fig. 3 Buchman with French foreign minister Robert Schuman, Caux conference center, September 1953. Photo: Peter Sisam, Oxford Group Archives.

once insisted to Corderoy, and he said the same to Peter Howard.[137] But few felt confident enough to give it to him.

In the light of the potential dangers as well as the possibilities associated with the practice of guidance, it is perhaps surprising that no larger spiritual manual, introducing people more systematically to the nature of discernment and how to distinguish between the right and the wrong kind of inspiration, was written in the OG or MRA. It would be wrong to suggest that this was because Buchman's supporters thought there were no dangers in the practice of guidance. People were well aware of the problems associated with impulsive decision making. In fact a side effect of the emphasis on unity through guidance was that the "checking" of decisions sometimes took a long time, as people tried as far as possible to coordinate their thinking on issues or actions. Indeed, some thought that the culture of checking was at times too strong and that it made creative, bold action more difficult.[138]

The reason why no systematic spiritual manual was written was probably connected to the fact that in the OG and MRA the sharing of testimony was generally given greater weight than formal teaching and that people were often content to get inspiration from texts written outside the movement. Most OG and MRA accounts of how guidance worked were embedded in people's stories of change and were more anecdotal than analytic. That is not to say that some of them were not interesting or well crafted. A vivid example of this kind of literature was British pilot Edward Howell's *Escape to Live* (1947), an account of how the author turned to guidance in escaping from a German prisoner of war camp in Greece, stressing in particular the connection between surrender to God and knowledge of his will.[139] Yet works of a reflective as opposed to a descriptive or campaigning nature were relatively rare. Not a natural writer himself, Buchman could not have filled this gap.

Some solid, thoughtful attempts to explore or explain the practice of guidance were made nonetheless. Streeter's *The God Who Speaks*, the last two chapters of which were written under OG influence, was perhaps the closest thing to a more thorough, intellectual presentation of the subject, although it was theological rather than practical in emphasis.[140] *When Man Listens* (1936), by Methodist minister Cecil Rose, was a practical introduction to the subject that was widely used in the OG and MRA.[141] An Anglican priest, Jack Winslow—who was on the edge of the OG in the 1930s—wrote a guide to the morning quiet time, *When I Awake* (1938), that was targeted mainly at people with connections to the church and that explored listening to God in the context of the wider process of contemplative prayer and intercession.[142] Later, Charis Waddy, a woman central to MRA's postwar engagement with the Islamic world, produced a short reflection, *The Skills of Discernment* (1977), that drew on Christian, Muslim, and other sources and that accommodated the "unexpectedness of the Spirit of God" within a balanced treatment of the subject.[143]

The idea of guidance was also creatively, if briefly, interpreted by the French Catholic existentialist Gabriel Marcel, who became involved in MRA in the late 1950s. Marcel stressed the importance of "letting-go" in the act of the quiet time, arguing that people who surrendered themselves spiritually in some way transcended themselves. He also suggested that it was not essential to believe that people were listening to God in their quiet times—although he said that he had no trouble doing that—stating that "transcendence" was a good term to apply to what was happening, in that it expressed the principle of what he called the "going beyondness" that was at the heart of the practice.[144]

Marcel's interpretation of the quiet time, addressed as it was to a French intellectual audience, was another example of how those involved in the OG and MRA tried to adapt their message to different kinds of people. Buchman's supporters understood that the concept of guidance often needed further explanation if it was to be comprehensible to people. Sensitivity to different cultural traditions, Christian and non-Christian, was needed. A detailed knowledge of local languages was sometimes required. In Papua New Guinea, for example—where the OG had considerable impact in the 1930s—the moral struggles within people were interpreted as a conflict between good and bad spirits, and a Papuan word "davalia," which meant "finding," was used for listening to the good spirit's directions.[145] The assumption was that the Holy Spirit could speak to anyone. The challenge was to express this in a way that people from different traditions and backgrounds could understand.

3
Personal Work

Buchman was always enthusiastic about the subject of "personal work," or "life-changing," as he sometimes called it. It was here that the fourth of the absolute standards, love, came into focus for him. Personal work was meant to be the outcome of a real love for people, he believed. In this connection he liked some of the poetry of the Irish Protestant missionary to India, Amy Carmichael. At MRA gatherings he used to recite her poem "Kindle Our Love," the first line of which was "Father, forgive the cold love of the years," in combination with the first verse of "A Passion for Souls," which opened with the lines "O for a passionate passion for souls! / O for a pity that yearns! / O for the love that loves unto death! / O for the fire that burns!" The poems probably encapsulated for him the kind of affection he always thought was needed if evangelistic work was to be effective and done on the right basis.[1] Yet he also thought that love needed to be informed by the wisdom of the Holy Spirit. "All true diagnosis begins with God," he said in China, adding, "When we go into the life of that other person it is the God directed movement and not man made [*sic*]."[2]

Buchman's desire to try to help people spiritually was visible even in his teens, for he wrote in one high school essay that it was not the football star who was the true hero, but anyone who saved a fellow student from the "snares of hell."[3] His interest in personal work was also evident at the time of his visit to Northfield in 1901, for he decided at that time to make winning people for Christ a life objective. En route home from the conference, he tried this out on a porter named George, at the New York City station, telling the man that he had to be a Christian. It was a "crude" attempt at evangelism, Buchman recalled, and the result of it was unclear, but it had the merit of breaking the ice on a new life's work.[4] Returning to Northfield the following year, he was particularly impressed by hearing the story of a student who had spent six months helping another college student learn Greek, with the hope of ultimately winning him for Christ—which he was successful in doing. Buchman cited this in an article that he then wrote for the Muhlenberg College magazine, in which he proposed five conditions for effective personal work: cultivating a love for fellow men, studying their needs, living lives above reproach, exercising a natural and unconscious influence, and constant Bible study and prayer.[5]

The culture of college evangelism clearly played an important role in channeling Buchman's thinking about personal work. For example, writing about the practice of personal evangelism in his *Muhlenberg* article, Buchman recommended a pamphlet by Charles K. Ober and John R. Mott and a book by H. Clay Trumbull, which were then influential in student Christian circles.[6] The ideas of Henry Wright and Henry Drummond would, of course, subsequently shape Buchman's thinking too. The first book based on Buchman's methods, Howard Walter's *Soul Surgery* (1919), cited the importance of Wright, Drummond, Trumbull, Mott, and Ober in advancing the practice of personal work.[7]

Buchman's thinking about personal work, as it had coalesced during his time at Penn State and just after, was evident in some articles he published while in Asia. Writing in 1916 in the organ of the South India United Church, he emphasized that "individual work for individuals" was Christ's main method of work, lamenting that many Christian workers were so preoccupied with administrative duties that they had no time for real contact with people. Moreover, he suggested that many Christian workers approached evangelism in the wrong way. For example, he said that the method of asking people whether they were saved or not might help some people, but it would repel others. What was needed was a much more specific sense of a person's needs.[8] Similarly, in a 1918 article for the bulletin of the China Continuation Committee—a central organ for coordinating Protestant missionary outreach in China—Buchman drew attention to the way in which Jesus had crafted his message to meet the particular needs of individuals, stating that the world was hungry for men and women who could understand others. What was needed was what he called "personalization" and "spiritualization" in every department of Christian activity. Too often Christian workers failed to diagnose the specific sin that kept a person from faith.[9]

These ideas underpinned Buchman's talks at Kuling in 1918. He told his audience there that the most influential converts in every country were won to Christianity through one-to-one work. People needed to prepare themselves properly for personal conversations. "I prepare as carefully to meet one man in interview, as for a sermon to four hundred people," he declared.[10] Work done that was not personalized would be wasted, he thought. "Don't throw eye medicine out of a second-story window" was a catchphrase he sometimes used in stressing the need for a more accurate diagnosis of a person's troubles.[11] Different strategies had to be adopted for different personalities. He liked a phrase attributed to Drummond that reflected this: "If you fish for eels you catch eels; if you fish for salmon, you catch salmon."[12]

The gathering at Kuling was intended by Buchman to be what he called a "personalized conference"—and he saw this as a distinctive innovation. His aim was to structure proceedings around trying to meet people's needs personally. In practice this meant dispensing with meetings that revolved around inspirational talks and replacing them with a more informal, conversational framework in which people were encouraged to share how God was active in their lives or how they were falling short in their spiritual journey. People who were expecting great speakers to lift them would be disappointed, he warned. The reason for the failure of missionary conferences, he said, was that they were not based on "life." He meant by this that contributions from participants should grow out of their more immediate religious experiences rather than theory. "The thing we need to market most of all is experience that is not memory," he said.[13]

Buchman was not against preaching or speaking as such. For example, at Kuling he referred favorably to Henry Ward Beecher's *Yale Lectures on Preaching* (1872).[14] But he thought that the problem with speeches was that they often failed to engage with the particular needs of an audience. He said elsewhere that the problem with most conferences was that their programs were "superimposed." Instead, speakers needed to be chosen on what he called "the basis of life."[15] Writing to Murray Webb-Peploe in 1921 he said, "In personal evangelism one proceeds naturally on the basis of life without super-imposing." The problem with many conferences, he said, was that people tried in what he called "human ways" to "accelerate spiritual results," and consequently they failed to have a real, lasting influence.[16] Later in life he suggested that at Sunday services it would be better to have fifteen men talk rather than one, evidently preferring the idea of the communal sharing of experience to just one person preaching.[17]

Buchman also wanted the meeting at Kuling to be small enough for deep conversations to take place. He had initially hoped to restrict attendance at the conference to about fifty people, although in the end the number totaled nearer one hundred.[18] He also deliberately planned the gathering so that it would last for well over a week. He said that a conference should ideally last at least ten days, citing his own experience at one of the Northfield conferences, where he had apparently been critical of proceedings at the beginning, before changing his mind and moving to a more honest view of himself after a week. In addition,

Buchman warned of conferences that became overrun with meetings—so that they turned into a kind of "Christian vaudeville."[19]

Buchman thought that many missionaries in China were not engaged with the inner lives of the native population and thus did not really know the country they were living in. In his mind one of the aims of the Kuling conference was to try to rectify this by creating a space for a deeper kind of encounter between Westerners and Chinese. Buchman also wanted to counter the view that personal work, while effective in the United States, was inapplicable in China. "You will never know the real China . . . unless you are willing to untie the bandages of the people around you, dead men about you," he told his missionary audience.[20] He also hoped that a deeper level of personal work could lead to a missionary outreach that could affect China as a country and not just draw the Chinese into Christian circles.

The main vehicle for the expansion of the FCCF and the OG in the interwar period was the house party, and this was effectively the same thing as the personalized conference. Indeed, Buchman named the first house party to take place after his breakthrough at Oxford in May 1921—which took place at Trinity Hall, Cambridge, in August of that year—a "personalized Conference."[21] He was still using the same vocabulary in a letter to Sam Shoemaker a couple of years later, when he talked of the need for a "carefully thought through, personalized conference" in the United States.[22] House parties, then, were effectively an expression of this concept. Some of the early house parties were small and intimate, involving a few dozen people at most. But in the 1930s they became much larger. For example, roughly five thousand people attended the Oxford house party of 1933; a three-day demonstration at the British Industries Fair in Birmingham in 1936 attracted as many as twenty-five thousand people; and up to one hundred thousand attended a series of Whitsun meetings in the Netherlands in 1937.[23] Personalization was still the aim, but the expansion of the work to this extent clearly posed new challenges.

The postwar MRA conferences, like the OG house parties, also had much in common with the conference at Kuling in 1918, even if, again, they were much larger.[24] Although important political figures sometimes spoke at Caux and Mackinac, meetings rarely contained scripted presentations and were often quite informal. Indeed, they were usually given shape immediately before they actually took place in "set-up" meetings, where the Holy Spirit's wisdom was sought about who should speak and what they should say to ensure that the content of meetings was relevant to those actually in the audience. Speaking at Caux in 1954 Buchman contrasted what he called the "conference with a cure" with the "old type of conference," in which people read papers out loud.[25] Clearly, the ideas about conferences that he had first expressed in China continued to inform his thinking after 1945.

Buchman's emphasis on personalization was closely linked to a belief that the Holy Spirit himself operated in a personalized kind of way. On the basis of the encounter with "Tutz" at Penn State and other episodes, Buchman came to the conclusion that God could reveal exactly who might be most ready to respond to a spiritual challenge. There was a sense that people were in some way "prepared" for their encounters with him, he said. "Here is God, and here are you, and here's the other person, prepared for you."[26] It was an idea that was central to Buchman's spirituality until the end of his life. "I have been wonderfully led to those who were ready," he said years later.[27]

In this connection Buchman had a personalist understanding of the very nature of the Holy Spirit. He once said in the late 1920s that the Holy Spirit was not an "electrical current" that could be tapped to work any machine a man wanted, but a "Person" working with other persons, a person working in individuals as they faced up to absolute standards and became sensitive to his action in the lives of others.[28] The result of this was that Buchman also believed that people could have a personal relationship with the Holy Spirit. He evidently felt that he himself had such a relationship, for he once said that he came to know the Holy Spirit as "light, guide, teacher and power."[29]

Buchman also stressed the importance of listening to others in personal work. Talking too much was not the way to help people, he said.[30] He was much impressed by a postcard sent to him in 1921, with a caption beneath the face of a man: "God gave a man two ears and one mouth. Why don't you listen twice as much as you talk?"[31] Choosing the right moment to raise an issue was also important. At Kuling Buchman reported an episode in which he was asked to help a young ordinand who was suffering from insomnia. He suggested to him that the underlying problem was that he was stealing other people's sermons and passing them off as his own. But he said this only after taking the man to New York and ensuring that he had a long sleep and a good breakfast. In other words, Buchman challenged the man only when he felt he was ready for it. According to Buchman, the young man admitted that his sermons had been plagiarized and began a recovery.[32]

Buchman was also keen to try to establish what he, Sherwood Eddy, and Wright called a "point of contact" with the other person: an opportunity for conversation on moral and spiritual issues.[33] At Kuling Buchman said that conference participants should develop a "natural point of contact" with one another.[34] Gaining a point of contact was also the first of a series of suggestions for personal work that he and Eddy formulated while working together.[35] Years later, he told an American woman, "The thought comes strongly that the first step will be to pass on to others what you discover. That's a natural point of contact."[36] Buchman clearly thought that the sharing of personal experience was always a possible point of contact. Indeed, he sometimes advised people not to go beyond their own experience in talking about the spiritual life.[37]

At some point during his trips to Asia, Buchman's thinking about personal evangelism also came to focus on what he called the "five c's": confidence, confession, conviction, conversion, and conservation. Walter's *Soul Surgery* was structured around these five stages. The idea was that in winning people to Christ, it was necessary to gain their confidence, bring them first to a confession and then a conviction of sin, encourage their conversion, and finally support them in their new lives.[38] Another of Buchman's formulations, from the same time, was borrowed from Drummond. At Kuling he argued that there were stages in what he called "the scheme of salvation": at the lower end there was the "groping of the soul for the light," then the "glimmering light," then "the growing faith," and then the advent of a more formerly Christian stage, in which a person worked things out "in fear and trembling."[39] Buchman had probably recently read Drummond's "Spiritual Diagnosis," because his understanding of the nature of spiritual growth was clearly modeled on the one that the Scottish writer had outlined in his essay.[40]

Interestingly, Walter wrote in *Soul Surgery* that Drummond's "Spiritual Diagnosis" had marked the beginning of what he called the "modern movement of scientific evangelism."[41] Certainly, the title of Walter's book itself sent out the message that Buchman and his colleagues were trying to bring a "scientific" methodology to the evangelistic enterprise. Buchman himself liked using the word "laboratory" in such a way as to suggest that there was a scientific dimension to his work. For example, he used to describe his time at Penn State as a "laboratory" for testing his principles.[42] He also wrote to Wright in 1918 that he was using his own "laboratory experiences" in his work in China.[43] In addition, one of his courses on evangelism at Hartford was called a "clinic," implying that the spiritual truths being imparted there were verifiable in a scientific kind of way.[44]

Buchman also used a medical analogy to justify his habit of using examples of personal work from his own life to illustrate the nature of evangelism. In his view it was not egotistical of people to speak of their own experiences of personal work. No one would accuse a doctor of being self-centered if he spoke of his patients, he said; the matter was comparable to personal spiritual work. While acknowledging that some people did embark on personal work in a spirit of egotism, he also insisted that it was necessary for people to forget themselves if they were to win people for Jesus.[45] At a house party in 1922, he used another medical image: "What people today want is the knife. [People] want soul surgery—a physician of souls. People today want you to get at their particular sin, and the trouble today is that we do not know the power of the Holy Spirit."[46] The use of scientific vocabulary was to remain in MRA culture well after Buchman's death. For example, Garth Lean subtitled his spiritual autobiography, *Good God, It Works* (1974), an "experiment in faith," thereby suggesting that religion, like science, could be explored through the experimental method.[47]

There were, of course, other evangelists who tried to explain their work in scientific terms. For example, Charles Finney used to call on preachers to be more scientific in their methods.[48] Likewise, some of those attending the World Missionary Conference in Edinburgh in 1910 wanted to see a "science of missions."[49] The idea that religious experience could be classified had also become popular through the influence of William James's *Varieties of Religious Experience* (1902), a work that Buchman almost certainly knew about.[50] But there was a tension here. The kind of personalization that Buchman wanted to see in evangelism ran somewhat counter to the methodology of the natural sciences. In one of his speeches in China, he warned his listeners of the danger of becoming "professional," and yet his stress on the need for greater thoroughness in personal work could easily be termed a call for professionalization.[51] His disappointment with the missionary community in China may have been at the root of his vocabulary in this context.

If Buchman used scientific and medical analogies to describe his work, he also took the view that some people needed medical help in a more formal sense. The actor Phyllis Austin—the wife of Bunny Austin—who was drawn into Buchman's work in the late 1930s, recalled an occasion in 1939 when Buchman was asked to see a young man with physical and mental problems. At the meeting that transpired the man stared vacantly ahead of him. After he had gone, Buchman said, "I'm afraid he's a cracked vase and needs medical help."[52]

If "sharing" was another word for confession in the OG, it was also used to refer to the process by which people shared their own experiences with others to try to help them. "Sharing as witness," Julian P. Thornton-Duesbery called it, emphasizing the importance of people getting guidance from the Holy Spirit about what it was appropriate to share.[53] F. B. Meyer had once said that preachers should tell people on Sundays what they had told him during the week; in other words, evangelism should be an outgrowth of real contact with people. Buchman was impressed by this and perhaps by Meyer's own tendency to share personal problems and failures with others.[54] Telling stories became central to the way in which Buchman did personal work. It was a nonprescriptive way of awakening a response. Drummond used to say that in evangelism appeals to the imagination were more likely to be effective than appeals to reason.[55] Buchman's emphasis on story telling can be seen as reflecting a similar perspective.

From his own life Buchman often told people the story of his experience at Keswick or described other episodes where he thought he had sinned and then repented. He once said that he drove his own sins "like a team of horses," because they provided entry points into the heart of the other person. Honesty about himself could elicit honesty in others.[56] He also regularly used the story of Bill Pickle's change.[57] He encouraged other people to share their stories too. On one of his visits to Westminster College, Cambridge, in the early 1920s he was challenged by the church historian, P. Carnegie Simpson, as to the advisability of having young men talk publicly about their sins and their victory over them. His reply was "Fresh fish every morning, Dr Simpson; fresh fish every morning."[58] He meant, of course, that the best argument for the Christian life was up-to-date religious experience. Changes in people's lives were "miracles," he once said, and he was keen for these miracles to be publicized as widely as possible.[59]

Buchman's use of story telling was important in the way that the OG itself came into being. When he came to Oxford in 1921 he was invited to attend a meeting of a debate society known as the Beef and Beer Club, which took place in Christ Church College. He remained silent throughout the proceedings, until he was invited to contribute at the end. He then recounted stories of change from the lives of two Cambridge undergraduates. According to the account by Loudon Hamilton, a Scotsman who became Buchman's first full-time supporter in the United Kingdom, Buchman avoided conventional religious phrases in his remarks, relying on the stories themselves to communicate his message. The effect was considerable, particularly on Hamilton himself. Breakfasting the following morning with Hamilton and his roommate, Buchman told another story, this time about a young man who had stolen money. This provoked Hamilton into recalling a recent dishonesty in his own life. His conscience aroused, Hamilton started to become interested in Buchman's message. He had consciously turned away from God at the Battle of Passchendaele, but a decision to turn back to God soon after his meeting with Buchman reawakened his faith.[60] When Buchman visited Oxford a year later to encourage the growing interest in his work, his methods were similar. At one occasion where he was asked to speak, he avoided argument and concentrated on telling people about what he saw as the reality of God's power. "I didn't question their beliefs. I told them of the power of the Holy Spirit," he reported.[61]

The emphasis on telling stories was linked to a larger determination to avoid using conventional religious vocabulary. People in the OG dispensed with the vocabulary of "conversion," talking instead of the need for "change."[62] Words like "sanctification," "consecration," and "salvation" were to be avoided, Buchman believed, because people did not really understand them. Prayers embarked on too soon might also create resistance in people or put them off if they were too long.[63] The decision to organize meetings in the form of house parties, often in nonreligious settings like colleges, hotels, and country houses, where people from well-educated backgrounds felt at home, reflected the same concern. It was, as Daniel Sack suggests, a creative adaptation of an elite social practice for religious purposes.[64] Ever eager to reach the unchurched, Buchman wanted to take religion out of its familiar, ecclesiastical setting.

In other words, there was a constant attempt to present religion as something natural—replicating and reinforcing Buchman's desire to present the idea of "guidance" as natural. The very manner with which Buchman communicated his message reinforced this. It seemed, at least to some, unforced. Hamilton cites being impressed by Buchman's "ease and naturalness" at mixing with people.[65] The apparently natural and not overly religious atmosphere that he encouraged was appealing. John Roots, then at Harvard, was impressed by the fact that the first house party he attended, in winter 1923–24, was not religious in a traditional sense, and he was also struck with the "transparent honesty" of the atmosphere.[66]

Buchman's impact in the interwar-era universities cannot be attributed to his spirituality alone. The concerns and atmosphere of the 1920s were also a factor. In the United States Buchman met a postwar desire for excitement and new experiences in a way that did not involve abandoning religion altogether.[67] In Britain World War I had eroded traditional certainties and left a climate of disillusionment. This was certainly felt in the makeup of the Beef and Beer Club in Oxford, where many of the members were ex-army officers of roughly twenty-three to twenty-four years old. Yet behind the cynical poses, there was much soul searching going on. The religious climate at the university was changing, with Anglicanism's dominance being challenged by a growing religious pluralism, yet there was still much interest in religion.[68] For some Buchman seems to have offered a nondogmatic way of recovering a lost sense of meaning. His emphasis on the social dimension of Christianity also appealed to a generation keen to prevent the possibility of any future war.

The same was true after World War II, when—in Europe and the Far East, for example—MRA's emphasis on rebuilding shattered societies was an important reason for its attraction. But it was in the interwar period in particular that Buchman had his greatest successes with young people. Although MRA still sought to enlist students into its work after 1945, sometimes successfully, its outreach became less focused on the universities than it was in the interwar period. The combination of spiritual training and adventure that it offered was also increasingly available through other religious organizations after World War II.

Buchman once prayed to be "super-sensitive" to people, and he clearly had the ability to discern people's needs or anxieties at some level.[69] Henry Van Dusen even goes as far as to suggest that he was "psychic" in diagnosing people's problems. If occasionally he made mistakes about what was troubling somebody, it was not often.[70] If this discernment was a spiritual gift—as Buchman's supporters thought it was—it was also the result of a careful attentiveness to people. Buchman was like Drummond in thinking that people often sent out subtle signals about the nature of their problems.[71] He said in China that people revealed their moral weaknesses by their inefficiencies, forced activities, criticisms, refusals, silences, and antipathies. He also suggested that they would try to conceal these weaknesses from others. People would attempt to "throw dust in your eyes when they begin to feel that you are on their track," he said.[72] This was one of the reasons why he generally avoided trying to defend his faith at a doctrinal level: he thought people often raised intellectual problems with Christianity when they were trying to cover up their real needs.[73]

Buchman was constantly on the watch for signals about people's underlying problems. For example, he thought that a person's tone of voice was revealing. He once said to Rajmohan Gandhi, one of the mahatma's grandsons who started to work with MRA in the late 1950s, "Something is wrong with you. I could feel it in your voice." Gandhi confessed that he was not in his best form and that he had been trying to please people too much.[74] Buchman also paid attention to people's faces. Begbie claimed that Buchman even knew the facial indications of particular sins.[75] He once told a man whom he had accused—correctly—of committing adultery and who asked him how he had been able to figure this out, that the evidence for it was "all over [his] face."[76] He also thought the relationship between "heart, face and bearing" was an interesting study. A person's eyes were also revealing. Talking at Kuling, he said that dishonest people often exhibited an "eye that wavers" and that dishonesty also resulted in people looking at others with a "small eyeball" and a "squinting of the eye."[77]

Buchman tried to use his own experiences of temptation as a bridge of understanding with the other person. They enabled him to empathize in some way. According to Bunny Austin, he thought that the best insurance against temptation was to assume that one day he would encounter someone with the same problem and would need to be able to meet the person's need.[78] Sometimes he also seems to have used feelings occurring inside himself as a way of interpreting what was happening in the other person. He once said that when he had a particular temptation, he took it as an indication that someone he was going to meet that day would have the same temptation.[79] This was clearly unusual, but there was possibly some overlap here with the charismatic tradition. John Wimber, the founder of the Vineyard Christian Fellowship that emerged some decades after Buchman's death, believed that he could sometimes discern people's specific physical ailments through what he was experiencing in his own body.[80]

There were in fact a number of similarities between Buchman's work and the emerging charismatic movement, particularly in their common stress on the possibility of immediate guidance from the Holy Spirit. For example, what Wright and Buchman called "luminous thoughts" were in essence very similar to what Wimber and others—drawing on Saint Paul—called "words of knowledge."[81] There was arguably also something in common between Buchman's emphasis on the Holy Spirit and the Alpha courses later used by some evangelists with a charismatic emphasis.[82] Overlaps between the two currents might partly be accounted for by the fact that they both drew inspiration from the Keswick tradition and Wesleyan spirituality.[83] Yet while there were "proto-charismatic" elements in the OG, Buchman's tradition did not stress the possibility of miraculous physical healing to the extent that the charismatic movement did.[84] The kind of healing that it promoted was more psychological than physical. On the other hand, a couple of American doctors involved in the OG and MRA wrote books on the link between spiritual and physical healing.[85]

There was, in fact, at least one story of physical healing associated with Buchman. In Saratoga Springs in November 1942 Buchman had a serious stroke, from which he nearly died and which left a permanent mark on his health. Thereafter he normally walked with a stick, and he often suffered chronic pain from hemorrhoids.[86] At one point during his convalescence, Buchman was having his shoes cleaned by a shoe shiner. Signe Strong recalled that "as the man worked he kept looking up into Frank [Buchman]'s face. . . . When it was all finished and Frank had said goodbye, the man looked at Frank again and said, 'I was blind, but while I was working on your shoes I could see again.'" Buchman replied, "God hasn't done that for me yet."[87]

Perhaps because of his experience at Keswick, Buchman was particularly sensitive to the importance of people becoming free of bitterness. While this was always an important element in OG spirituality, it came—for obvious reasons—to be accentuated in MRA after World War II, when trying to heal the wounds of the war became one of the movement's central tasks. Buchman himself brought this into focus when, on arriving at MRA's newly acquired conference center at Caux in July 1946, he said, "Where are the Germans? You will never rebuild Europe without the Germans."[88] Since at that time few Germans were allowed out of Germany and there was a lot of hostility toward Germany in Europe, it was an awkward question.

Buchman's tendency to focus issues by asking questions, and his interest in helping people become free of hatred, was then evident in 1947, when Irène Laure, secretary general of the Socialist Women of France, came to Caux. Laure, who had been a Resistance leader in Marseilles during the war, had vowed never to stay under the same roof as Germans and was distressed by the presence of a German delegation at the conference. During her visit she was asked by Buchman what kind of Europe she expected to create. "How can you expect to rebuild Europe if you reject the German people?" was what he said, according to one account.[89] The result was that she decided, after some inner turmoil, to make a public apology to the Germans in Caux for her hatred of their country. It was an unexpected act that led on to a deeper dialogue with members of the German delegation. Laure said later that Buchman's question to her had been a "challenge in love," remarking that it would not have had a positive effect on her if he had expressed pity or sympathy for her.[90] It was an episode that was to be often recounted by MRA workers in subsequent decades. It symbolized the sort of apology, honesty, and mutual forgiveness that they sought to promote. It was also to be the most well known of a number of examples in the movement's history where the "victim" of oppression became the first to initiate a process of reconciliation.[91]

Another aspect of Buchman's approach to personal work was his directness. There was often a robust quality about his dealings with people. Morris Martin recorded him as saying, "Some of you have never graduated from the school of collision. You never collide. Remember our work is the collision of a living with a dead soul."[92] OG and MRA events were supposed to have the same challenging quality. Buchman said in 1937, after a weekend in The Hague, "It is not enough to give [people] a nice weekend. We had a sticky weekend. The Holy Spirit got tired of it."[93]

An early example of one of Buchman's "collisions" was a letter he wrote in China to the president of Penn State, Edwin Sparks. He told Sparks that he did not seem to be a really happy man and lacked real joy in his religious life. He was too diplomatic—to the point of dishonesty—and financially so scrupulous as to be "penurious." "There is a note of unreality somewhere. Your interest is commendable and far exceeds that of others I know, but it does not ring quite true," he said. The letter was prefaced with a quotation from the Book of Proverbs (27:6), "Faithful are the wounds of a friend," through which Buchman tried to signal that the criticism came with affection.[94] How Sparks responded is not clear.

Possibly the most famous of Buchman's "collisions" involved his relationship with Peter Howard, who had first encountered the OG in the summer of 1940 after co-authoring the famous attack on appeasement, *Guilty Men* (1940).[95] Howard, who was working at the time for Lord Beaverbrook's *Express* newspapers, had the idea of doing a scoop on Buchman's work but was instead drawn into it, subsequently producing a string of books in its defense.[96] After the war he became MRA's most visible spokesperson. But in the late 1940s his relationship with Buchman deteriorated. According to his own account, Howard had some challenging thoughts in his quiet time that he was resisting, and Buchman, sensing this, refused to work closely with him for some years. Howard, who was pretty thick-skinned, eventually responded to the treatment, in the sense that he decided to make a fresh decision to surrender his life to God. After the relationship was restored, Buchman said to Howard that he always had to be ready to risk his relationships with people.[97]

Buchman also had a combative relationship with T. Willard Hunter, who began working with Buchman in the late 1930s. Hunter recalled that Buchman trenchantly told him that he was a "stubborn and bull-headed Minnesotan" and that if he did not change, he should find something else to do. According to Hunter, it was only after surrendering his life to God and setting aside human effort in trying to create a better world—which took place in 1940—that he "stepped into equality with [Buchman]."[98] Hunter was implicitly referring to the fact that some of the people around Buchman were in awe of him, and his point was that it was only following a wholehearted decision to put God first in his own life that he became free from his own fear of or dependency on him.

Fig. 4 Buchman speaking at the Mackinac conference center, June 4, 1952. *Front left*, Senator Eugénie Eboué from France; *front right*, Irène Laure with her husband, Victor; *back right*, Peter Howard. Photo: Oxford Group Archives.

According to Michel Sentis, a young Frenchman who helped to develop MRA's links with the Catholic Church in the 1950s, the people who found Buchman most difficult were the ones who wanted his approval.[99] If that is true, Howard and Hunter found a spiritual independence that made it possible for them to work with Buchman as equals.

Buchman's readiness to confront people was often expressed in relation to apparently very small matters. Talking of Buchman's uncompromising attitude to what he saw as evil, Howard wrote, "He never lets one thing pass, whether in the kitchen or a conference."[100] This was evident in his attitude to money. For example, he was once critical of a young English supporter, Roger Hicks, for making phone calls when he could have saved money by writing letters and for staying too long on the telephone when making long-distance calls. He even warned him against leaving thumbtacks behind when he packed Buchman's bags.[101] Buchman's decision to tackle people over what might be seen as tiny matters was because he saw them as symptomatic of bigger character problems, and it was the bigger problem he was trying to address. Sometimes, it seems, the issues he actually raised with people were inaccurate. Howard recounted an incident in which Buchman criticized him for being less than his best at a party that he had attended in Berlin. When it was pointed out that he was not actually present at the party, Buchman responded by saying, "What's that got to do with it?"[102] He evidently thought that the fact that he had made a mistake did not invalidate his assessment of Howard's character.

If in some cases Buchman's "collisions" had a positive outcome, there were other examples where people rejected Buchman's authority or corrective and moved away from his work. In the early 1920s, for example, Buchman clashed with Robert Collis, a former Cambridge University student. Collis, an Irish rugby international who had played a central role in organizing the house party at Cambridge in August 1921, fell out with Buchman after a joint quiet time in which Buchman told Collis that he had received a "clear message from God" that he should give up smoking. Unfortunately, Collis had the opposite guidance, and the difference led to a rift between the two men.[103]

Buchman's relationship with a Swiss colleague, Philippe Mottu, was also complicated. Mottu had worked with the Swiss Foreign Office during World War II and had built up links in Berlin with those who were subsequently involved in the plot against Hitler in 1944, such as Adam von Trott zu Solz. The idea of creating an MRA conference center in Switzerland, which would be dedicated to the reconstruction of Europe, had originated with Mottu, and he played a role in gathering the funds for purchasing the center at Caux that came to fill that function. He himself worked full-time with MRA for a number of years before distancing himself from the movement after Buchman's death.

Mottu had a high regard for Buchman. But, as his memoir indicates, he became afraid of crossing the MRA leader and would quickly swing from adulation to criticism of him. In letters written in 1947, he explained that he needed to find an independence and liberty regarding Buchman's attitude to him and wondered if some of the people around Buchman had not been hypnotized by him. On at least a couple of occasions, he felt that Buchman wrongly accused him of certain failures. The Buchman depicted in his memoirs was thus a man who was erratic and sometimes dictatorial.[104] For his part, Buchman clearly thought there were spiritual issues at stake in Mottu's character. He probably believed that it was necessary to deal with him in the manner that he had treated Howard and Hunter—for Mottu also had a forceful personality. For example, he wrote to Mottu in 1961, encouraging him to take time away from MRA work. He needed, Buchman suggested, to get at the "false things" in his nature that had made him "unpredictable and at the same time, in the eyes of many, indispensible [sic]."[105]

Buchman was obviously a person who could be stubborn and difficult to resist. He sometimes spoke to people abruptly or lost his temper with them. According to one of his colleagues, life around him was a mixture of Christmas Day and Judgment Day.[106] In his biography, Lean suggested that he did not take criticism easily, taking the view that if some of his closest colleagues had been more ready to challenge him, his leadership would have been enhanced.[107] Yet Howard saw Buchman's energy and strength of personality as assets without which MRA would not have been possible. "Many hated Buchman's pace, his unreasonableness, his blazing resolve to hack through and crack on.... And it was and is the hope of our work," he said after Buchman had died.[108]

Buchman would not have gained the support and affection of some very able people if the more forceful elements in his personality had not been balanced by other qualities. For example, Strong remembered him as a sensitive person who frequently cried when he was moved.[109] There was sometimes a "deep stillness" about him, according to the young American John Wood, who was one of Buchman's main aides after 1945, and he would sometimes sit with people who had been shocked or bereaved without saying anything, leaving the silence to express his empathy.[110] He often treated people gently. He felt, for example, that Cuthbert Bardsley, a future Anglican bishop who was involved with the OG in the late 1930s, had been put off the movement by an OG supporter who had teased him in a cruel way. He remarked privately in 1940 that Bardsley had a "feminine nature" and that he had to be won by "affection and inclusion."[111] The case reinforces the sense that Buchman's approach to people was influenced by what kind of personality he thought they had.

Most of Buchman's interactions with people were in fact thoroughly ordinary. The content of his innumerable letters, for example, was generally commonplace, often containing news that was designed to feed people's sense that they were part of a larger team and international endeavor.[112] There was also a lighter element, reflected in the fact that there was sometimes a lot of laughter in the meetings he organized. "You will get more people changed by pulling their legs, than kicking their bottoms," he once remarked.[113] "Brevity," "sincerity," and "hilarity" would be present at a meeting he was planning to chair in Mackinac in 1944, he announced.[114] His sense of humor was something he had prayed for, and it came—he thought—as a spiritual gift. According to Strong, he had prayed for it daily over the course of at least a year before it was given.[115]

As he saw it, Buchman was trying to enhance people's sense of their own significance. For example, while visiting Berlin in 1936, he wrote on his calling card for the elevator operator at his hotel, "To Max—friend and fellow-fighter."[116] Sometimes his advice was unexpected. Although not a smoker, Buchman told a Swiss manufacturer who wondered if he should stop making cigars that he should be making the "best cigars" in the country.[117] He also believed that people sometimes had good instincts that were expressed in the wrong way, and he wanted to find a way of channeling those instincts in what he thought was a more creative direction. In this connection he often focused on the potential he saw in people rather than dwelling on their weaknesses. This tendency was exemplified by his dealings with a German communist, Max Bladeck, who had been drawn into MRA following a visit to Caux in 1949 but sought to leave a couple of years later following a scandalous episode in which, under the influence of alcohol, he had publicly embraced a woman who was not his wife. Hearing of Bladeck's lapse, Buchman sent him a cable stating that the biggest sinner could become the greatest saint and that he had faith in the "new Max."[118] Bladeck and his wife subsequently joined Buchman's campaign in India in 1952–53, and the story of his involvement with MRA was often presented as an example of how communists could change.[119]

Buchman saw himself as trying to release the creative potential in people. He once said that he had devoted much of his life to "pulling the cork for bottled-up people."[120] Personal work, he also suggested, meant the "unfolding of the possibilities that are in men."[121] Sometimes he thought the key to this lay in a person having a new spiritual experience. For example, he wrote to George Stewart—the co-author with Wright of a couple of books on evangelism—in 1921: "I have coveted for you a larger service. I feel that you have not found your full area capacity. You need a second touch."[122] He also thought that sometimes people had gifts that they were not using. For example, in 1940 he asked Alan Thornhill, an Oxford University college chaplain who was then working with him, what he was writing. This question resulted in Thornhill writing *The Forgotten Factor*, a play about how MRA principles could help address industrial unrest, which was widely used by MRA during and after the war, and he went on to write many other plays.[123] Yet Buchman's predictions were not always realized. He once told Lean that he would write the plays that the world and MRA needed, but Lean never wrote any plays, although he did become a successful writer.[124]

Buchman also expected others to do the kind of personal work that he was doing. At the beginning of one term at Oxford he told his student supporters that they should try to change the most difficult person in the college.[125] He thought the spiritual gifts he had were open to others. "If you listen to God he

Fig. 5 Buchman with former German communists Max Bladeck (*left*) and Paul Kurowski (*right*), Kashmir, spring 1953. Photo: Richard N. Haile, Oxford Group Archives.

will give you the secrets of men's lives," he said in China. Only sin could prevent a person being a miracle worker.[126] In the 1950s he said that unless his team were in "daily and God-filled touch with people," they would not touch the problems that they were facing. "Do not lend yourself to any programme that is not aimed at changing people," he declared. Lamenting that many of his colleagues lacked a "strategy" to win people, he advised them to go "straight into the difficulties" of the people they met. At the same time, he warned against salesmanship and pressure and insisted that he himself had never tried to "influence" anybody. People should act with conviction and in unity with their colleagues, he said.[127]

Buchman also once said that there was something morally wrong with people who were not winning people to Christ. "If one is not winning people for Christ, one is sinning somewhere along the line," he suggested.[128] On one occasion in the 1950s, he complained that a number of his supporters had not changed anybody during the previous couple of years.[129] Whether he meant in these comments that people should be bringing people to formal Christian commitment is doubtful, for he did not generally seek to convert people from the non-Christian religions to Christianity. More likely, he simply expected people to see the fruits of their spiritual work reflected in the lives of others in a real way. "Do you expect total commitment to be the result of your work with men?" he asked his team. A "drastic and deep love" was needed if their personal work was to go deep enough, he insisted.[130]

Buchman consciously tried to train people to do personal work. An ability to "read" people was part of the equipment for any personal worker, he thought. "You should read fewer books and more men," he told Thornhill.[131] He also encouraged his team to memorize stories of change from people's lives and to be ready to recount them whenever the opportunity arose. In addition, he tried to put his supporters into situations where he thought they could learn how to do personal work. For example, in 1935 he wrote to B. H. Streeter, suggesting that he be in contact with the Danish head of the YMCA, Falk Hansen, who he thought was self-righteous and undercutting the OG in private conversations. If Streeter was ready to give Hansen a spiritual challenge, Buchman declared, it might have a profound effect on him: "Draw him out, and then give him a daring challenge. . . . Lure him along, then at the right moment land the fish." He concluded with a flourish: "Have him grilled and served with granola."[132]

At the same time, it was important for supporters of the OG and MRA to avoid allowing a desire for success in doing personal work to cloud their motives. In a culture where effectiveness in helping others was considered a sign of spiritual vitality, it was always possible that people would try to be good "life-changers" to establish a reputation for holiness or to advertise their importance to the movement. The answer to this kind of problem, Buchman believed, was for people to let go of any selfish desires they may have had for personal achievement or impact. To a sportsman who complained that he was unable to help people, he cited some lines four times from a nineteenth-century hymn by Henry Francis Lyte, "Jesus, I My Cross Have Taken," about the importance of letting go of false ambition: "Perish ev'ry fond ambition, / All I've sought, and hoped and known. / Yet how rich is my condition, / God and heav'n are still my own."[133]

Buchman always emphasized the importance of spiritual accountability. A one-man endeavor was a "false principle," he wrote in his guidance in 1924, and a few years later he said that no one could be fully obedient to God who worked alone.[134] One of his favorite maxims reflected this: "It's the banana that leaves the bunch that gets skinned."[135] People needed fellowship with others for training, spiritual support, and direction, he thought.[136] He also believed that in teamwork people would find that their different gifts complemented one another. He told Mottu in 1937 that he and Martin might work well together: "You have dare, and Morris has caution. . . . Each supplies what the other lacks: that is the fellowship!"[137] Buchman's vision was for a community led by the Holy Spirit. Indeed, in a book of 1935 the Anglican clergyman R. H. Murray likened the OG to the Montanists, Franciscans, Friends of God, Jansenists, Methodists, and Tractarians in this respect.[138]

An early example of Buchman's emphasis on spiritual work in small groups was when at Penn State he started the practice of meeting with a small group each day for the "morning watch." On these occasions, the reading of the Bible preceded a time of listening to God and the making of plans.[139] Then, in Asia, as an alternative to Eddy's emphasis on big platform speeches, he created a small team from some of the students he had met at Hartford, although in the end that dwindled to Buchman working alone with the YMCA missionary Sherwood Day, who then worked closely with him in the interwar era.[140] The personal work groups that he organized in China in preparing for Eddy's visits also reflected the same emphasis on fellowship.

At the same time, Buchman initiated the practice of taking small groups of supporters on journeys with him. Something of this was already taking place in China when Buchman took men like Day with him. The visit he made to the United States in early 1921 with Godfrey Buxton and Webb-Peploe reflected a similar pattern. But this way of operating was applied more ambitiously in 1924–25, when Buchman took what he called an "apostolic group" of young men on a world tour that included visits to countries in Europe and the Middle East, India, and Australia. Day, Shoemaker, Loudon Hamilton, and three others agreed to join him for all or part of the journey, which lasted roughly nine months. It was an early example of Buchman using international outreach as a means of training individuals. He wrote, before leaving, that the purpose of the journey was to "train" the younger people, and in his correspondence with Shoemaker about the trip, he told him that he needed a "year's discipline in a team" to help him develop.[141] What Buchman hoped for in community life was partly expressed in his response to a visit he made during this journey to the Dohnavur community in India, which had been set up by Carmichael. Buchman wrote to one of his American backers, saying that Carmichael's community was a kind of "School of Life," which could be a model for his own work. "We need a demonstration centre with living miracles all about us with reality as the keynote," he declared.[142]

The journey of 1924–25 led to an impressive range of contacts for Buchman and his team. At the same time, it was not an easy experience for those concerned, for tensions emerged in the group, sometimes over what the younger travelers thought was an authoritarian manner by Buchman, but probably also arising out of the tensions that were inevitably likely to accompany a small group traveling together for a long time. At one point, there was a painful conversation in which people's reactions to one another were aired: an example of the kind of honesty that Buchman encouraged, even if on this occasion he was on the receiving end.[143] Yet if there were difficulties, it did not stop Buchman from believing that involving people in campaigns was a key way of helping them. For some of the younger people, the journeys or campaigns that he organized then or in subsequent years involved an exhilarating combination of spiritual uplift, international travel, and encounters with foreign dignitaries. The life of faith was thus portrayed, and experienced, as an adventure. This was deliberate. Buchman noted in his guidance in 1924 that in a "selfish, sex-mad world," sin had come to seem very attractive. The challenge was to make the life of faith more appealing. "God must be made attractive and interesting," he said.[144]

Training did not take place only on campaign. After 1945 MRA supporters often lived together in large houses—some of them given by wealthy families involved in the movement. Community living thus became a central means of training people. There were also more focused occasions for team building and spiritual input. Perhaps the most important of these was a three-month retreat that took place beside Lake Tahoe in the Sierra Nevada mountains in 1940. During this gathering, which was eventually attended by several hundred people, meetings took place every morning in which Buchman explored aspects of the spiritual life and often challenged people about their character weaknesses—sometimes in public. For many of those attending, the time was formative. One British supporter, Reginald Holme, recalled that the event led to the creation of a "force-in-being, like a regular army, capable of fighting anywhere anytime"—the military metaphors reflecting the OG's insistence that the spiritual life involved a kind of battle. Holme also suggested that those present, many of whom had individual religious experiences, had at this time a kind of "corporate experience of Christ" in which they became newly committed to one another.[145]

Training people, in Buchman's mind, meant trying to encourage them to take greater levels of responsibility. When six Oxford students from the FCCF decided to go to South Africa in 1928, he separately told each of them to be the person in charge. They discovered this only once they were aboard ship. It was a way of making a point about the need for each person to take responsibility for the whole group.[146] Buchman thought that many of his team depended too much on the initiative of others: "Most of you live on the spiritual initiative of a few people. Those few pay the cost of an enlarged vision and leadership. The rest just chatter." The root of this problem, he said, was "unresolved areas in personal lives."[147] He wanted instead to see everyone going all out for God at the same time. Using a horse-racing analogy, he once said that he wanted "all [his] fine horses to run all out together, neck and neck."[148] Buchman obviously wanted to try to expand people's understanding of what responsibility entailed. Howard wrote, a couple of years after Buchman's death, "Buchman paid me the compliment for a long time before he died of holding me responsible for anything that went wrong anywhere in the world concerning our work, regardless of whether I knew anything about it or not."[149]

Another area where Buchman's attitude to team building and fellowship was evident was in his approach to relationships. He was often insistent that demanding or exclusive relationships were to be avoided. At the Kuling conference he had warned of the danger of what he called "absorbing friendships" and "crushes."[150] In this case his comments were probably an allusion to homosexuality, and they provoked a strong negative reaction from some of those present, which was an important reason why his time in China ended in a cloud.[151] Yet Buchman was wary of exclusive or sentimental relationships of any kind, believing that they had a tendency to distract people from what God wanted them to do. "Sentimental relationships are the death of spiritual life," he once said.[152] Flirting, too, was discouraged in MRA culture.[153]

Buchman talked in some detail about the nature of love in the Netherlands in 1937, telling his team there that some of them were getting involved in romantic tangles that were sapping their spiritual energy: "Fall in love by all means, but don't take the time you do and spray it all over the place. Some of you are out of power from three to five months. You have an absorbing friendship that keeps you out of power for three years." "Guided love," he said, was one of the "most wonderful things in the world," but he warned that if it was unguided it would take a "tremendous toll." More generally, he stressed that friendships ought to be based on the "fullest affection," talking at the same time of what he described as an "expulsive love where there is real fellowship." He meant by this that people's relationships should be based on the kind of honesty where people were not afraid to challenge each other. At the same time, he also noted, "You sometimes need to draw people to yourself and on a fairly human level." Here the point was that some people were not ready for a more spiritual relationship and had to be drawn into the work in another way.[154]

At Kuling Buchman had talked about people who were "temporized on top"—meaning by this that they were always trying to keep people happy.[155] The desire to please others rather than God was something that Buchman particularly associated with homosexuality. Pressed once on what he meant by homosexuality, he replied, "Parroting to please. Sameness."[156] He also associated it with relationships of domination.[157] As Lean indicates, the meaning of these points was not always clear, because when Buchman criticized homosexual behavior, people sometimes thought that he was talking about physical homosexual activity, when in fact he was often referring to the sentimentality or dependence that he saw in the people around him. In this connection Buchman was sometimes suspicious of weak men and powerful women. He believed that the phenomenon of homosexuality in men could often be ascribed to the influence on them of strong women. Much depended on the right kind of mothering in childhood. "It goes back to the mother, to train the mother," he said in 1937.[158]

This kind of thinking may explain why Buchman led a meeting in Caux in 1950 aimed at "bossy and heady women."[159] "Bossy women make cowards of men. Impure men make bossy women," he said a few years later.[160] He expected women to be feminine in a relatively traditional way. At the Lake Tahoe retreat he tried to express this visually by asking a group of people, "Why is a woman like a peach?" He held a peach in one hand and a prune in another, declaring that too many of the women there were like prunes in the sense that they did not really reflect the life of God.[161] Buchman may himself have found strong women difficult, for during an argument at Kuling he told one of his co-organizers, Ruth Paxson, that he never took orders from a woman—although he apologized afterward for the way he had treated her.[162]

Married men in MRA were certainly expected to have the strength of character needed to give leadership in their families. Conversely, women were encouraged to help their husbands to take leadership. For example, Buchman once told Phyllis Austin what little time he had for spoiled, selfish, and bad-tempered women and the effect they had on their husbands—implying that she was like that herself.[163] One of Howard's plays, *Through the Garden Wall* (1963), depicted a wife coming to realize that she had dominated her husband in an unhealthy way.[164] There was also a current of thought in MRA that tried to provide an alternative to the emerging feminist concept of sexual liberation and that was given particular expression, some years after Buchman's death, in *Freewoman* (1977) by French author Claire Evans.[165]

On the whole, Buchman's main work at a pastoral level was with men rather than women. He took the view that in addressing what he called "trenchant issues," it should be done by "men for men and women for women."[166] Yet he also worked closely with some women and often gave them a lot of responsibility. In the interwar period, he sometimes confided in the young Canadian, Eleanor Napier Forde, the first woman to work full-time with him and author of one of the OG's earliest booklets on guidance.[167] In the postwar era Laure was a central figure in developing MRA's strategy with Germany.[168] Buchman also once said that women were good at personal work because their instincts about people were "surer than men's and more developed."[169]

A related issue, and a key component in Buchman's strategic vision, was the family. The family was, in Buchman's mind, meant to be a key place for nurture, spiritual outreach, and hospitality. Buchman thought that an effective marriage should be a creative partnership and that husbands and wives should ideally embrace the same calling, even if their roles were different. The family was seen as a place for learning the right values. For example, discussing purity in 1953, Buchman emphasized that if parents did not talk with their children about morality, they would absorb the wrong kind of values from society.[170] Buchman also believed that God could guide people as to whom they should marry, and people in the OG and MRA regularly sought God's wisdom on who their life partners might be. Many, indeed, sought Buchman's own discernment on this, a circumstance that highlighted the extent of his spiritual authority in the movement.[171]

Buchman often tried to address difficulties in family relationships. He warned that disunity in the home was a source for disunity in the nation, but a new home, rooted in a unity under God, could be a source of inspiration to many. "Out of one new home can come a hundred new homes," he suggested in 1938. Every home could be a center for "life-changing."[172] In Mackinac in 1944 he heralded a family of four that he said had become "one unit," when it had previously been divided. The family context could also be the key for the international context, he said, "The man who could say he was wrong at the breakfast table can, with equal grace, acknowledge his sin at the conference table."[173] "No secrets, no fights and no bluffing," was his recipe for a happy marriage.[174]

The emphasis on unity in the family was indicative of an important strand in OG and MRA spirituality. As Ian Randall has observed, there was a "relational" emphasis to Buchman's work.[175] Quiet times in the OG and MRA often produced thoughts about the building or repairing of relationships. For example, the first thought that Theophil Spoerri had, as he experimented with the quiet time in 1932, was "go down into the street!" He understood this to mean: "Go down from your position as a professor, spectator and observer, and do something with people. Expose your life to men, make your faith real and your ideas actual." In other words, Spoerri felt himself being invited to reach out to others. A by-product of this was that his own family benefited from him being more available to them.[176] Similarly, Paul Tournier had the thought in one of his early quiet times that he should start listening to his wife. It led later to his writing books about the importance of mutual listening in families and the contribution of women.[177]

Couples who worked full-time with MRA were sometimes expected to be as mobile as single people. An ability to travel was important for the expansion of the work, but it also sometimes led to difficult choices for parents with children. For example, some parents who worked outside of their own countries or traveled with MRA campaigns left children in a specially created school at Caux. At times this worked very well. Some children, however, found the long separations from their parents difficult, and some parents later wondered if their families had been apart for too long.[178] It was an example of how the challenges of "remaking the world" and the campaigning culture that came with it were not easy to reconcile with the demands of domesticity. It was also sometimes difficult for those working closely with Buchman to find time for family holidays. Perhaps Buchman's bachelor status made him less sensitive to these issues.[179] But he was also a frail man in later years and could not always see how to run the movement without the presence of some of its younger leaders.

In these matters MRA had much in common with some Christian missionary groups in the challenges it faced.[180] Like many missionaries, MRA workers believed that they needed to live in a sacrificial way if their work was to be fruitful. The world's needs called for a radical personal response. In practice this meant being ready to live abroad and to operate without much financial security. Yet it was not always easy to distinguish between those acts of sacrifice that could credibly be understood as helpful or good and those that were in some way misplaced and that might have unhappy consequences for others. Buchman and his team hoped that through guidance and accountability people would make wise choices.

Buchman believed that purity in sexual behavior was a matter for married people as well as single, an issue that became more topical as the first generation of OG and MRA workers married and had children. It was important that married couples were living "in power," he said.[181] Strong recalled that at the Tahoe retreat Buchman talked to both nonmarried and married people about the importance of purity.[182] In this context, Buchman was critical of the growing acceptance of contraceptives in society. He essentially held the view taken by most mainstream Christian denominations in the early twentieth-century that contraception ran counter to God's plans for procreation. In keeping with his own general emphasis on living in spiritual power, he saw a link between the use of contraception and the loss of power. In 1937 he called contraceptives a "cheap plaything," declaring that he had seen whole groups of people lose their spiritual power ("slain") by using contraception.[183] So he said in 1940, "Let the Holy Spirit be your birth control—and this is free!"[184]

It is possible that Buchman thought that abstinence except for the purposes of having children was an ideal for married couples. He once said that his views on birth control and abstinence were similar to those of Gandhi, and Gandhi came to believe that a commitment to chastity in his own marriage had helped to give him the strength to pursue his battle for nonviolence.[185] But one of Buchman's American colleagues, Kenaston Twitchell, expressed what Lean considered to be Buchman's philosophy less definitively, and in a way that put responsibility on married couples themselves to decide what they thought was right—as long as it fitted in with what was "natural": "A single man or woman finds in the discipline and freedom of absolute purity complete satisfaction and the free use of every energy and affection. The married man or woman finds exactly the same freedom in this redirection of instinct, along with whatever natural use of it God may direct."[186]

According to Strong, Buchman assumed that wherever celibacy or periodic abstinence appeared, a rich culture would grow up around it.[187] His basis concern was that the sexual dimension of marriage should be as much surrendered to God as any other. He evidently thought that people who were self-indulgent within marriage would not be able to help people who had problems with sexual sin outside it nor have the energy for the kind of unconditional spiritual outreach that he thought was needed. A related factor was that much of MRA's international outreach was staffed by married couples, and if they chose to have a lot of children it was bound to affect their mobility. In this context, if contraception was morally wrong, abstinence became an obvious possible solution.

A culture certainly developed in which the virtues of abstinence were much emphasized—although it is difficult to generalize across a movement that had expanded so much. Some people's experience of this was evidently liberating.

Lean suggests that those who chose a path of abstinence out of genuine conviction found that it brought them a greater freedom rather than a sense of strain.[188] On the other hand, there may have been occasions when the stress on purity in marriage became exaggerated and complicated for some couples. In 1954 the Catholic commentator Arnold Lunn—while praising MRA's emphasis on discipline—compared MRA practices with Catholic ones by saying, "I find married couples whose conception of marital relations is more austere than ours, perhaps too austere."[189]

For all his emphasis on linking spiritual power with sexual abstinence or restraint, it is hard to know exactly what Buchman said privately to couples when discussing these issues. It is clear that he wanted them to discover the link that existed in his mind between purity and spiritual vitality. On the other hand, he may have been conscious that his unmarried status made him less suited to giving advice in some situations. In 1942 he told a British serviceman who thought that there was lack of spontaneity between men and women at Mackinac, "I am sometimes sad I never had guidance from God to get married—I might have been able to help more."[190] His responses were not always prudish. Hunter reports that he encouraged women whose husbands had a roving eye to counter the problem with greater seductiveness.[191] In certain circumstances he does not seem to have been against remarriage—even while being very opposed to divorce. In 1940, on hearing that the son of an old friend was getting married, he did everything he could to make the ceremony and reception a happy one. It was the man's fifth marriage and the woman's fourth.[192]

There was thus a sense that while Buchman had strong views about what was right and wrong, he tried to avoid responding to situations in a formulaic way. His responses to people's needs were often unpredictable. There was also an artistic, as well as logical, side to Buchman's mind. He had taken painting lessons in his youth, and a strong visual imagination was sometimes evident in the analogies he used about the spiritual life.[193] Perhaps these artistic instincts influenced Buchman's way of dealing with people, for he clearly believed that an element of creativity was needed for effective personal work.

4

Theological Questions

As Buchman's approach to personal work indicated, he was eager to avoid approaching people with preconceived ideas. F. B. Meyer once said that Christianity was "not a creed, but a life."[1] Buchman's view was similar. He saw his work in terms of "the propagation of life, rather than the propagation of a plan."[2] Method was necessary but also dangerous. "I believe wholeheartedly in method, but there is a great danger in method," he said at Kuling, noting that a great many Christian workers were being "fooled by method."[3] "I have no method. With each person it is different. It is not really a method, it is a principle of life," he said a few years later.[4] This emphasis on life was an important feature of Buchman's thinking and one that was connected to his understanding of the Holy Spirit. The Holy Spirit was essentially the source of the kind of life he was trying to promote. He once expressed something like this in a letter to Douglas Mackenzie at Hartford: "I conceive my first mission to be a programme of life under the sustained guidance of the Holy Spirit."[5]

Buchman was not primarily a theologian, and he stressed that he was not in any way proposing some new revelation about divine truth.[6] His core teachings were not complicated, and he wanted them to be simple enough to be comprehensible to everyone. He even once wrote of the "sin of not putting a message so that it is understandable by everyone."[7] At the same time, he did have theological assumptions. At one level, these were quite traditional or conservative, as illustrated by his attitude to scripture. His approach to the Bible was essentially precritical in the sense that he generally used it in a literal way to support his evangelistic work. In his courses at Hartford, in which the Bible was often quoted, he often emphasized its role in helping people learn how to deal with individuals. But he did not—according to a critic of his time at Penn State—read what modern scholars were saying about it.[8] Biblical authority was important to him. "Whenever I depart from Christ or Paul I am wrong," he said in the early 1920s, and he responded to a student who claimed that Plato was superior to the Bible by declaring that he found his norm in the Bible rather than Plato's *The Republic*.[9]

Throughout his life Buchman was drawn to passages in the Bible that referred to God communicating with and leading his people. Unsurprisingly, he was particularly drawn to the Acts of the Apostles. He often recommended the Whitsun story in the second chapter of Acts, for example. Indeed, Acts was arguably the OG's most important reference point.[10] He also drew inspiration from the Jewish prophets. For example, at meetings in Caux in 1947 he cited verses from Isaiah, Amos, and Habakkuk that referred to listening to God in some way and read Ezekiel 2:1–5, a passage that touched on God communicating with people. The prophets were "very modern for today," he said.[11] It is possible to read his own quiet times, with their references to social and political as well as personal issues, as an attempt to be prophetic himself. Moreover, by linking the OG and MRA to the Jewish prophets, he was clearly placing his work in a prophetic tradition. MRA was "recapturing, revitalizing [and] reliving" the message of the prophets, he said in 1939.[12]

In terms of his underlying doctrinal outlook, Buchman was in fact quite orthodox. The Anglican modernist H. D. A. Major praised the OG for avoiding "blood theology," and it is true that the movement's emphasis on experience gave space to churchmen like B. H. Streeter, who questioned substitutionary or sacrificial interpretations of the atonement.[13] In reality, though, as his descriptions of his experience in Keswick in 1908 indicated, Buchman's understanding of the cross was traditional in the sense that he believed in a literal sense that Christ had died on the cross for the sins of humanity. Furthermore, he stressed the importance of salvation through the blood of Christ throughout his life. For example, in 1943 he insisted that MRA took the reality of sin, and Christ as the cure for it, seriously. "You must have that emphasis on morals plus the saving power of Jesus Christ," he said.[14] He liked quoting the verse from John's First Epistle: "The blood of Jesus Christ cleanseth us from all sin," quoting it even to people who were less likely to be religious. Once in Caux after the war he used it as the title for a meeting when the audience contained a number of miners from the Ruhr.[15]

Buchman also saw his work in terms of expanding the influence of Christ in the world. "We are in a global effort to win the world to our Lord and Saviour, Jesus Christ," he said just before returning to Europe in 1946.[16] Later, a few months before he died, he said that he lived to make Jesus Christ "regnant" in the life of every person he met.[17] He also talked about Jesus himself in very personal terms. For example, he loved and would cite Charles A. Miles's devotional hymn "I Come to the Garden Alone," containing the lines "He walks with me, and he talks with me, and tells me I am His own."[18] This sense of the reality of Christ's presence obviously had its roots in the Keswick episode, but it had been reinforced by subsequent experiences. Notably, following his stroke in 1942 he said that he had seen the "glory" of the other world: "I saw the outstretched arms of Christ, and they were marvellous."[19]

Buchman did not shy away from bringing this focus on Christ into the wider MRA culture, even though the vocabulary of MRA was less overtly Christian than that of the OG. In the 1950s Buchman encouraged members of the MRA team to bring people to what he called a "mature experience of Jesus Christ."[20] A team gathering of 1951 concluded with the singing of two famous evangelical hymns: "Rock of Ages" by Augustus Toplady and "Jesus, Lover of My Soul" by Charles Wesley.[21] Jesus "Just Exactly Suits Us Sinners," Buchman told a Mackinac audience in 1956.[22]

In Buchman's mind there was also a link between Christ and the Holy Spirit that reflected traditional Christian understandings of the Trinity. In a speech on the "War of Ideas" in 1943, Buchman declared that when people faced their sin and found new life through the saving power of Christ, they would then experience the "dynamic" of the Holy Spirit. This combination of features was, he said, the "programme for the Church today."[23] According to the theologian Klaus Bockmuehl—who saw Buchman's theology as thoroughly mainstream—Buchman's essential teaching lay in these three areas: acknowledgement of sin as revealed by absolute standards, regeneration of humankind and the world through the cross of Christ, and guidance by the Holy Spirit.[24]

Alongside the traditional aspects of Buchman's theology, there were also more liberal elements. His approach to evangelism involved addressing the conditions of nonbelief in people rather than trying to change their beliefs. He assumed that once a person had been freed from sin, belief would follow. Experience rather than doctrine was thus emphasized. "We must recapture the power of personal religious experience," he said in 1938.[25] There was little room here for formal apologetics, and it was one of the features of the culture of the OG and MRA that it produced few publications aimed at directly engaging with the war of ideas in intellectual terms.

Buchman's liberal side was also evident in his attitude to the non-Christian religions. Whereas he assumed that the recovery of belief in people from Christian cultures would normally lead them to Christianity, he treated people from non-Christian cultures differently, not expecting them to convert to Christianity but suggesting that they take their own religious traditions more seriously. This might explain his readiness, at Penn State, to question Blair Buck's adherence to Confucianism, while later being more enthusiastic about other spiritual traditions. But there was probably an evolution in Buchman's thinking here too, as he was increasingly exposed to non-Western cultures from 1915 onward.

In later years Buchman was keen to dissociate the OG and MRA from one particular religious outlook. So, at the Congress of Faiths in London's City Temple in 1937, he said that the OG was not itself a faith but a "fire through all the faiths" and that it never took people "from faith to faith."[26] MRA, he said a couple of years later, was to be a "common denominator" for everyone, regardless of party, race, class, creed, point of view, or personal advantage.[27] There was, of course, a kind of minimalist theology present here. Buchman liked the idea that MRA could be seen as the "ABC of the answer," and at a very basic level his emphasis on God and absolute moral standards did amount to a kind of theological ABC.[28] But to distance themselves from any one particular creed, MRA workers sometimes insisted that MRA was not a religious organization as such. For example, in an MRA funding application to the Ford Foundation in May 1959—which was unsuccessful—it was stressed that MRA was not a religious organization, although this was somewhat ambiguous, for people representing different religious traditions were then listed as involved.[29] The point was clearly that although MRA strongly emphasized the importance of faith, it did not espouse any one religious viewpoint.

Buchman's openness to the non-Christian world was in many ways a product of the calling to "remake the world" that he believed God had given him. This task was by its nature so big that it invited the contribution of people of all faiths. Implicit in it too was a challenge to Christians to let go of control of the process. The task went "beyond the grasp or control of us Christians," Finnish MRA worker Paul Gundersen recalled.[30] Buchman intended MRA to be a means of bringing people together for this larger global endeavor. Speaking in California in 1948, he described it as the "good road of an ideology inspired by God" on which all could unite, declaring that Catholic, Jew, Protestant, Hindu, Muslim, Buddhist, and Confucianist could all travel on this good road together.[31]

This call for co-operation can be seen partly as a response to a particular situation: the urgent need for postwar reconstruction in many countries and the threat of expansionist communism. It was not a theological statement that the world's religions should be seen as equivalent but a practical call for people to learn from one another as they engaged in common tasks. Buchman wanted to create an environment where people from different traditions could listen to

God without the threat of proselytism, although he did not thereby intend to prevent people from talking openly about the central tenets of their faiths. The call for greater unity was also perhaps a response to the changing makeup of MRA itself. People of many faiths were attending the Caux conferences by the late 1940s. For example, over one hundred Muslims from ten Islamic countries visited Caux in 1949.[32]

Among people of non-Christian backgrounds, Buchman had a special respect for Mahatma Gandhi. He first met him in February 1916, when he spent three days on his own with him in Madras, and they remained in touch over subsequent decades.[33] After Gandhi's death Buchman stated that he had been a "very close personal friend" of his.[34] During a visit to India in 1924, he wrote of Gandhi to a friend: "The sphere of [Gandhi's] usefulness will be sainthood and a compelling one at that."[35] Clearly, Buchman did not see sanctity as the exclusive preserve of Christians. On the other hand, he perhaps sensed certain specifically Christian qualities in the Indian leader, because he once told a group of people in Caux that Gandhi was "more of a Christian" than some of them realized, highlighting his enthusiasm for Christian hymns.[36] On hearing of Gandhi's death in 1953, he is reported to have said, "He lives. His spirit lives for ever."[37] Buchman believed that Gandhi's philosophy was vital for modern India, and he lamented that there were people who claimed to be followers of Gandhi but did not live by his principles.[38] India needed a lot of "little Gandhis" who could carry his thinking to the people of India and the world, he thought. Such work was part of India's "great mission."[39]

The implication of Buchman's appreciation of Gandhi was that he was also respectful of Hinduism. He was certainly willing to draw on Hindu spirituality. In 1952, during the MRA tour of India at that time, he laid a wreath at the place where Gandhi was cremated, with the flowers being arranged in the form of Hindi words that had also been Gandhi's last words, "Oh God"; later during the same tour he had guidance to mention the *Gita* in a conversation with the Maharaja of Mysore.[40] This respect for other religions was also evident in Buchman's approach to Islam. For example, he said in 1955 that the Muslim world could be a "girder of unity for all civilisation."[41] Again, in 1959, he wrote to Mohammed V, king of Morocco, "The hour is late, but with the help of Allah we will win."[42] Buchman also tried to use his ancestry in this connection. He believed that his family was related to Theodore Bibliander, a professor of theology who had succeeded the Swiss reformer Huldrych Zwingli at the academy in Zurich in 1531 and who published a Latin translation of the Koran in 1543. Whether Buchman was indeed related to Bibliander is not clear, but he referred

Fig 6 Buchman meeting Mahatma Gandhi, India, 1924. Photo: Oxford Group Archives.

enthusiastically to the supposed ancestral link with him in a letter to the Shah of Iran in 1959.[43] Buchman was also keen to highlight the contribution of Jewish spirituality. Speaking in California in 1948, he cited verses from Isaiah and the Psalms to emphasize what he called the "pristine contribution of the Jews."[44]

Buchman's approach to people of other faiths was exemplified by an episode often cited in MRA literature, which involved the Muslim president of the Northern Territories Council of the Gold Coast (Ghana), the Tolon Na. At an

MRA conference in 1954, the Ghanaian was unexpectedly asked by Buchman when he had last stolen something. He was so shaken by the question that he "prayed to Allah" for help and decided to put right as far as possible the dishonesties he had committed in his life since childhood.[45] Buchman evidently approached the Tolon Na as he did everyone else, asking him a question that he thought brought a particular issue into focus for him. Typically, Buchman also used stories in his interactions with people from other faiths. On a visit to Teheran in 1953, he had a meeting with the Iranian prime minister, Mohammed Mossadegh, where he told him stories of fathers and sons becoming different, with Mossadegh's own son standing beside them.[46] Clearly, Buchman made no attempt to convert these men to Christianity. Others who saw him on a regular basis confirm that there was no hidden agenda to convert. Rajmohan Gandhi, who was often in Buchman's company, either with others or on his own, recalled that never once, directly or indirectly, did Buchman suggest that he should embrace Christianity.[47] Christian MRA workers who were operating in non-Christian cultures adopted a similar approach. Service rather than conversion was regarded as the priority.[48]

Yet people from non-Christian religious or spiritual traditions were probably attracted to Buchman as much for the personal qualities they saw in him as for the inclusivity of his ideas. Some of them clearly thought he was a source of great wisdom. When the Stoney Indians, a branch of the Sioux people, made him a blood brother in 1934, they gave him the name of A-Wo-Zan-Zan-Tonga, which means "Great Light in Darkness," and declared, "The Great Spirit will look with love and compassion on you when He calls you to the Happy Hunting Grounds."[49] On arrival in Egypt in 1952 en route to India he was visited on his first evening by Mohammed Neguib, the first Egyptian prime minister after the country's independence in the same year. Neguib consulted him about how to bring up his son.[50] Similarly, a month before Buchman's death, a group of six Buddhist monks, representing the Presiding Abbots' Association of Burma, arrived in Caux to celebrate his birthday, suggesting that a man like him came only "once in a thousand years."[51]

Buchman also sometimes collaborated with people who had no particular religious or spiritual affiliation. For example, during MRA's effort to promote industrial harmony in postwar Europe after 1945, Buchman worked closely with the leader of the French textile unions, Maurice Mercier, who was outside any religious tradition.[52] Buchman seems to have made no direct attempt to convert nonbelievers, although the faith-based culture that was a feature of MRA was clearly an implicit challenge to agnosticism or atheism. In a supportive statement about Buchman made at the time of his eightieth birthday, Paul Kurowski, a German communist who encountered MRA in the late 1940s, said, "Frank Buchman never tried to convert me. He never tried to answer my anti-religious points of view. He just had faith in the best in me."[53]

People were also drawn into MRA who had not yet come to endorse all of Buchman's views. More generally, and perhaps obviously, not everyone who spoke at MRA assemblies was "changed" in any formal sense. Buchman often encouraged people to contribute their reflections, whatever stage they had reached on their spiritual journey. He had long wished to avoid creating a kind of Christian club that was inward looking in character. In a comment of 1921, which reflected his later thinking as well, he said, "The group I have got to form is not one with other Christians, but with interesting sinners."[54] "We are going to have Communists this morning—some of them changed, some of them changing—speak to us," he announced one day in Caux in 1950.[55]

The roots of Buchman's open-minded attitude to other faiths or beliefs partly lay in his approach to personal work. His emphasis on spiritual practices rather than beliefs meant that his message could easily be adapted to non-Christians. It also had roots in the culture of the American YMCA, where John R. Mott's ecumenism was so influential. Indeed, Buchman's work can arguably be understood as an offshoot of the international ecumenism that Mott pioneered and perhaps of the wider evangelistic impulse given expression at the World Missionary Conference in 1910. The YMCA itself had an interest in Asian religion. Howard Walter, for example, had been assigned by the YMCA to specialize in the study of Islam.[56] In its outreach into non-Christian cultures, the YMCA welcomed non-Christian participation, even if control remained in Christian hands.[57] Buchman built on this practice, but also went beyond it. In places like India and Japan MRA came to be run by non-Christians, even if at times Europeans and Americans remained closely involved with the work there. Beyond the YMCA, however, Buchman's thought reflected the growth of a wider ecumenical current in twentieth-century American religion. MRA was not unlike the many special interest groups that grew up outside a denominational framework to work on specific objectives, particularly after 1945.[58]

The case for placing Buchman in an international ecumenical context is reinforced by the fact that he attended one of Henry Lunn's ecumenical conferences for Christian leaders in Switzerland in 1930.[59] In addition, he was a friend of the Swedish archbishop and ecumenist, Nathan Söderblom, founder of the Life and Work movement.[60] Both Buchman and Söderblom were aware of Europe's growing encounter with non-Christian religious cultures. Interestingly, they were also both admirers of the Sikh Christian and mystic Sadhu Sundar Singh, who made a strong impression on religious audiences when he traveled to Britain and America in 1920. Buchman himself had helped to organize the visit of Singh to the United States, spending a month with him and recommending him for his saintly qualities.[61]

Writing to Söderblom in 1931, Buchman argued that the OG could help to make the ecumenical vision a reality. Inviting the Swedish cleric to a house party in Oxford, Buchman observed that many ecumenical leaders were concerned that the spirit of unity they longed for in the wider church was not present in their own immediate circles. It was to answer this problem through "meeting people's deepest needs," Buchman said, that people of different generations were gathering in Oxford. He also talked of the way unity in people's home lives could be seen as a precursor of the kind of unity that could take place at an ecclesiastical level.[62] While Buchman endorsed the ecumenical vision, he saw his own work not so much as trying to make it happen in a formal way but as enabling people of different sides to have the kind of spiritual experience he thought could make greater unity possible.

The desire to appeal to as wide an audience as possible and the expansion of the movement beyond its Christian heartlands meant that from the 1940s onward references to Christ became fewer in OG and MRA literature.[63] The word "God" itself was sometimes removed from MRA vocabulary if it seemed problematic. Speaking to Buddhists, Peter Howard talked not of God but of the "universal force in the heart of every man." At the same time, even in non-Christian cultures, a Christian message was sometimes presented. For example, *A Cowboy's Christmas*, a modern presentation of Christ's nativity, was put on in December 1952 during the MRA campaign in India. The effect was considerable. A Christmas Day presentation of the play to a multireligious audience resulted in hundreds of people filing past a crib after the performance.[64]

The historian of British evangelicalism, David Bebbington, has argued that the OG's approach to evangelism was based on a strategy of "maximum inculturation."[65] It is true that the OG constantly sought to interpret Christianity in the light of contemporary culture. The same could be said of Buchman's attitude to non-Christian traditions. He wanted to reexpress the heart of his own faith in language that could be understood by people from other religions. But if "inculturation" is here understood to have meant a tactic for the Christianization of the non-Christian world, then Bebbington's interpretation would not be accurate. There was an emphasis on Christ, certainly, but not on Christianity as such. In a letter to Mackenzie in 1918, Buchman observed that his work in

Japan was being done in the spirit of the Japanese Christian leaders who had once told Henry Drummond, "Tell [the church at home] that Japan wants no more doctrines. Japan wants Christ."[66] Buchman differentiated between Christ and Christianity. "The Group wants to transform organised Christianity into an organic fellowship of Jesus Christ," he said in a letter of 1936.[67]

There was also a sense in which Buchman believed Christians had something to learn from people with other beliefs. For example, talking about MRA's postwar outreach, he wondered if Marxists, with what he saw as their openness to new things and readiness to die for their beliefs, might be the ones to pave the way for a new dimension of moral and spiritual living.[68]

It is clear that Buchman wanted to distance himself from promoting a Christian work as such. But when asked in the late 1930s what the difference was between the OG and MRA, he would sometimes answer that if MRA could be thought of as the passenger cars of a train, the OG was its engine.[69] The implication was that the deeper Christian roots of the OG needed to inform and give energy to MRA's wider social outreach. But it would probably be a mistake to read too much into this. The metaphor was likely more a working illustration of the different strands of his work than an ideological statement. It points, though, to the fact that Buchman was engaged in projects that were slightly different and that to some people would have seemed contradictory. He was trying to deepen the Christian experience of certain individuals, while at the same time reaching out to as wide an audience as possible. He hoped, of course, that in doing the former he would be giving life to the latter.

Buchman's theological assumptions did not go down well with everyone. To some conservative evangelicals it seemed that there was little room in Buchman's thinking for the uniqueness of Christ or the atonement. For example, the Oxford Evangelical Fellowship came down publicly against the group in 1932, and in 1958 an editorial in *Christianity Today* complained that MRA's teachings were syncretist.[70] Some religious commentators also thought that Buchman's ideas could be reduced to a kind of moralism and that he promoted a natural theology.[71] MRA workers from Christian traditions clearly saw things differently. Alan Thornhill, for example, once observed that the movement was involved in "enlisting everyone in a common purpose, without falling into the dangers of syncretism." He acknowledged that there was an element of paradox in MRA's approach but argued that the Gospel itself contained paradoxes, suggesting that when dealing with living people, truth was bigger than formulas. "I see no contradiction in the fact that MRA is truly Christ-centred, and yet that there is room in it for all men everywhere," he said.[72]

A clue as to how Buchman was able in his own mind to reconcile a Christ-centered view of the world with an appreciation of other faiths can be found in his experience at Keswick. In one of his accounts of the episode, he described his experience of surrender by saying, "I was the centre of my own life. That big 'I' had to be crossed out." Buchman would often talk to his colleagues about the need for people to have an "experience of the Cross," by which he meant something similar to what he had gone through: a "crossing out" of a person's "I" or ego and its replacement with a will wholly given to God.[73] If the surrender of self is understood to have been the central element in Buchman's Keswick experience, then it is possible to see how he could approach people from non-Christian traditions so generously. All people could choose to surrender themselves to God, whatever their faith backgrounds.[74]

MRA can thus be understood as Buchman's attempt to universalize his experience at Keswick. By talking of the cross of Christ as an experience rather than a doctrine—the "Cross of Christ lived in reality"—he was stressing that it was not essential to be talking about Christ in order to be living in his power.[75] During an OG campaign in Denmark in 1935, the bishop of Copenhagen, Dr. Hans Fuglsang-Damgaard, questioned Buchman as to whether Christ had received sufficient emphasis in an OG meeting. Buchman responded by saying that when he had visited the bishop the previous week, the bishop had not told him that he loved his wife.[76] The implication was that those who talked about Christ the most were not always those who loved him most. "Relate all your activity to Christ, though that doesn't mean you will always have to be talking about Christ," he once said.[77] Buchman evidently thought that a person could have an inner experience of the Spirit of Christ without converting to Christianity. He seems to have been suggesting something like this when he said, in 1959, "Whether it is Jew or Gentile, democratic or Communist, it is an experience all can have."[78] Indeed, one of Buchman's British supporters, the Oxford graduate Michael Hutchinson, once explained there was an assumption by people in MRA—and he was clearly referring to Christians here—that whenever the Holy Spirit spoke in someone's heart, Christ was there also.[79]

In Buchman's mind the reach of the Kingdom of God was clearly broader than the Christian church as such. He also thought that it was not easy to describe. Speaking to colleagues in the Bavarian town of Garmisch-Partenkirchen in the late 1940s, he said, "The Kingdom of God is symbolic of a definiteness of experience directly observable by someone else, but not easily described. What is observable is a peace, a confidence, a recovery of freedom, and spontaneity of thought, of will and of nerve. It is not joinable. You have to experience it for yourself." He also said that he experienced at Keswick the "restorative and recuperative processes of God" and that MRA was "such a moment" in the life of anyone. The future of MRA, he said, lay in such moments occurring in different lives, in different countries, with the outcome being felt at a national level.[80]

Buchman's approach to nonbelievers and people of other faiths obviously had major theological implications. Tellingly, however, he showed little interest in trying to explore them or to defend MRA at a doctrinal level. In some ways, his approach was replicated in ideas developed by Catholic theologian Karl Rahner after Buchman's death. Rahner's suggestion that there existed "anonymous Christians"—believers who were in their spiritual orientation Christian, if not their doctrines—had much in common with Buchman's conviction that the signs of the Kingdom of God were often visible outside the Christian church.[81] Yet if Buchman would probably have endorsed such thinking, he would have been cautious about the implicit Christian paternalism in such vocabulary. It is certainly hard to see him articulating his message in terms of the fulfillment theology that was widespread at the time of the World Missionary Conference in 1910, which saw Christianity as the natural fulfillment of all that was best in the other religions.[82]

Buchman's approach to theological questions was reflected in his attitude to the Christian church. Buchman was sometimes uneasy with what he saw as the ecclesiastical priorities of the churches. One reason he clashed with the missionary community in China was that he did not wish to work through exclusively ecclesiastical channels. He probably thought that the church in its traditional form was destined to pass away, for he had guidance in the summer of 1919 that a new order was coming in Christian work, the basis of which was to be a "Holy Spirit–directed life."[83] This skepticism about traditional religion at times pervaded the OG and MRA as well, for they sometimes saw themselves as doing the work that they believed the churches were failing to do.[84]

In the mid-1930s attempts by some in the Church of England to draw the OG under its wing failed in part because Buchman did not want his work to become the property of only one group. The Holy Spirit could not be limited like that, he thought. To one proposal he objected that hitherto there had been no chair of the OG except the Holy Spirit.[85] Impatient with denominationalism, he once lamented that many people found it hard to get away from "preconceived ideas" and to "see Christ in other confessions." He said in 1937 that the church of the future would be "above confession."[86] There was also a sense in which his spirituality ran counter to ecclesiastical structures that emphasized priestly authority. Borrowing a phrase used by a member of his team, he recommended to one Caux audience the concept of "the spiritual priesthood of all believers."[87] In ecclesiastical terms his work was essentially a movement of the laity. Indeed, Franz König, the cardinal archbishop of Vienna who became supportive of MRA some years after Buchman's death, identified his work as a "lay apostolate."[88]

Although Buchman had a significant following in the Church of England, he also aroused considerable suspicion among some Anglicans. This was revealed in 1955 when a working party of the Church of England's Social and Industrial Council came out with a report on MRA suggesting that, among other matters, it lacked a serious engagement with theological questions, its members could easily become psychologically dependent on the movement, and its approach to social change was utopian. Not everything in the document was critical, and the report was not formally adopted by the Church of England; however, it was clearly a damaging assessment. Yet it was also contentious. The leadership of MRA thought that the working party had been prejudiced against MRA from the outset and that MRA had not been given an adequate opportunity to make its case. In addition, the working party itself was not fully united in recommending the report.[89]

MRA's postwar relationship with Catholicism was also difficult, primarily because the Vatican was worried that MRA was promoting syncretist ideas and also because for a time it thought—mistakenly—that MRA was secretly structured around a religious hierarchy. So, in 1951, it issued a warning that Catholics should not take part in MRA meetings except with special permission, nor take offices of responsibility with MRA, and it sent out a similar warning in 1957. Furthermore, the future cardinal Suenens of Belgium published a book, warning that MRA was promoting religious indifferentism.[90] These criticisms made life difficult for MRA in some countries. It was not easy for MRA to work in Italy, for example. It was less affected in France and Germany, in spite of the presence of large Catholic populations there.

Many senior Catholics were in fact impressed by MRA and publicly endorsed Buchman's message. These included the German theologians, Karl Adam and Werner Schöllgen, and the prominent American layman, Joseph Scott.[91] Moreover, some in the entourage of Cardinal Montini of Milan, the future Paul VI, were intrigued by MRA, especially by its record of dialogue with communists in Italy, and there was a gradual, if cautious, improvement of relations over time. Catholics who did endorse MRA evidently saw common ground between MRA spirituality and their own. For example, at the end of the 1940s a group of roughly ten Catholic supporters of MRA, priests and laypersons, put together an informal defense of MRA teachings about the quiet time, stressing the essential healthiness of MRA's thinking and stating that Catholic concerns were more a matter of vocabulary than substance.[92]

More personally, Buchman did not share the anti-Catholic attitudes that were widespread among American Protestants of his time. He wrote to an English Jesuit in 1933, "Our principle has always been to send all Roman Catholics back to their Fathers for confession," while also adding that the OG allowed individuals to decide for themselves which church to go to.[93] He admired the Catholic Church in many ways. He thought, for example, that it was a bulwark against communism.[94] He was also impressed with Catholic teaching, for he said in 1948, "The Catholic has the teachings of Christ in [their] fullest conception—the Body and Blood of Christ." Yet he said at the same time, "Give the Catholics the Holy Spirit," perhaps believing that a personal encounter with the Holy Spirit was lacking in some of them.[95] Buchman did not himself place special emphasis on the Eucharist in the way that the Catholic Church did. But he was not indifferent to it. To one supporter, who was seeking the kind of "experience of the Cross" that he frequently talked about, Buchman recommended Holy Communion.[96]

Buchman probably became more attuned to the importance of spiritual authority in the Catholic tradition over time.[97] His Lutheran training, which led him to believe that a priest was effectively a master in his own parish, may initially have prevented him from fully understanding the structures of the Catholic Church, and in particular the pressures on Catholic priests from the wider hierarchy whenever they tried to develop links with non-Catholic groups like MRA. At least that is how Michel Sentis saw it. In dealing with François Charrière, the bishop in whose diocese the Caux conferences took place, Buchman—according to Sentis—was inclined to blame difficulties on problems in Charrière's character rather than on the pressures arising out of his accountability to the church hierarchy.[98]

If Buchman's later thought suggests that he was more concerned with national rather than ecclesiastical renewal, he certainly understood himself to be doing the work of the church in the broadest sense. Indeed, Bockmuehl argued that his entire life consisted of dialogue with people within the church.[99] His primary interest, however, was in whether or not a particular church was in practice under the control of the Holy Spirit. He sometimes felt that the "Church was an enemy of the Church."[100] The church was meant to be revolutionary. "I believe with all my heart in the Church, the Church aflame, the Church on fire with revolution," he said in 1943.[101] He evidently felt that the churches of his time lacked a realistic engagement with world issues when compared with contemporary politicians. Talking in Caux in 1947 he said, "The Churches don't sound the note yet. The statesmen do. They have to. They face facts."[102]

Buchman often stressed that he did not wish the OG or MRA to compete with the churches; and many theologians and thinkers of different denominations found this convincing.[103] But there was a tension in Buchman's thinking here, for he once also said that the OG contained the spirit of the church. Lawson Wood recorded him as saying, "I believe in going to church on Sunday morning. That's what we want to bring back to Britain again." Yet at the same time he said, "The Oxford Group is the church. . . . The church fathers said that the church is where the Holy Spirit is. Don't let us lose that." He also reacted to the idea that the church and the group were different. "The Oxford Group is the church at work," he insisted.[104]

Clearly from these perspectives, Buchman's network was indeed the church to the extent that it was a vehicle for the Holy Spirit. In practice, OG and MRA activities did for some people perform some of the functions of a church, in the sense that they created a culture that provided a framework for spiritual fellowship, accountability, and action.[105] In postwar Britain national MRA meetings were for many years scheduled on Sunday mornings, and this of course kept members of the MRA team from attending morning church services—implying to some that MRA was in competition with the churches. Yet Buchman's Christian supporters always remained members of their traditional denominations, sometimes actively so, and in this sense the movement did not become sectarian.[106]

Buchman's attitude to the church was one of the reasons behind a split in the American branch of the MRA work in April 1941. The base for Buchman's work in the United States in the interwar period was Calvary Church in New York, an Episcopalian parish where Sam Shoemaker had become rector following his participation in the world tour of 1924–25. Shoemaker continued to be closely involved with the OG until 1941, when Buchman's supporters were asked to leave Calvary Church. For Shoemaker a central reason for the separation was that he thought MRA was moving away from the tradition of operating within the framework of the churches. There were probably personal reasons for the split too. Garth Lean, at least, suggests that Shoemaker—who, like Buchman, had a strong personality—did not always want to accept Buchman's authority.[107] Buchman was very upset by the division. But MRA's growing engagement with people from non-Christian backgrounds would probably not have been possible if it had remained tied to an ecclesiastical framework, so some kind of separation might have occurred anyway.

Buchman's attitude to the church, and his use of stories of change as evidence for the Gospel's effectiveness, provoked contrasting responses from theologians. Karl Barth, for example, in an article of 1937 suggested that there was a fundamental difference between the OG and the church. The OG, he said, had a tendency to judge the truths of Christianity by results, that is, the numbers of people who had been changed. This contained a subtle kind of humanism, he thought; the church's authority should come from Christ, through scripture and not through the apparent effectiveness of its work in the world.[108] B. H. Streeter came to the OG's defense, arguing that the effectiveness of the group in making the truths of Christianity real to large numbers of people was a sign that the Holy Spirit was "manifestly at work" at work in it. Streeter also differentiated between what he called the visible and the invisible church. If Barth was right that the OG was not formally a part of the former, there was much to be said for seeing it as part of the latter.[109]

The irony here was that at a purely theological level Buchman's outlook was probably closer to that of Barth than that of Streeter. T. Willard Hunter, at least, thought that Buchman and Barth had in common a belief in the divinity of Christ and the objective authority of scripture.[110] Moreover, Julian P. Thornton-Duesbery wrote in 1932 that the OG held "spiritual kinship" with anyone who in their experience was realizing the truths that had been proclaimed by Barth and his school.[111] Buchman would probably have agreed with Barth in saying that the Gospel did not need stories of change to prove its validity, for he once said, in a letter to the Swiss Reformed theologian, Emil Brunner—who was involved in the OG in the early 1930s, "The Gospel is its own defence. It does not need the bolstering of men's device. Let us be willing to live and courageously witness what we preach, that we are sinners saved by grace."[112]

Buchman, however, was looking for a kind of Christian work that went beyond ecclesiastical revival. Here his thinking was again similar to that of Drummond, who once called for a class of mission work that was "not wholly absorbed with specific charges, or ecclesiastical progress, or the inculcation of Western creeds" but whose outlook went forth to the "nation as a whole." The emphasis would be not so much on the church as on the Kingdom of God.[113] It was a good expression of what Buchman was later striving after. He once said to his team that he wanted them to live with the program of reconstructing nations uppermost in their minds.[114] Writing in the foreword to the French edition of *Remaking the World*, Robert Schuman—a devout Catholic—seems to have

Fig. 7 Buchman with New Testament theologian B. H. Streeter, Oxford, mid-1930s. Photo: Arthur Strong, Oxford Group Archives.

seen MRA as reflecting this kind of vision, for he commended Buchman's work for providing "teams of trained people, ready for the service of the state."[115]

One of Buchman's most important statements about the need for a more revolutionary form of Christianity was a speech he gave in 1938 in the Swedish city of Visby on the island of Gotland, titled "Revival, Revolution, Renaissance."

It was sometimes held up in MRA as indicative of an expansion in Buchman's thinking, although it less contained new ideas than was a synthesis of the thinking of previous years.[116] In this speech Buchman suggested that many Christians wanted the OG to campaign for what he termed "revival." In his mind, however, the concept of revival was too much associated with ecclesiastical renewal in the narrower sense. He obviously thought that there were people within his own team whose religious outlook was too rigid and who failed to appreciate that something more radical was needed to address the deteriorating world situation. "The next step is revolution," he declared, calling on Christians to counter destructive forms of revolution with a revolutionary program of their own. Buchman warned that the kind of anticlericalism that had been seen on the Left in the Spanish Civil War would be repeated elsewhere if Christians did not become more radical. Two kinds of revolution were on offer, he thought. "How many churches are in ruins in Spain today? That is revolution—very uncomfortable. The point is this. Are the Christians going to build a Christian philosophy that will move Europe? Are you the kind of Christians that can build that revolution?" He challenged Christians to be more wholehearted: "There were some people in the Acts and the Gospels who gave everything. There were others who did not give everything. Even in a revolution some people want an amount of padding around them. I want to ask you this morning whether you want to be that kind of a revolutionary. If so, there may be a comfortable place for you behind the lines. But somewhere on the battlefront we will have the real revolutionaries."[117]

As the Visby speech indicated, Buchman believed that the spread of communism was linked to failures in the Christian churches. He said much the same elsewhere. In a letter of 1936, he linked the Russian Revolution with the weakness of the Russian church. The church in Russia had been "bereft" of the Christ it sought to bring, he said.[118] The need, then, was to create a Christianity that could meet the challenge of militant socialism. Buchman was not alone in trying to mobilize Christians by using a more revolutionary vocabulary. For example, Sherwood Eddy, who had moved away from YMCA pietism toward socialism since working with Buchman in Asia, published his own *Revolutionary Christianity* in 1939, in which he sought an amalgam of Marxism and Christianity.[119] If Buchman's version of Christian revolution was less left-wing than Eddy's, the two men shared a conviction that Christianity needed a more radical edge.

Buchman's increasing focus on the state and society rather than the church in the 1930s was reflected in some comments he made about OG outreach into

Scandinavia in the mid-1930s. In planning campaigns in Norway and Denmark in 1934–36, Buchman wanted to start by having contact with the countries' leaderships rather than going through traditional prayer meetings with their ecclesiastical associations. In discussing the Danish campaign of 1935, he was critical of a group meeting that had taken place in January 1935 without his blessing, which he thought had conveyed an overly ecclesiastical picture of what the OG was trying to do. He said that he wanted to begin with contacts with the prime minister and other national leaders: "That's where we have to begin in that nation. . . . We don't want to go in on the old basis." In discussing a projected campaign in Sweden, which in the end did not take place, he said, "My present thought is to try to go to Sweden when I can see the country together at a single function."[120]

Yet, deeper even than revolution, Buchman said at Visby, was what he called "renaissance," which he interpreted to mean the "rebirth of a nation."[121] Exactly what this involved, and how it differed from the idea of revolution, is not clear, but Buchman was evidently dissatisfied with his work at some level and sought a bolder expression of what was needed. To his Dutch supporters, following their successful house party in 1937, he said, "You have arranged excellent house-parties. But now we must see where we are in the perspective of international problems. You must be able to bring about a national renaissance in your country."[122]

This emphasis on the need for "renaissance" was replicated after World War II. Buchman said in 1948 that there was no other way than the "voice of God," with the Holy Spirit leading the way, and that "this revolution [would] result in renaissance."[123] In a speech at Caux a couple of years later, which showed again that Buchman was searching after a fresh expression of Christianity, he said that what was being offered at the conference center was a "new mold . . . something entirely different . . . something so different that it has never been attempted." He defined this new way as "renaissance," remarking that some people were trying to fit their "old mold" into something that could be called "renaissance."[124] Exactly what Buchman meant here is not clear, but in criticizing people who were attached to what he called the "old mold," he may have been suggesting that some Christians were failing to realize that MRA was not a religious enterprise in the traditional sense. "Life-changing is passé," he also once said in the late 1950s.[125] Again this is slightly obscure, because Buchman never ceased believing in the importance of personal work. He was probably again stating his desire to break out of a traditional evangelistic framework and to focus his attention on national as well as personal renewal.

As Buchman's call for a new mold indicated, there was a "modernizing" tendency in OG spirituality. People like Streeter who came from a liberal modernist theological background did not feel out of place in Buchman's work. To a certain degree, people in the OG understood themselves to be modernizers. "Let us be Moderns with God," declared the author of a key summary of OG spirituality.[126] Buchman himself once said, "Whatever you do, relate it to modern life."[127] Buchman's belief that ideas should not stand still was illustrated in his attitude to MRA itself. In his comments at Garmisch-Partenkirchen in the late 1940s, he said that the MRA fellowship could look forward with zest to the "adventure of receiving further disclosures." He meant by this that MRA was not a static concept. In the same spirit, and somewhat mischievously, Buchman sometimes insisted that he had not founded MRA at all, but only "discovered" it. He did not wish to identify MRA with himself.[128]

At the same time, it is also clear that Buchman never wanted to reinvent traditional Christian theology and morality, and in this sense he was not a modernist at all. This was another of the paradoxes at the heart of Buchman's theological position. He was orthodox on Christian doctrine and morality, while also wanting Christian thinking to evolve. Perhaps a way to disentangle the tension—if that is possible—is to say that while Buchman's theology changed little, his interpretation of the relevance of that theology, and how it could speak to the world of his time, was constantly shifting. "We must learn to put our truth differently," he said in the 1930s.[129]

Buchman believed that the presentation of truth by Christians was often too theoretical. Already at Penn State, in a series of observations about his work, he stated, "We want intellectual presentations, but they must contain convictions." He also wrote in his notes, in reference to some person or issue, "Too clever—bovine versus divine," the phrase once again illustrating his wariness of what he saw as intellectualism.[130] It was to be a recurring point in his thinking. After World War II, he said that the priority should be to put the "Holy Spirit first and the intellect second."[131] In a sense, the primary signal of a healthy spiritual life in his mind was not so much right thinking as a rightly directed will. Belief could not be separated from moral character. The Holy Spirit was "caught, not taught," he once observed, pointing to his conviction that evangelism came best not so much through the presentation of a set of doctrines as through the spirit of God-led people.[132]

Buchman's thinking on these matters had been shaped or reinforced by his experiences at Hartford Theological Seminary. Writing to Shoemaker in 1922, he said that the nature of theological seminary education as then conceived was inadequate. It was the task of every member of the faculty to promote "life" in such a way that it resulted in personal and social salvation, he suggested. Personal work in the broadest sense could not be relegated to a set of lectures on the subject but was the "whole purpose of theological seminary training." This was not happening.[133] He obviously envisaged the possibility of universities themselves coming under God's leadership, because he said a few years later, in 1934, that it was in God's plan to see the Holy Spirit "guiding the policy of a university."[134] In 1927 he wrote to H. Alexander Smith, stating that he was a "God-chosen instrument" for demonstrating what true education could become when Jesus was the central figure and where the Holy Spirit was present to lead. He added that Thomas Arnold, the nineteenth-century English headmaster of Rugby School, was a man who in his time had successfully revolutionized education along these lines.[135]

Some of these points were also present in a letter Buchman wrote to Brunner in 1932. Buchman complained to the Swiss theologian about what he saw as the inadequacy of much of modern theology: "The great conception of how to present Christ as He ought to be—the regnant Person and Power in the midst of the modern world—is lacking." More than that, he said, many theologians lacked a deep experience of what they were trying to convey—something he thought they needed if their theology was to be right: "If the Holy Spirit is once in control of our thinking as well as of our lives, it is remarkable how intelligent He is in giving our theology its correct perspective."[136] He evidently believed that Brunner's personal religious experience lagged behind his thinking, for a couple of years later he suggested to him that he had given people a "safe theology" as compensation for a lack of "victorious personal faith" in his own life. He wrote—referring to his own experience at Keswick—that it was only a deeper experience of the cross that had healed his own resentment; "a correct theology [had been] of no avail."[137] Brunner himself, in a subsequent defense of the OG for its practical missionary work, said something similar: many people had a correct knowledge of theology without it actually affecting their lives.[138]

Buchman ultimately thought that men like Brunner were inclined to judge people according to the correctness of their ideas rather than fight for a change in their lives. This was illustrated by a letter he wrote to Brunner justifying the OG's role in organizing a visit to London in October 1933 by the controversial Nazi bishop, Joachim Hossenfelder. Once the Nazis came to power, Buchman believed that the right strategy was to try to win them to a deeper, Christian perspective, and he saw Hossenfelder's visit in that light; it was a way of trying to change him at some level. The OG was widely criticized over the episode, including by Barth and Dietrich Bonhoeffer.[139] Brunner, too, was worried by it, complaining that Hossenfelder had damaged the reputation of the group. Buchman responded to Brunner by saying that the issue of the OG's reputation was insignificant compared with the opportunity that the visit had given to try to give the Nazi bishop a touch with what he called "real Christianity." He also suggested that Brunner himself was meant to be a model for this kind of authentic Christianity: "What might it mean for the future of Germany, if by the grace of God [Hossenfelder] could see a maximum message of Christ incarnate in you." In Buchman's mind, then, Brunner was meant to be a life changer as much as a thinker. Hossenfelder's visit to Britain was not in fact a success, mainly because it seems the German cleric made little effort to engage with concerns of his hosts.[140]

Buchman believed that the best way to help theologians in their spiritual lives was to avoid getting drawn into theological discussions with them and get them into action. For example, when he took Streeter with him on a tour of Denmark and Sweden in 1935, he paid little attention to the pamphlets the scholar offered him, concentrating on—according to their chauffeur—the "inspiration of the new Streeter" rather than his academic theories.[141] Buchman probably wanted to introduce Streeter to a wider circle of people, because he thought that people's thinking evolved as their experience of the world expanded. He once told Theophil Spoerri that there was a hesitant quality in his life arising out of a lack of perspective. He was not sufficiently exposed to people who controlled world situations.[142] "The art is to enlarge people's viewpoint," he believed. Typically, he also linked intellectual problems to moral ones. He said of one theologian that he was unable to distinguish between the causes of a disease and its symptoms and that this was rooted in a desire to have the approval of other people.[143]

Theologians involved with Buchman's work sometimes came to downplay the purely academic side of theology. Streeter's intellectual journey was an example of this. His encounter with the OG strengthened a conviction he had always had that matters of faith could not be comprehended by reason alone. At the beginning of *The God Who Speaks* he stated that in the previous two years—the period of his involvement with the OG—he had come to see "more clearly than before" the limitations inherent in any purely intellectual approach to religion.[144] Seeing the OG's impact on individuals led him to believe that although his work of relating religion to modern knowledge had been important, there was a more pressing need to make Christianity real to society as a whole and not just to scholars.[145] L. W. Grensted was another who under OG influence stressed the need for theology to be more than an academic discipline. Notably, in his book *The Person of Christ* (1932)—written at a time when he was closely involved with Buchman's work—he insisted that theological truths could not be proved on logical grounds alone and that religious experience was central to Christianity. He also declared that the Christian interpreter should seek "divine guidance" in everything that he wrote.[146]

Some people argued that the OG stressed the experiential side of its message too strongly—to the detriment of the theological or intellectual dimension. Grensted's *The Person of Christ* was criticized on these grounds by Charles Raven, for example. Raven accused the Oxford theologian of abandoning the task of real intellectual endeavor in his book. Challenging issues were explained away with reference to religious experience, he complained.[147] Buchman's supporters generally responded to criticisms of this kind by stating that their primary concerns were essentially practical rather than theoretical in character—they wanted to make faith and moral standards a reality in people's lives, and they wished to avoid trying to develop a distinctive theology of their own. They also thought that the experiential rather than doctrinal emphasis of their work had the advantage that it allowed people with different opinions to get involved in the movement without immediately being confronted with a set of doctrines that they were required to endorse.

It would be wrong to call Buchman anti-intellectual. It is true that he did not like to philosophize and in that sense could be impatient with theory. Moreover, he did not have the instincts of an intellectual. On the other hand, the amount of time he invested in figures like Brunner, Spoerri, Streeter and Thornton-Duesbery suggests that he had high regard for academics. It was more that he wanted ideas to be rooted in personal experience—especially in the area of theology. Connected with this, he thought that the mind could not be artificially separated from the will and that the two worked best when rooted in commitment to God. In addition, he wanted intellectuals to find new ways of expressing old truths and to be able to communicate them to the wider public. He was, as Hunter suggests, a kind of "mystical pragmatist."[148] He did not so much dismiss traditional theological concepts as try to craft their expression to meet the particular needs of individuals or groups. As he wrote to Spoerri, "I think it is a question of what a person can swallow. That does not minimize the full value of food."[149]

5
Strategy and Organization

In OG and MRA spirituality, the quiet time was partly intended to provide a reflective space in which people could try to look at the needs of others and the world from the Holy Spirit's perspective. It was thought that the Holy Spirit had a strategy or plan for humankind that people could try to cooperate with. A prayerful quiet time would give them the inspiration to do that. Buchman was often critical of people who he thought lacked a sense of strategy. In the 1930s, for example, he expressed regret that certain church leaders seemed to lack a sense of the "strategy of the Holy Spirit."[1] To have an inadequate plan or no plan at all was a "sin," he said in 1936.[2] His idea of such a strategy would certainly have a national impact. "Tolerate no activity that doesn't have national significance," he said to his team in 1937.[3] To stop at the level of personal revival was "inferior thinking."[4]

In Buchman's mind the OG and MRA themselves were intended to be instruments in God's strategy for the world. The kind of movement that he envisaged had already been evident in the early 1920s. He talked at that time of creating a worldwide movement of "peripatetic evangelism," involving small groups of men and women moving continuously around the world, touching individuals and then binding them into close-knit fellowship groups.[5] The same concept was then expressed slightly differently in a transatlantic broadcast of 1936, when Buchman talked of the need for a "supernational network of live wires across the world to every last man, in every last place, in every last situation." Leadership would be given "not through one person, but through groups of people who [had] learned to work together under the guidance of God," he said.[6] To cite Theophil Spoerri, Buchman foresaw small teams of people living under the guidance of God and acting as "formative cells of history."[7]

These teams would be integrated into a wider whole. The OG was to be a "world organism," Buchman said in 1938.[8] The strategic outreach of the OG and

MRA was thus to be characterized by small teams of people operating under God's guidance within different countries, as well as in collaboration with other national teams across the world in a more international endeavor. Accountability of local teams to the wider work was to be expected. Just as Buchman was keen for individuals to work in teamwork with others, he was also anxious to ensure that OG- or MRA-inspired movements did not remain confined to the national or confessional contexts in which they first emerged.[9] In this connection, Buchman often tried to foster moral and spiritual renewal in particular countries by bringing in international teams from the outside. This was the method used in most of MRA's most effective outreach programs or campaigns. Yet balancing the needs of local teams and the international work was not always easy. If T. Willard Hunter is right, for example, the launch of MRA in the United States led to a decline in local teams, as their purpose increasingly undergirded Buchman's own endeavors.[10]

As Buchman conceived it, MRA was meant to be a "force" that was "trained and on the march" and that had the answer to "individual and national selfishness."[11] Buchman also called it a "super-force," by which he meant the "force of an all-powerful God working through men."[12] He clearly envisaged it as a movement with a powerful influence, because he once said that it belonged on the "editorial page."[13] The challenge for the OG and MRA was to step into a larger framework of thinking. "How many people are in the grip of the next thing?" Buchman once asked, obviously concerned that people's mental horizons were too short-term.[14] He encouraged his supporters to see their work in pioneering terms. He was fond of some lines from a hymn that had been adapted from the poem "Pioneers" (1865) by American poet Walt Whitman: "All the past we leave behind: / We take up the task eternal, and the burden, and the lesson. / . . . so we go the unknown ways," and he used to encourage people to repeat the lines out loud.[15] It was yet another example of how Buchman's spirituality, and the language in which it was expressed, carried the imprint of American culture.

Buchman also talked of his supporters as being "apostles" of a new international order. In this context he wanted them to have the "leisure to do the thinking adequate for nations."[16] At conferences and on campaigns he tried to make this practical by organizing meetings, often before breakfast, in which quiet times took place and people were encouraged to share their ideas about outreach and strategy. The atmosphere of such meetings often made a strong impression on people. For example, John Wood recalled the "vibrancy" of the sharing sessions that took place during the OG campaign in Jutland, Denmark, in 1935, at which forty to fifty people were regularly present.[17]

Buchman regularly felt a sense of urgency about the work of the OG and MRA. At Visby he said that he was interested in how to save a "crumbling civilisation."[18] MRA was a "race against time to remake men and nations," he said a year later, and he had guidance in late 1940 that the next six months were going to be critical for the history of the world. At the same time, he also sensed that many of his team lacked the same sense of concern, for he warned them, "You don't get the urgency of world events—they don't move you."[19] In the 1950s the sense of urgency remained. He wanted, he told people, to be in touch with the Holy Spirit about the "very serious situation" in the world.[20] In this kind of context, a central question for him and his team was always where God wanted them to concentrate their forces to have maximum impact.[21] Buchman also thought MRA's own future depended on it having a coherent strategy: "Live a strategy—or you will damn the work," he said at one of the postwar MRA conferences.[22]

In a sense, MRA was an evolving concept. MRA regularly "recreated" itself in response to changing circumstances, Daniel Sack observes.[23] Buchman's methods were always subtly changing. For example, if the house party was the central vehicle for the expansion of the work in the interwar period, in 1939 Buchman turned to the mass meeting as a way of publicizing his message in the United States. The most notable example of this was an MRA meeting at the Hollywood Bowl in July 1939, attended by thirty thousand people. Buchman was still hoping, and indeed believed, that war could be avoided. There was a chance, at this point, that MRA could have turned into a mass movement. However, in 1940, once it became clear that the war could not be prevented, Buchman turned away from large-scale initiatives and started to build up his own team in a more intensive way, for example through the retreat at Lake Tahoe.[24] Then, after the war, the conference centers at Mackinac and Caux became rallying points for a larger international work, with plays and musicals becoming in many cases the first point of contact with audiences. If the methods were changing, there was also in some ways an evolution of tasks. For example, Buchman called for "moral re-armament" in the late 1930s, because he felt that the concept offered an alternative to war; after the outbreak of war, he presented it as a vital component in national defense.[25] But in 1943, in response to the ideological conflicts of the decade, he started to call it an ideology. It was one of the advantages of moral re-armament as a concept that it could be presented in different ways as circumstances evolved. The emphasis on strategy brought with it a belief in a certain ideological flexibility.

Behind the evolution of the organization and its concerns, however, the personal emphasis remained central. "What a strategy God gave—it was people, people, people," Buchman once said, recalling his time at Penn State.[26] "I am frankly out to win the leaders or to create the leadership that will change present day conditions," he wrote in a letter of 1928, comparing himself in this regard to the English evangelist Lord Radstock, who had been famous for his outreach to the Russian aristocracy in the nineteenth century.[27] Changed individuals could change the world, he always thought. This was summed up in a slogan he used in his BBC broadcast of November 1938: "New men—new homes—new industry—new nations—a new world."[28]

The advantage of this kind of person-led approach was that it could be adapted to any situation. This did not mean that Buchman believed that everyone had exactly the same calling. There was a belief in the diversity of vocations in the OG and MRA. Full-time workers were always encouraged to think through what sphere of life, or region of the world, they were called to focus on. But "personalistically working fellowships" remained central to the underlying vision of the movement, wherever it was at work.[29]

In practice Buchman's approach meant that he was always looking for people who he thought could bring a new dimension of thinking into the world. "God-prepared instruments are there. One step enough for me," he said in the 1950s. He thought these instruments were often particular individuals, so the aim was to discern who specifically they might be. He had come to believe that the destiny of countries often turned on relatively small issues and that the generation of new spiritual life in one or two individuals might genuinely alter the trajectory of a nation's history. The task then was to find the "convinced personalities" and "men of conviction" in each situation.[30] For example, he told some of his supporters who were going to South Africa in 1929 that they should think of the ten men in Africa who, if they changed, would have the greatest influence on their countries. "Convert the editors, M.P.'s, Cabinet Ministers, the Administration. They will travel on the team," he said.[31] Similarly, visiting Morocco in 1954 at a time of rising nationalism, Buchman talked of the "mining of men" and "quarrying for leadership."[32]

If the aim here was to foster new leadership, it was also to bring a spiritual element into the leadership that people were already giving. For example, in 1936, following a meeting with Henry Ford in Detroit, Buchman wrote to the industrialist to encourage him to accentuate the spiritual dimension of his work: "I am particularly impressed with your feeling that God has been guiding you during all these years and it certainly is evident to me that He has been preparing you during it all, for a leadership that is way out beyond anything you have yet experienced." Buchman clearly wanted Ford to expand his concept of what he could achieve, for he suggested that Ford's organization could be secure only when the message of a "God-guided industry" had been taken to the whole world.[33]

There were plenty of other examples of a similar approach. Unlike some leading American statesmen, Buchman felt no visceral hostility to the idea of empire, although he was critical of the attitudes of cultural superiority that sometimes accompanied it. So he once told Stanley Baldwin that he could become "the authoritative voice for the rebirth of the [British] Empire."[34] In 1940 he suggested to the former Russian prime minister, Alexander Kerensky, that, in contrast to Marx, who had preached a doctrine of hate, he might adopt a "doctrine of love" that could rebuild "whole nations."[35] Whether this was realistic at this stage in Kerensky's career was probably not important to Buchman; the point was to enhance Kerensky's vision of how his life might be constructively used.

Buchman tried to give people role models for the kind of leadership he thought they could give. For example, in 1960, writing to the governor general of newly independent Nigeria, Nnamdi Azikiwe, he singled out Abraham Lincoln as a possible role model for him, saying that he could play the "role of Abraham Lincoln" in Africa.[36] Azikiwe had first encountered MRA during a visit to London 1949 at a time when he was president of the nationalist National Council of Nigeria and the Cameroons, and he retained a close connection with the movement in subsequent years.[37] Buchman was a strong admirer of Lincoln's legacy and elsewhere suggested that America needed a lot of "little Lincolns."[38]

Buchman and his team were also often keen to encourage people who tried to resist communism. This was evident in their contacts with the nationalist Chinese in the late 1940s. Like many American churchmen and missionaries, MRA workers were generally supportive of the Chinese nationalist cause in the late 1940s, although they believed it could have had a more liberal emphasis. As the Maoist forces advanced, attempts were made by the MRA group in Washington to get the Truman administration to reaffirm its moral commitment to a free China and give its message in the region a stronger ideological emphasis.[39] Similar efforts were being made to reach out to the Chinese leadership—with some success. For example, General Ho Ying-chin, who was briefly prime minister of China in the spring of 1949, met Buchman while heading a Chinese delegation to an MRA assembly in Niagara Falls in early 1947 and became enthusiastic about the ideological contribution he thought MRA could make to his country.[40]

Buchman's connections with some of the Chinese nationalist leaders resulted in 1956 in him receiving a decoration from the Republic of China (Taiwan), with the citation reading, "The tenets of Moral Re-Armament are in conformity with the traditional principles of Chinese ethics and philosophy."[41] Buchman wrote to Chiang Kai-shek at that time, saying that Chiang had a God-given gift to inspire confidence and faith in people and that this arose out of his faith in God and in his country, mentioning also that he was a "prophet voice."[42] This did not necessarily mean that Buchman approved of all of Chiang's policies; it was more that he saw his hostility to communism and his faith—Chiang became a Methodist in 1928—as something to build on.

Buchman tried to prepare carefully for his meetings with people, and he sought to get guidance beforehand regarding how he should approach them and what he might say that could help or inspire them. Hospitality was planned in the same way. An example of this occurred during the Tahoe retreat in 1940, when Buchman met two estranged farming brothers from the Sierra Nevada and invited them to dinner. Prior to the meal, he spent two hours preparing the event. No detail in the planning, cooking, and serving of the meal was overlooked, Bunny Austin recalled, reporting that it led to the ending of the long-running feud between the two men.[43] Buchman's preparation for meetings with national leaders, and his letters to them, often involved the same effort.

Hospitality always had a central strategic role in Buchman's outreach. His emphasis on personalization was evident here. Whenever he gave parties, they were arranged around particular individuals, in the sense that the food and entertainment were prepared in the light of who was attending. Alan Thornhill, after watching Buchman in action in Sarasota, Florida, in the winter of 1943–44, reported that the parties Buchman hosted all had a distinctive purpose: "The arrangement of the room, the seating of the guests, the special food, the special song, the last arrival from an army camp or from Canada, all had their part in the total impact." Parties were as "carefully planned as an invasion," while being "free and flexible." The aim was that people would leave with their spirits lifted, having experienced a "new freedom." Impressed by what he saw, Thornhill talked of how a community might be "wakened" and a nation "touched" simply through the impact of a tea party.[44]

Detailed planning also went into the meals at the larger conferences. In Buchman's later years at Caux a dining room was set aside for him, where lunch and dinner parties were held. These were usually for about twenty people, with seating arrangements carefully selected to encourage interesting or spiritually helpful conversations.[45] A feature of such occasions was that Buchman sometimes encouraged members of his team to read out poems that they had written for particular people. This was intended to be a creative and, perhaps, lighthearted way of passing on spiritual encouragement.[46] Buchman once said that the secret of his success was a "tremendous attention to detail," and certainly his approach to hospitality indicated a man who believed that little details mattered.[47]

Hospitality was often mixed with story telling to try to create the right combination of welcome and spiritual challenge. This strategy was illustrated in 1959 by Buchman's meeting with Saburo Chiba, chair of the Security Committee of the Japanese Diet and a former student at Princeton. The meeting took place at Buchman's home in Tucson, Arizona, a place that was rented for him in the last few years of his life because it was thought that a warmer climate might improve his health. Chiba spent the day with Buchman and some of his team and was treated first to a long breakfast, at which stories of change from around the world were told, then a walk in the garden, and finally—according to Peter Howard's enthusiastic report—a "Japanese meal, perfectly cooked." As Chiba was leaving, Buchman said, "I had one thought for you early this morning. . . . The world will walk into your heart." He seems to have thought that Chiba could become a more open and generous person, and he found, after a carefully planned day, a way to say so. Chiba responded by stating that for the first time in his life he had found God. It was a good example of the detailed planning that went into some of Buchman's encounters.[48]

Chiba's subsequent letters to Buchman confirm that the meeting in Tucson did indeed have a considerable effect on him. At the time Chiba was much exercised by the threat of communism, and in this context he subsequently floated the idea that a network of leaders should be created worldwide who would make MRA their ideology. He raised the issue himself in a meeting with Konrad Adenauer in January 1961. Buchman was clearly intrigued by the suggestion, because he himself wrote to Adenauer summarizing the idea and suggesting that Adenauer's wisdom and support were needed for what he called a "nation-saving advance."[49] Chiba subsequently played a central role in the founding of an MRA center in Odawara, Japan, in 1962.[50]

Entertainment on a yet larger scale was sometimes used. A good prewar example of this was at the time of the Abyssinian Crisis in September 1935, when the Czech minister of foreign affairs, Eduard Benes—who Buchman had first

Fig. 8 J. A. E. Patijn, foreign minister of the Netherlands, speaking at a League of Nations lunch, September 15, 1938. *Extreme right*: Buchman alongside the Norwegian parliamentarian Carl Hambro. Photo: Arthur Strong, Oxford Group Archives.

met at the League of Nations in 1926—gave a dinner for Buchman and his OG supporters to meet delegates to the League of Nations in Geneva.[51] Buchman had a low opinion of the league, believing that it was not what he called "God-arched," and the aim of the dinner from his perspective was to try to revivify the organization by bringing a moral and spiritual dimension into its deliberations.[52] Nearly five hundred people attended. Once again there was an element of story telling in the occasion, for some of the OG representatives who spoke emphasized in a very personal way how the group had changed their lives.[53]

Similarly, in September 1938, following an OG house party in Interlaken, Switzerland, another large dinner took place at the league, hosted by, among others, the Norwegian parliamentarian, Carl Hambro, and the Dutch foreign minister, Dr. J. A. E. Patijn. In his speech, Patijn brought up a recent dispute between Belgium and the Netherlands that had come before the International Court in The Hague and had been decided in the Belgians' favor—much to the annoyance of the Dutch. Patijn then explained that OG principles and a desire to do God's will had helped him to respond generously to the Belgian success and that this had helped to stem hostility toward the Netherlands in Belgium.[54] It was a typical OG story about how a change of attitude in a political leader could bring people together. It was also an example of how Buchman was trying to move the location for sharing and telling stories of change from an ecclesiastical or small group context to a political setting.

Story telling was sometimes accompanied by music. During an MRA audience with Ramon Magsaysay, president of the Philippines in 1956, Buchman got his team to tell stories about their lives. This was followed by music from the Colwell Brothers, an American musical group involved with MRA at the time.[55] MRA meetings after 1945 were often punctuated by carefully chosen music, designed to provide a change of pace and an alternative form of spiritual uplift. Buchman was keenly aware of the place of the arts in shaping society, even if he had little time for attending cultural events himself. He once said, following a visit to see the film *Gone with the Wind* in 1940, that cinema had a tendency to put things in an "abnormal way."[56] He wanted something different, believing that the arts were often the best means of presenting a vision of what moral and spiritual change could entail.

From his youth Buchman had been interested in theater. Plays, which Buchman thought of as "weapons" in MRA's spiritual battle and which were a means of promoting an MRA narrative in an easily accessible form, first started to be extensively used by MRA during World War II.[57] Notably, *You Can Defend America* (1941), a variety show that stressed the moral dimensions of national security, was shown widely in the United States in the early years of the war, often to audiences involved with industry. For example, in 1942 it played to large audiences in Detroit and was shown at the Annual Convention of Steelworkers in Cleveland, Ohio. Henry Ford was one of those who attended.[58] After 1945 drama was widely used to try to portray a vision of social reconciliation and hope. Like Thornhill, Howard wrote many of the plays used on campaigns. For example, his musical satire on the Cold War, *The Vanishing Island* (1955), which featured two warring states moving from enmity to cooperation, became the vehicle for an ambitious international campaign in 1955–56 known as the Statesmen's Mission.[59] In Britain the Westminster Theatre in London's West End, bought for MRA in 1947, put on plays as part of the movement's national strategy.

In keeping with the emphasis on personalization, plays were sometimes staged just to reach one person. For example, when the Statesman's Mission came to Finland in late 1955 with *The Vanishing Island*, the timing of the visit was arranged so that the play could be put on for the Burmese prime minister, U Nu, who was visiting Helsinki on the way back from a trip to Moscow. It worked out as planned. A special morning showing was arranged at short notice at the Swedish Theater on November 6, which was attended by the Burmese leader.[60] U Nu came to have a high regard for MRA.[61]

The emphasis on theater reflected that fact that MRA was attempting to express its truths in contemporary form. Theater was influential in the postwar world. Musicals like *Oklahoma!* (1955) were popular in the United States and Europe, and in the 1950s a new generation of radical playwrights generated a lot of debate in Britain. MRA artists and writers thus tried to be sensitive to cultural developments. A similar attempt to imitate contemporary cultural forms had already been evident in the 1930s, when some OG occasions or publications featured the kind of pageantry being deployed by the European dictatorships. For example, the OG magazine, *Rising Tide*, which came out in nine languages, with a print run of 1,630,000 copies in 1937–38, had a photograph on the front cover of youths marching in line carrying banners.[62]

Sometimes unlikely playwrights were found. On the basis of receiving what he described as "very definite directions" from the Holy Spirit, Buchman suggested to a group of Africans in Caux in 1955 that Africa could speak "with an answer" to both East and West in the form of a play.[63] He had in mind what he called an "*Uncle Tom's Cabin* for modern Africa." He had been impressed by seeing a theatrical version of Harriet Beecher Stowe's antislavery novel when he was a boy; he said that he could still picture the famous episode from it in which the escaped slave, Eliza, went over the icy river to escape her pursuers.[64] He wanted to see something similar, which could influence political leaders in the way that the original novel had helped Lincoln in his battle against slavery.[65] The result was the play *Freedom*, which was later turned into a film, about an African country undergoing decolonization, in which both imperial and nationalist leaders experienced a spiritual change of heart. It was to be one of MRA's most successful artistic initiatives, reaching large numbers of people across Africa in both stage and film versions.[66] It was often targeted at countries experiencing major ethnic divisions or going through a process of transition. For example, in the period preceding Congolese independence in June 1960, it was put on in some of the country's provincial capitals, and a showing was also arranged just before independence day for the newly elected prime minister, Patrice Lumumba, and seventeen of his ministers.[67]

Buchman wanted to publicize stories of people changing as widely as possible and have them recounted at the highest political level. He believed there was a biblical sanction for this. In his Visby speech, he responded to a Swedish journalist who had attacked his methods as "American-style publicity" by citing the King James version of Isaiah 52:7: "How beautiful upon the mountains are the feet of him that bringeth good tidings, that publisheth peace." Here, according to Buchman, the Bible specifically endorsed the role of publicity, and he challenged the tendency for the media to be dominated by bad news.[68] "For too long we have breathed the atmosphere of problems," he once said.[69] He wanted to surround people with news of what he thought were solutions.

In this context, Buchman and MRA were often blamed for exaggerating their successes. It was one of the central charges made of Buchman and MRA by Tom Driberg that they had a tendency to manipulate stories and headlines to inflate the level of their influence.[70] Certainly, postwar MRA was always keen to present its side of the story in a positive way. Howard was particularly attuned to the way the press worked and saw the presentation of media stories about MRA's outreach as an essential element in the battle of ideas. Buchman had the same view. He said of one Danish journalist in 1935, "He is not apt to understand understatement."[71] It typified a conviction he held that there was no point in underselling the reality of God's power. If God was the source of what MRA was doing, then it would have been wrong to hold back in saying so.

Buchman's postwar speeches were peppered with enthusiastic endorsements of MRA by well-known figures, often in connection with the supposed impact it was having in particular countries.[72] There is no reason to doubt the veracity of these statements. But their accuracy about the influence of MRA was often hard to gauge, one way or the other, which pointed to a wider issue. MRA made much use of personal testimony in its publicity, and this sometimes made it vulnerable to the charge that the evidence it was using to assert its significance was too subjective to be convincing. At the same time, proving the reality of its impact was never going to be easy, for the simple reason that the kind of change it was seeking—originating in people's motives—was not easy to quantify.

A circumstance here is that when Buchman told stories or passed on news, he emphasized different things to different audiences. For example, his experience at Keswick was sometimes reexpressed to link it with a new situation or issue. For example, speaking in 1948 about the dangers of materialism, Buchman announced that at Keswick God had showed him the cost of his "pride" and "materialism."[73] In other accounts of his story, Buchman rarely—if ever—mentioned materialism, but in this case he used the concept as a way of connecting MRA's postwar ideological outreach to his earlier experience. It highlights the fact that when Buchman related a story his concern may sometimes have been less with presenting a precise historical account of what happened and more with trying to draw out, and find new ways of expressing, what he saw as the underlying spiritual message of the episode in question. This emphasis on adapting stories to audiences led to a wider MRA tendency to present its history differently in diverse situations. David Belden notes, for example, that in later years MRA spokespeople downplayed the movement's evangelical origins to try to make its message more acceptable in new religious contexts.[74]

The strategy of trying to address particular situations by both working with and trying to develop key individuals was systematically applied in a number of contexts. It was, for example, a central feature of the OG's prewar work in Europe. A good example of it involved Carl Hambro, who was twice secretary of the General Assembly of the League of Nations and who was initially drawn into the OG by reading *For Sinners Only*—although he never identified himself completely with it. Following the OG dinner at the league in 1935, Buchman took Hambro on a speaking tour of the United States, in which Hambro stressed to some well-connected American audiences what he saw as the moral and spiritual dimensions of the crisis in the world. In Buchman's mind part of the aim of this was undoubtedly to try to build on the leadership potential that Buchman had sensed in the Norwegian. A postwar example of MRA's deployment of key individuals in its larger strategic outreach involved Irène Laure. In early 1949, roughly a year and half after her apology to the Germans in Caux, Laure embarked on an eleven-week speaking tour of the Federal Republic, where she spoke at up to two hundred public meetings, including ten of the country's eleven state parliaments. In a vivid example of how personal testimony was used strategically in the OG and MRA, Laure apologized on every occasion for the hatred that she had formerly harbored.[75]

Laure's tour of Germany was part of a wider MRA plan to try to bring a moral and spiritual dimension to the reconstruction of that country. International MRA teams visited and lived in Germany for some years after 1945, and a number of plays were used as a focus for the action, among them *The Good Road*, a dramatization of the spiritual heritage of the West, which had been originally shown to audiences in North America.[76] At the same time, Buchman obviously wanted people to think not of just how Germany could be helped but how Germany could come to help others, for he suggested in Caux in 1947 that a "mighty movement of God's Holy Spirit" could be born in the country that would have great influence elsewhere. There was room for the "intellectual life of Germany" to go out to the whole world, he said.[77] Buchman's aim here, according to John Wood, was to emphasize Germany's future and potential rather than its past and guilt.[78]

This outreach into Germany was linked to a wider continental strategy that involved promoting German-French dialogue, in particular through bringing German and French politicians and trade unionists to Caux.[79] Buchman's links with Adenauer and Schuman played an important role here. Adenauer had been sufficiently impressed by his visit to Caux in 1948 and other links with MRA to encourage the staging of plays such as *The Forgotten Factor* and *The Good Road* in Germany. He clearly thought that MRA could help to counter the spread of communism, because he wrote to Buchman in 1950, mentioning that in the context of the spread of totalitarian ideas in Germany, the Ruhr would be a good platform for the demonstration of MRA thinking.[80] The two men remained on good terms until Buchman's death.

Schuman had become interested in MRA through hearing of its attempts to improve industrial relations in northern France. He met Buchman for the first time in August 1949—shortly after a brief tenure as prime minister. Subsequently, at a dinner in October 1949 Buchman passed on to Schuman the names of a number of prominent Germans who had been to Caux and whom he thought the French foreign minister could work with. Adenauer was one of them. Then, before Schuman's first meeting with Adenauer in January 1950, he wrote to the German leader recommending the Frenchman for his awareness of the difficulties facing the German government and his readiness to cooperate. Typically, his letter contained an emphasis on the guidance of God and the importance of unity rather than specific policy issues: "If we can get together and have a common mind under the guidance of God, then He can give the answer to the extremely difficult and seemingly insoluble problems which present themselves."[81]

Buchman's touches with key individuals in France and Germany were accompanied by a more systematic attempt to bring influential figures from the two countries together at Caux, a fact indicating that MRA was trying to influence a whole elite rather than just selected individuals. The numbers involved were considerable. A total of 1,983 French citizens and 3,113 Germans came to the Caux conferences between 1946 and 1950. These included from France 17 members of the government, 200 trade unionists, 207 industrialists, 35 clergy, 30 representatives of the media, and 100 educationalists. From Germany, there were 82 members of the government, 400 trade unionists, 210 industrialists, 14 clergy, 160 representatives of the media, and 35 educationalists. In a venture that involved what could be called a kind of "parallel diplomacy," the aim was to create an atmosphere that was conducive to honest dialogue. In making this possible, Edward Luttwak argues, MRA did not invent the Schuman plan, for responsibility for that lay with the politicians. It did, however, contribute to its realization.[82]

If postwar Europe was a central focus of MRA's strategy, so too was the Far East, and in particular Japan. After 1945 a lot of effort was put into trying to reach the Japanese elites with MRA philosophy. Prominent Japanese first attended MRA conferences at Riverside, California, in 1948 and at Caux in 1949 and 1950. According to Basil Entwistle, a young American who was central to MRA's work in Japan, the outreach involved three main aims: to restore Japan's place in the community of nations, including healing hurts and divisions arising from the war; to demonstrate an alternative to class war by raising up a healthy leadership in industry and in socialist parties and trade unions; and to create a determined minority that would seek to strengthen the moral foundations of democracy.[83]

Buchman's involvement with the Japanese elites went back to August 1916, when he visited the country during his first spell in Asia. One of those who worked closely with MRA in the 1950s and 1960s was Masahide Shibusawa, the great-grandson of the first viscount Shibusawa, the influential Japanese industrialist. The viscount had helped to host Buchman's visit in 1916.[84] Buchman's link with the Shibusawa family was an example of how his involvement with certain countries grew out of connections with particular families, often over more than one generation. Buchman once said, "I maintain friendships"—doubtless referring to the long-lasting nature of his relationships with people.[85] He might have said the same about the amount of time he invested in certain families.

One of Buchman's most important initiatives in relation to Japan was a response to what Moscow was doing. Buchman and his MRA supporters were very conscious of Soviet attempts to influence the Far East and keen to counter them. On being told that 500 delegates from the Seneindan, a Japanese youth organization with more than 4 million members, had been invited to go to the International Youth Festival in Moscow in 1957, Buchman and his team issued a counterinvitation for them to visit Mackinac and the United States, guaranteeing return air travel and a month's stay. This was accepted after a narrow vote by the Seneindan Central Executive, and a group of 104 young Japanese were then hosted by MRA in the United States, accompanied by 50 senior Japanese figures, 30 from the Philippines and 20 from Korea.[86]

With his focus on individuals and their potential to change countries, Buchman spent a lot of time simply trying to meet the right people. It was for this reason that he started to attend international conferences in the 1920s, the first of them being the Washington Disarmament Conference in 1921 and the second the League of Nations in 1926. Throughout his life he was grateful for new opportunities for outreach. After attending a funeral in 1951, his guidance was "You were right in going to the funeral. It let loose a host of openings. God be praised."[87] On some occasions, particularly in earlier days, he even encouraged his team to travel first class to maximize opportunities for networking—although that was not typical, because Buchman was very careful with money.[88] Good networking might enable a person to establish connections with people from all sections of a society. Speaking of how to influence metropolitan life, he once said, "You have got to feel into [sic] every form of life in a city," adding that in this context the newspapers were tremendously important.[89]

Buchman also thought it was important to be in the right place at the right time. During the UN conference in San Francisco in 1945, Buchman took a table near the door of the restaurant of the Fairmont Hotel, where many delegates were staying, and met people over lunch or in passing. In the course of time, friends at the conference arranged for *The Forgotten Factor* to be put on as part of the schedule of events.[90] The strategy at the conference thus evolved out of a fluid social situation, where Buchman could follow the leading of the Holy Spirit—as he interpreted it. Good timing and obedience to the Spirit were clearly linked in Buchman's mind. In January 1956, following mass at Milan Cathedral with his team (350 of them) and a visit to Archbishop Montini, Buchman declared, "The God-timed plan of the Holy Spirit is always effective."[91]

The carefully planned nature of Buchman's outreach at international conferences was also reflected in 1951, again in San Francisco, when Buchman and some of his colleagues were present for the conference at which a peace treaty was signed between Japan and some of the Allied powers. The conference convened in an atmosphere of tension, heightened by reservations from Australia and New Zealand and by a Soviet decision to reject the proposed treaty and boycott the conference. In the light of the then prevailing distrust of Japan, Buchman's aim at the conference was to try to enable Japanese delegates to get to know Asians, Americans, and Europeans. Consequently, senior members of the Japanese delegation, some of whom were already friendly with MRA, were invited to meals in the restaurant of the Mark Hopkins hotel, which had a spectacular view over the city, and introduced to guests from the United States, France, Vietnam, Ceylon, and other countries.

More generally, delegates to the conference were invited to the local Geary Theater for showings of *Jotham Valley*, an MRA musical that depicted the reconciliation that had taken place at Tahoe between the feuding brothers from

Fig. 9 Japanese foreign minister Mamoru Shigemitsu (*seated left*), presenting Buchman with the Order of the Rising Sun (second class), Tokyo, May 1956. Standing behind Shigemitsu is Niro Hoshijima, speaker of the Japanese Diet. Photo: Oxford Group Archives.

Nevada. All this involved careful planning. Howard, who was with Buchman at the time, wrote to his wife that he had a daily meeting with Buchman after breakfast before going on to the conference meetings.[92] Quiet times were always a feature of such planning sessions. If the effect of all these initiatives is hard to measure definitively, it was the kind of work that gained Buchman a reputation among political leaders. Schuman was impressed enough by MRA's links with Japanese leaders to say to Buchman on the final day of the conference, "You made peace with Japan before we did."[93] It was for this kind of work that the Japanese government decided to decorate Buchman when he made a visit to the country in 1956.[94]

Some have suggested that Buchman was too strongly impressed by social status.[95] From early on in his life, his reports and letters were so full of references to the apparently important people he was meeting that he certainly laid himself open to the charge of name dropping. But it is hard to argue that engaging with the rich and famous was his primary aim. If, in Europe and the United States, the leadership of the OG and MRA was, broadly speaking, in the hands of university-educated people of middle- or sometimes upper-class backgrounds, there was also a solid sprinkling of working-class supporters and a serious outreach into poorer areas, for example in the prewar East End of London. MRA was the "ordinary person's opportunity" to remake the world, Buchman once suggested.[96] People who were outside the corridors of power had a contribution to make. Buchman's outreach did indeed sometimes come about through the conviction of unexpected people. For example, the OG's work at the League of Nations, which culminated in the visits to Geneva in 1935 and 1938, originated in the conviction of an elderly Scottish widow in 1931.[97] Buchman also sometimes challenged people in authority in a way that runs counter to the idea that he was trying to curry favor with them. For example, in one of his conversations with Sun Yat-sen in 1918 he directly challenged Sun over his recent divorce and relations with women. "[Buchman] was the only man who told me the truth about myself," Sun is supposed to have said.[98]

There were also politicians whom Buchman showed no desire to meet. For example, he responded to a suggestion that he should meet British prime minister Anthony Eden by stating, "It is not our job to help lame dogs over stiles." Before the outbreak of the Suez Crisis in 1956, he warned that the inability of Eden and others to "handle people" was inflaming Middle Eastern politics. He evidently thought that a character weakness was the underlying problem, for he called Eden a "defeated man."[99] Whether this view was based on some information about Eden's life or simply on the basis of an instinct about him is not clear. He obviously sometimes reacted to people at a gut level. Another figure about whom Buchman was scathing was Lord Mountbatten, viceroy of India at the time of Indian independence and partition in 1947. He attributed some of the chaos surrounding partition—which he called the "greatest fiasco in world history"—to weaknesses in Mountbatten's character.[100]

Buchman emphasized to his colleagues that what he saw as the forces of evil had a strategy too. At the Kuling conference, he cited Luther as saying that he never went into the pulpit without being conscious of the presence of the Evil One there. Saint Paul, in Acts, seemed to start a revival or a riot wherever he went, and that was a good example for Christian workers, he also observed.[101] From early on Buchman stated that people could expect persecution if they followed God, and in his letters to people he often warned them of the existence of subtle forms of opposition.[102] For example, he wrote to Sherwood Day in 1919, "The subtle designing forces which have endeavoured to black [sic] us are still at work."[103] He clearly thought that opposition often came from within religious circles. He took encouragement, for example, from a chapter in a popular biography of Henry Drummond by the religious author Cuthbert Lennox, titled

"Misunderstood," which described how Drummond had been criticized by other Christians over his theology.[104] He also once warned that spiritual opposition would increasingly emerge inside the OG team itself, just as it had done among Jesus's followers in the person of Judas.[105] At times, he seems to have welcomed opposition, and he certainly recommended it to others. He once told Thornhill that he needed persecution for his own spiritual development; and he used to say that persecution was the "fire that forged prophets—and quitters."[106]

Concerted opposition on a world scale could also be expected as a consequence of MRA's global outreach, he said in 1956; it was the outcome of the "effectiveness of the working of the Holy Spirit." For example, he thought—rightly—that Driberg was often instrumental in mobilizing hostility to MRA. In 1940 Driberg had been a key figure in exciting controversy over the fact that some British MRA workers had not enlisted for the war but were concentrating efforts on trying to raise local morale.[107] Buchman and his team took the view that their morale-boosting activities, replicated in the United States, were essential for the war effort, while their opponents accused them of draft dodging. Later, during the mid-1950s, Buchman thought—probably on the basis of instinct rather than direct evidence—that Driberg was in some way responsible for the Social and Industrial Council report on MRA of 1955. Driberg was a "clever article," he said privately before the publication of the report; church people were "duped" by him. He added, however, that Driberg would be "confounded" by the working of the Holy Spirit.[108]

Right or wrong, Buchman often interpreted opposition as originating in a deeper moral and spiritual weakness in an individual or people rather than arising out of a straightforward disagreement with some aspect of his message. He linked what he called "false propaganda" with people who lived "upside-down."[109] The challenge of MRA might stir people's consciences in an uncomfortable way, he said in a speech in 1948, and thus might be open to misinterpretation by people who wanted to escape it.[110] Since Buchman often thought that opposition to his work was rooted in moral weakness rather than honest intellectual difficulty, he generally did not try to answer criticisms directly. The best policy, in his view, was to press ahead with what he thought God had called him to do and let the fruit of his work be its own witness. He made this point in a letter in March 1936 to a Norwegian journalist, Fredrik Ramm, who became involved in the OG following a house party in Høsbjør in October 1934. "Keep the full light of the sun in mind, and forget shades, only so that the sun will shine the clearer," he said. Accusations against the OG might be given credence by the very attempt to answer them. The truth could be emphasized in such a way that the erroneous nature of criticisms would be obvious.[111] Similarly, he told an audience in Mackinac in 1944 that he preferred not to discuss matters with people critical of his work but instead offer changed lives as "the sufficient answer."[112]

In Buchman's view, a strategy was not something that could be exactly mapped out in advance. He once said to a woman whose life was planned out months ahead: "How can you say you're a Christian and know in advance exactly what you are going to do? Where is the opportunity for the leading of the Holy Spirit?"[113] The challenge was to let God run things rather than to be in control oneself. It was also a matter of drawing on God's strength rather than one's own. He told a young Swedish woman who felt that she was spiritually exhausted that her feeling of emptiness gave Jesus an opportunity to act in her life, citing lines from "Rock of Ages": "Nothing in my hand I bring, / Simply to thy Cross I cling."[114] Moreover, he once said that great advances were often preceded by a feeling of helplessness: "Again and again before a great advance I have found that God makes me feel [helpless], so that I never forget he does everything, and I do nothing."[115] He himself often felt exhausted in the last decades of his life, following his stroke. During the Indian campaign of 1952–53, he was once overheard saying, "Lord, I can't do it. I can't do it."[116]

In Buchman's mind strategies inspired by God often revealed themselves through processes, people, and events. Buchman's initiatives often evolved from one event to another in an unplanned kind of way. For example, the retreat at Lake Tahoe began when Buchman was offered a five-room cottage to have a break. Others joined him, staying in nearby accommodation, and soon a few hundred people were involved.[117] Likewise, MRA outreach also sometimes arose out of Buchman's friendships. For example, the work in Morocco came partly through Buchman's link with Schuman. Following his visit to Caux in 1953, Schuman asked Buchman's help in addressing unrest in Morocco, and Buchman then went to the North African country with a small group a year later.[118] In other words, the formation of a strategy was something that took place through a mixture of human thinking and what Buchman understood as divine prompting, as presented through quiet times, sharing, and circumstances.

Buchman's attitude to money reflected his hope that people could learn to be dependent on God. Like many evangelists, he believed that "where God guides, He provides." In his case, this meant that after his departure from Hartford he relied mainly on gifts from individuals to finance his work. He was never personally wealthy. His average bank balance for the 1920s, for example, was one hundred dollars, and he often gave money away. At his death he was the owner of his family home in Allentown, and two bank accounts, one containing a few hundred dollars and the other a few thousand pounds given to him at a recent birthday for the use of MRA.[119]

If an initiative was inspired by God, Buchman thought that money would be given to support it, and he sometimes embarked on a journey or project without knowing where all the money would come from. Talking of one of the OG trips to South Africa in the late 1920s, he said that although the prospective travelers had booked their passages, there was no money to pay for them until twenty-four hours before the ship set sail and that the money had then come in as a "spontaneous gift."[120] Occasionally, Buchman rejected the money offered him. In the early 1930s, and just prior to a campaign in Canada for which he needed funds, Buchman rejected a young colleague's offer of ten thousand pounds, which was the remains of an inheritance from his father, and accepted only a more modest two thousand pounds, after the colleague had guidance about how much to give him.[121]

Buchman thus saw the financing of his work as an opportunity for the development of faith in individuals. He wanted people to engage in actions that would throw them into dependence on God rather than aim at what seemed humanly achievable. He made this point in 1955 in a letter to MRA's assistant treasurer in the United States, Gilbert Harris. Responding to Harris's concern over whether MRA could afford some construction work it was doing at the Mackinac conference center, Buchman suggested to Harris that he should live in the dimension of what needed to be done rather than what could be done: "I am grateful for your business caution, but I want you to move with me and the people of America in the dimension of what needs to be done, not what we think we can do. I want you to help me always to live at the place where I rely not on what I have but on what God gives."[122]

Buchman was alert to the importance of money raising. Already at Penn State he had been keen to find people who could finance his work. Then, in the 1920s, he succeeded in developing a network of people who could be called on to give money when needed. Funding at that time came partly from certain New York women, in particular Margaret Tjader, founder in 1901 of the International Union Mission. Yet Buchman shied away from making public appeals for funds. In some ways the OG and MRA reflected the "faith missions" tradition in missionary history, associated with such men as Hudson Taylor, founder of the China Inland Mission. Like these earlier movements, the OG and MRA were interdenominational organizations that did not make public appeals for money.[123] Buchman's informal methods of money raising changed somewhat after 1945, when solicitations for money became more regular, but they were still targeted at the internal MRA fellowship.[124] There were no large external institutional backers. Ford, for example, gave Buchman only one thousand dollars, and Mrs. Clara Ford offered only two thousand.[125] But some of the first generation of Buchman's full-time workers came from comfortable backgrounds and had access to private incomes. In addition, costs were kept down by the fact that MRA full-time workers did not normally receive salaries, a circumstance that slowly began to change in the decades after Buchman's death, although practices were not the same in every country.

People attending MRA assemblies at Mackinac and Caux were not normally presented with a bill but invited instead to search their consciences as to what they could or should contribute. At meetings, however, people were sometimes asked to share their convictions about giving money, in the hope this would prompt others also to give. For example, in Caux in 1951 Buchman introduced a British businessman, Cecil Martin, who had decided to give money to MRA, with the words: "Cecil Martin had a conviction, and I thought if one man has a conviction, many more might get the same conviction."[126] In other words, the practice of sharing experiences to awaken a response was applied in financial matters, as well as in other areas of life.

Occasionally, Buchman spoke more urgently about the need for money. For example, he talked in Caux in 1952 of a deficit of 626,000 Swiss francs that needed to be covered, at the same time emphasizing that it would be through guidance that the money would be found: "It is a serious crisis.... Still the guidance has been when I heard the news, 'You must tell whoever is here, and it will come.' Now that is what we are here for." This kind of appeal was unusual. "It is a thing unheard of for me to do something of this sort in a public meeting," Buchman declared. He went on to say, in a forthright manner, that while there were people at the conference who could not pay the full amount, there were others who could do more.[127]

This financial crisis passed, but it was indicative of some of the problems that MRA faced as it expanded. The growth of the movement brought with it new organizational challenges. Buchman's attitude to organization was perhaps not unlike his attitude to doctrine; he thought it could become restrictive if it was not rooted in spiritual life. "Growing life will burst the bonds of organisation. Life can't be poured into old bottles," he once said.[128] A rhyme that Buchman was fond of using, which expressed his tendency to downplay the institutional side of the OG and MRA, was "It's not an institution; it's not a point of view; it starts a revolution by starting one in you."[129] Buchman did not want MRA to be an organization or movement in any traditional sense. He hoped instead that it could be a kind of family. Introducing a meeting at Caux in August 1952, he emphasized that it was "just a family gathering."[130] In the same month he said, "God's idea is to have a community here under the guidance of God's Holy Spirit [so] that each one does the maximum he is able to do for the community."[131] The conferences at Mackinac and Caux were mainly staffed by volunteers, a fact that led Buchman to describe those gathered there as forming a "classless society."[132]

A key element here was that Buchman wanted people to experience what it might feel like to participate in a global collective or family. Certainly, the chance to be part of a kind of worldwide community was one reason why some people were drawn to MRA. Gabriel Marcel, for example, was particularly impressed by this aspect of Buchman's work. He thought that Buchman's most important "discovery" was the idea of creating a "world community" in a practical rather than a technocratic sense, explaining that he felt at Caux the presence of a "real world conscience."[133] The decision by William Conner to give his short anthology of quotations from Buchman in the 1950s the title "Builder of a Global Force" reflected a similar belief that Buchman's distinctiveness lay in his attempt to bring some kind of global spiritual community into being.[134]

In a speech in Caux in 1947, Buchman tried to articulate the kind of community he had in mind. "People come to me and say: 'Now what is your organization?' We have no organization. You never sign a paper. You can never resign from our work because in that sense you never join. It is an organism. You don't join; you don't resign—you live a life." He went on to say that personal change was the condition of being part of it: "You change—if you want to; and if you don't want to, why that's alright too. Probably sooner or later we part company, but you part the company. Nothing on our side." Buchman concluded by saying, "I simply mention that because a great many people never understand why 12 or 13 hundred people live together in utmost harmony. Doesn't anything go wrong? The Committee went wrong."[135]

The committee Buchman was referring to here was the board of the hospiz at Overbrook. Buchman's wariness of organization probably went back to the events of 1907, when he thought the trustees of the hospiz put cost accounting above human need. It was certainly present while he was working with the YMCA in Asia, when he concluded that many missionaries had lost the ability to engage with people at what he thought was a deep enough level. At the end of his time there, in March 1919, he warned against people becoming "job-centric" rather than "man-centric."[136] This was probably in his mind when, the following year, he turned down an approach by John D. Rockefeller Jr. to administer an ambitious, nondenominational missionary venture, provisionally called the Interchurch World Movement, on the grounds that he did not want something that was too large-scale or organized.[137] Two decades later, following his stroke in 1942, he concluded that the organizational element in his previous activities had been too strong. He told Ray Purdy, "[Jesus] showed me where I was going wrong. I had been organising a movement. But a movement should be the outcome of changed lives, not the means of changing them."[138]

Sometimes, perhaps, Buchman's worry was about a certain kind of mentality rather than organization as such, for MRA's conference centers and larger campaigns could not have been run without good coordination and administration. For example, internal communications were often excellent. OG and MRA leaders on different continents regularly wrote detailed letters to Buchman and one another about their activities, and this made the management of sometimes very ambitious projects possible. But such reporting mechanisms, effective though they often were, were not formalized as such. Indeed, informal procedures were generally the norm in the work, especially in its more formative stage. For example, the OG and MRA usually operated without statutory obligations, regulations, and membership fees. They also often relied on a strong volunteer culture and rarely had officers in a formal sense. In many ways this informality served the movement well and probably gave it extra flexibility. But, as Morris Martin argues, the relatively ill-defined nature of the decision-making structures meant that sometimes it was not clear who was responsible for which decisions, and this became more of a problem as the movement expanded.[139] Inevitably, MRA did over time develop some more typical organizational features, as people donated money or property that had to be managed. MRA was registered slightly differently from one country to another, according to local charity law. It was not a process that Buchman found easy. Possibly he did not foresee some of the administrative challenges that running a large movement would entail.

Buchman's capacity to give leadership to MRA in the last years of his life was affected by his declining health. His stroke, in particular, deprived him of energy. Philippe Mottu contrasted the Buchman of 1939, whom he described as "lively, active, petulant, and full of life and projects" with the man he met at the end of the war, who he called a "disabled old man, walking with pain"—although he suggested that the loss of exterior movement had led to a more intense interior life.[140] Buchman's health deteriorated further in the winter of 1957–58 when he experienced heart problems. He also had a growing problem with a hardening of the arteries—something that had happened to his father—and this was probably a cause of an increasing irritability. Health problems and old age probably affected his judgment at times. There were questions, for example, about his backing for an initiative to build expensive recording studios on Mackinac Island, a place that was cut off from the mainland by ice throughout the winter and early spring.[141] On the other hand, the amount that Buchman accomplished in his later years was impressive. Moreover, as late as February 1959 Paul Campbell remarked on how sharp Buchman was mentally, noting his "unfailing" memory.[142] He remained very alert to what was going on in the world, and in the MRA work, right up until his death—in Freudenstadt, in August 1961.

Partly as a result of his health problems, Buchman's leadership style also changed over time. He was increasingly dependent on others, and his views of the work and the world were sometimes mediated by his entourage. This was inevitable, but not always healthy, for in the last years of his life some of his ideas about people were formed secondhand. Furthermore, power sometimes resided with those who could claim they were close to him, and some close colleagues had difficulty getting regular access to him. The expansion of the movement also made it more difficult for him to be involved in all aspects of decision making. Buchman's poor health meant that, even before his death, the leadership of the movement was passing to others. He probably sensed this himself because, shortly before he died, he said, "Perhaps I have come to the end of my usefulness for the Group."[143]

In the months before his death Buchman expressed considerable unease with the state of MRA. He was particularly critical of some his older American colleagues. According to Garrett Stearly, Buchman thought that many of them had become "movement-minded, imitative of himself rather than God-led, [and] encased in an ideological form, instead of having freedom to follow the Spirit's new ways." This found expression in a series of meetings in which Buchman emphasized the need for people in his team to have a deeper experience of the Holy Spirit.[144] More generally he seems to have felt that something was not quite right with the movement. In fact, the late 1950s and early 1960s was not an easy time in MRA. Some memoirs about the period suggest that an element of introspection came into it. The assumption that organizational failings were the fruit of moral compromise at times created an atmosphere of pressure or criticism, as MRA workers sought to pinpoint in themselves or their colleagues the weaknesses that were holding them back.[145] This may partly have been a side effect of Buchman's own tendency to challenge people directly about their lives, as people who did not have his stature tried to copy his methods. Another issue was that it was not always easy to combine ambitious outreach programs and campaigns with the adequate nurturing of people.[146]

Yet MRA's difficulties were also a product of its success. In spite of its internal difficulties, it was an ambitious and expanding movement that had put down roots in many countries and had the capacity to organize campaigns in troubled situations at short notice.[147] What in the interwar period had been a network of people operating in a relatively informal way had become larger and more difficult to manage. Part of the new challenge was to try to resolve the tension between giving people or national groups the freedom to follow the leading of the Holy Spirit as they saw it and requiring them to be answerable to more formal structures. It was the kind of choice between spontaneity and professionalization that many movements have faced. Indeed, the rise, consolidation, and expansion of MRA, and the challenges facing the movement in its different phases, reflected growth patterns that could be discerned in other religious movements originating with a visionary leader.[148]

Buchman himself said little about how the movement should develop after his death. He did, however, predict that the work would come to be run by a "cabinet of like-minded friends around the world," although he also said that the work was not yet ready for that, and initially there would be one leader.[149] That was indeed what happened, for after Buchman's death Howard took over as his successor. But after he then died, while on a campaign in South America in 1965, a more collective form of leadership began to emerge.

With Howard's death, strains in MRA that had been concealed while Buchman and Howard were alive became apparent. The fact that MRA survived the death of these men indicated that it had not been held together by charismatic leadership alone. But it went through a troubled phrase. In particular, there were differences between the older cohort of full-time workers, who were essentially loyal to Buchman's original vision, and a younger generation of Americans who thought that MRA's message and methods needed to be updated and wanted to branch out in a different direction. The latter, headed by a new leader, Blanton Belk, launched a musical show aimed at youth called *Up with People*, featuring the music of the Colwell Brothers. It soon diverged from the wider MRA work, drawing into it MRA workers from a number of countries. The conference center at Mackinac, which was initially turned into a college, was sold.[150]

Although MRA was hit hard by this split, it remained active internationally, continuing to stress the guidance of God and absolute moral standards and to emphasize the moral and spiritual dimensions of social and political life. The Caux conferences globally, and the Westminster Theatre in Britain, continued to be a focus for its activities. In the United States a group of Americans connected to the international MRA network reestablished control of the MRA Board in May 1976, and in subsequent decades interracial reconciliation became a central concern of the work there.[151] An Asian MRA conference center called Asia Plateau was established in Maharashtra, India, in 1968. In the 1990s MRA moved slowly toward creating more formal mechanisms for the exercise of leadership, and it was renamed Initiatives of Change in 2001.

6
Politics and Ideology

If MRA was intended to be vehicle for changing the world, it was also an idea—although there was sometimes a confusion of the two concepts in MRA publicity.[1] It grew out of a desire on Buchman's part to articulate a vision for the world. This had been present in his mind at least from the mid-1930s onward. In December 1936, in response to the rise of Popular Front governments in Europe, he had suggested that what was needed was a "world Christian Front," and he added, "We must think what it means to be a world front."[2] The launch of MRA a couple of years later was effectively an attempt to articulate what such a front might mean. Buchman's aim was to generate a worldwide movement of moral and spiritual renewal that would avert war and bring a new spirit into national and international life. The process would begin with the individual, he typically declared: "It starts when everyone admits his own faults instead of spot-lighting the other fellow's." Anybody from any walk of life could choose to participate: "Every man, woman and child must be enlisted, every home become a fort." The result would be felt at a global level in the creation of a moral and spiritual force powerful enough to "remake the world."[3]

Buchman's thinking after the outbreak of war reflected a similar aspiration. In a series of world broadcasts in October 1939 he emphasized that "a new world philosophy is needed, a world philosophy capable of creating a new era of constructive relationships between men and nations." He hoped that MRA could be that world philosophy.[4] It was in the context of trying to formulate such a philosophy that in 1943 Buchman started to call MRA an "ideology." He was initially skeptical about the term but came round to believing that it had advantages. If Garth Lean is right, the term appealed to him because it hinted at a comprehensiveness of commitment that he thought "religion" had lost.[5] But it also allowed him to try to present MRA as a direct competitor to the totalitarian ideologies. In his "War of Ideas" speech of 1943, for example, he contrasted MRA's "positive message" with what he saw as the "negative" character of communism and fascism—specifically their "divisive materialism and confusion."[6] It was also a way of challenging Western leaders to look to the moral and spiritual values that he thought were essential if democracy was to function properly. MRA could be presented as giving democracy a moral root. "There is Fascism, and Communism, and then there is that great other ideology which is the centre of Christian democracy—Moral Re-Armament," he said in 1945.[7] In a general sense, Buchman and his supporters were trying to stretch the meaning of the concept of "ideology" to incorporate the very element that it hitherto appeared to lack: the spiritual component.[8]

Yet in talking about MRA as an ideology, Buchman was not talking about a set of ideas that could be understood in isolation from practical life. When, in a speech titled "The Good Road" in 1947, he presented MRA as an ideology for democracy—"democracy's inspired ideology," he called it—he explained it as "a life to be lived, a road to be followed." He was thus describing MRA as promoting a kind of spiritual journey rather than a doctrine: "Here is the good road. Anyone can travel it. Everyone must travel it—ordinary men and the statesmen alike. As we step out upon it, God becomes real."[9] It was yet again an example of how Buchman put an emphasis on practice rather than theory. The "good road" image was, of course, another way of trying to express what a world philosophy might look like, one that highlighted the experiential emphasis of MRA. Another image that Buchman used in relation to ideology was that of light; an ideology was a "global light" bringing "illumination" to the entire world, he suggested in Caux in 1954.[10]

At one level the use of the term "ideology" did not mean any change in the underlying message. When Buchman used the word, he really just meant a faith that could inform the entire thinking and living of an individual or people as a whole.[11] He thought that the Bible itself was a witness to ideological conflict. "The battle of ideologies was the granite of the Old and New Testaments," he said in 1943.[12] When he called in 1945 for an ideology that could "outmarch" the other ideologies, he explained what it meant in terms of the Holy Spirit ruling in the hearts and lives of people; a few years later he suggested that people needed to make "Jesus Christ" their ideology.[13] "Ideology" was thus a new metaphor for ideas that Buchman had always promoted.[14]

What Buchman and his team ultimately meant by the "war of ideas" was the struggle between moral and spiritual ways of living and thinking on the one hand and materialist attitudes and philosophies on the other. Buchman had already started to conceptualize this prior to endorsing the term "ideology."

Notably, in a broadcast of June 1940 Buchman called materialism "our great enemy," describing it as the "mother of all the 'isms.'" He also talked of tackling materialism "within our borders and within ourselves."[15] The struggle against materialism was then subsequently interpreted as a struggle between materialist and moral ideologies. At a press conference in India in 1952, Buchman summarized the differences he saw between the two: "In a materialist ideology the ultimate authority is a man or a party line, a human will, and the ultimate basis for change is force. In a moral ideology the ultimate authority is God's will and the basis for change is consent."[16] The idea that materialism was the main enemy was also present in some of Peter Howard's books. For example, in his book on MRA philosophy, *Ideas Have Legs* (1945), he said that "in the war of ideas, we fight against a spirit of Materialism. . . . The battle line in the war of ideas runs through every factory, farm, home and life in every land."[17]

While "ideology" was a metaphor for ideas Buchman had long held, its endorsement by MRA did point to the increasingly international nature of the movement's thinking and contribute to the growing deployment of a less overtly Christian religious vocabulary as compared with the interwar period. Initially, most MRA workers had no difficulty with the concept. The attempt to create a world philosophy made good sense to them in the context of World War II, and expressing it in terms of an ideology also seemed a good tactical move in the early Cold War. In the decades after the deaths of Buchman and Howard, however, people started to become less comfortable with it. While it seemed relevant in the face of the threat of communism, it was less suitable in other contexts. In addition, in the late Cold War some of the crimes of communism came to be blamed on the very notion of ideology. It was also difficult to defend the term to churchmen who did not think their Christian commitment was best describable in terms of ideology.[18] These were some of the reasons why the term started to disappear from the MRA lexicon in the 1970s and 1980s. There were some who regretted this, particularly from the older cohort of full-time workers. For example, in a memorandum of 1988 William Conner expressed a concern that in downplaying ideology, MRA might lose Buchman's vision for remaking the whole of society and settle for a "fire-engine" activity, involving the tackling of problem situations, which did not reflect the comprehensiveness of Christ's vision.[19]

Although Buchman had always been interested in social and political issues, it was only in the 1930s, in the context of the deteriorating situation in Europe, that his concern for nations started to become the focus of everything that he did. Unconvinced, for example, that AA—founded in 1935—was meant to be a major focus for his work, he once told Sam Shoemaker, that his own task was to deal with drunken nations, not drunken individuals.[20] The call for national and international change had become the overriding priority. "Begin on the basis of the nation, then bring on all the other things," he said in Caux in 1947.[21] Buchman's Christian roots, and in particular Anglo-American evangelicalism, had led him to believe that there was a spiritual battle going inside individuals. His focus on nations meant bringing that idea to bear on social and political life in general. Nations, like individuals, could be freed from their "prison cells of doubt and defeat," he said in 1938.[22]

Buchman probably had a natural instinct for politics; otherwise, it is hard to comprehend his influence in the political arena.[23] Yet he did not have a political program as such. He described MRA as nonpartisan, nonsectarian, and nonpolitical and beyond geographic division, racial distinction, party differences, and class conflict.[24] In fact, the OG was in many ways "anti-political" in the sense that it was looking for a nonpolitical way of addressing policy issues.[25] Buchman did not have a clearly defined political agenda beyond bringing change to politicians.[26] Although the OG and MRA became known for their contribution to the work of reconciliation, Buchman never thought that this was their primary aim. He said in 1933 that the OG's aim was "never to mediate" but to "change lives and unite them by making them life-changers."[27] In other words, social change was to be the fruit of changed lives. At the same time, Buchman also believed MRA thinking was essential for political life, for he once recommended his own collection of speeches, *Remaking the World*, and Peter Howard's *The World Rebuilt* (1951) as containing a "Magna Carta" for national life.[28] Moreover, if MRA did not espouse a particular political position, he did seek to apply its message about personal change and social unity in very specific contexts; its emphasis on the connections between religion, moral standards, and democracy can be seen, in a larger ideological sense, as political.

Buchman thought that any political system could be used for good or ill. The leader of a dictatorship as well as a democracy, if he turned to God and obeyed him, might have a healthy impact on his country. It would be wrong to assume from this that he thought that all political systems were of equal merit. Even in the monarchies—which he was generally very supportive of—he was aware that there were anachronisms. For example, during the abdication crisis in Britain in 1936, he wrote to a Swiss friend that the king's advisers supported an "archaic" system.[29] Likewise, he was obviously skeptical about czarism, at least in its final phase, because he once said that the system by which the czar could not go anywhere without massive protection had helped produce communism.[30] Yet he generally responded to problems in the political sphere not by calling for structural or constitutional change but by challenging people to embrace a new quality of living. For example, in 1934, at a house party in Banff, Canada, he warned that Nazism, fascism, and communism were totalitarian "isms" that could be met only by a Christianity that was equally total in its demands.[31] Buchman thought that changes in people would generate the motivation and unity needed to make healthy political reform possible, but he did not feel it was his role to agitate for such change himself. It was an outlook that led some commentators to believe that the OG lacked a social philosophy and failed to engage seriously with social evil. That was the view, for example, of John C. Bennett, co-founder with Reinhold Niebuhr of the *Christianity in Crisis* magazine and later president of Union Theological Seminary. Likewise, David Belden thought Buchman lacked an appreciation of how grassroots political action could be used to bring about social change.[32]

The focus on trying to change individuals, even if they were dictators, was central to Buchman's strategy in approaching fascism and national socialism.[33] Anybody, he believed, could have a life-changing experience of God. This approach was evident in the mid-1920s, when Buchman tried to develop a link with Benito Mussolini. Buchman wrote to the Italian dictator in February 1926, asking him for an interview and stating that his mission was the development of "constructive leadership" in different countries; he then sent him *Life Changers*, recommending it as suitable reading for his son. Then in October 1926 he heard Mussolini give an open-air speech in Perugia. Buchman was evidently quite impressed, for he wrote to a friend that he had said some "excellent things," citing in particularly some remarks the Italian dictator had made about his readiness to stand up against persecution. The Italian leader's emphasis on creating a democracy that was not subject to base or sectional instincts may also have appealed to him. Buchman also had an interview with Mussolini at that time.[34] Buchman's enthusiasm, however, was not long lasting. A few years later, when he was asked by Stanley Baldwin for his assessment of Mussolini, he replied, "He seemed to me a poseur."[35]

Buchman's connections with interwar Italy were limited. But he devoted a lot more energy to Germany. He was always interested in the country, even prior to the rise of Hitler—with his links going back to his visit there in 1903. Exposure to postwar German poverty had led him in 1921 to write that the Treaty of Versailles had been too drastic, and he talked at that time of the need to bring a moral and spiritual dimension to the reconstruction of Germany.[36] In 1927 and 1928 signs of what would become an OG team started to appear through the attendance of Germans at house parties in Britain and the United States. The rise of national socialism accentuated Buchman's concerns about the country and resulted in him trying to meet Hitler himself. A number of attempts to arrange a meeting with the Nazi leader took place in the years 1932–34, before Buchman decided in the summer of 1935—following a quiet time with German colleagues—that he should stop trying to get an appointment with him.[37]

Buchman was initially more successful in establishing a link with the Nazi SS leader Heinrich Himmler. He was introduced to Himmler by one of his German supporters, Anneliese von Cramon—a well-known churchwoman and former lady-in-waiting to Kaiser Wilhelm II's second wife, Princess Hermine Reuss. The two men met on several occasions in the mid-1930s, including at a lunch party at the time of the Nuremberg rally in September 1934—von Cramon arranged for Buchman to get invitations to the Nuremberg rallies of both 1934 and 1935—and for an interview in Berlin at the time of the Olympics in August 1936.[38] Buchman obviously hoped that Himmler might change and in the process help to introduce a new spirit and direction into German public life. But Himmler proved unreceptive. Surviving reports of conversations that Himmler had both with von Cramon and Buchman suggest that the OG's emphasis on the primary authority of God or Christ over and against the authority of the Nazi state was a key point of difference. Von Cramon accepted a job from Himmler for a period in the mid-1930s, organizing the social welfare of the wives and children of the SS men, but she was eventually dismissed when she refused to take an oath of allegiance to the Nazi party.[39]

The controversy surrounding Buchman's attitude to Nazism arose in particular from an interview he gave to William Birnie of the *New York-World Telegram* in August 1936, in which he was quoted as saying, "I thank heaven for a man like Adolf Hitler, who built a front line of defence against the anti-Christ of Communism."[40] Buchman's critics took this as evidence that he was a Nazi sympathizer. Among them Tom Driberg and George Seldes, the editor of the American leftist newsletter *In Fact*, condensed the statement into the phrases "Thank Heaven for Hitler" and "Thank God for Hitler," which Buchman was then often associated with.[41] Buchman never repudiated the interview, even though the press reports of it were apparently out of keeping with its real tone. He felt that the interpretation that was put on his remarks—that he was in some way pro-Nazi—was a deliberate distortion of what he was trying to say but he decided not to respond to it. His tendency to avoid replying directly to what he saw as ill-intentioned criticism doubtless influenced him. Talking privately to friends a year later, he insisted that his comments in the interview about how

God could use a dictator for constructive purposes in no way meant that he approved of that dictator.[42]

If that was the case, it needs to be asked why Buchman expressed himself in those terms. If T. Willard Hunter is right, his aim was not to express sympathy with Nazism so much as to reach out to Hitler to try to change him. Anybody could change, Hitler not excluded, he thought, and with that in mind he wanted to say something positive about him. He himself was concerned about the communist threat and thus picked on Hitler's anticommunism as something to build on. He seems to have thought that a humbler tone from the West, indicating that Western countries also needed to change, might also help to disarm Hitler. All this was part of a larger aim of trying "divert" Nazi energy into constructive channels.[43]

Buchman does seem to have been impressed by what appeared to be signs of national revival in Germany soon after Hitler came to power, even while being aware that the Nazi revolution was not a Christian one. At an OG meeting at Hatfield House in the United Kingdom in October 1936, chaired by the Conservative peer Lord Salisbury—an admirer of Buchman's work—Buchman came to the defense of the Nazi regime in some way. On the other hand, he emphasized to one of those present that he was far from approving the persecution of the Jews and in the *New York-World Telegram* interview declared, "Antisemitism? Bad, naturally. I suppose Hitler sees a Karl Marx in every Jew."[44] He clearly did not identify with the Nazis' racialist ideas. Daniel Sack suggests that he could be called a "soft fascist," in the sense that while fascism's call for an organic and unified society might have appealed to him, his social vision was never nationalistic, antisemitic, or violent.[45] Yet this is problematic, because fascism becomes a very vague concept when it is detached from its more sinister attributes.

There were a number of figures who thought that Buchman's approach to the Nazi regime was simplistic. Writing in 1934, for example, Dietrich Bonhoeffer suggested that the OG's attempts to try to convert Hitler reflected a failure to understand what was going on.[46] A few years later, Niebuhr also suggested that Buchman was naive about the Nazi regime and about politics in general. In his view the OG failed to realize that all power was to a certain extent anti-Christian and thus that it was unrealistic to believe that change in the hearts of leaders could bring about a fundamental shift in a society.[47] Interestingly, Buchman himself seems to have concluded that he misread Hitler in some way, for he said in 1940 that Hitler had "fooled" him—mentioning in particular the fact that he had hoped Nazi Germany would be a bulwark against communism.[48]

On the other hand, in the mid-1930s there were plenty of prominent people who were still uncertain about how to read Hitler's intentions. Even Winston Churchill, writing as late as 1937, stated that it was still impossible to make a final judgment on Hitler, noting that he had performed both "superb toils" and "frightful evils."[49]

Accusations of naivety about Buchman's response to Nazism need to be balanced against the general concerns he obviously had about the totalitarian regimes and comments he made indicating that he was well aware of the Nazi regime's more sinister side. For example, it seems that he was very shocked by the "night of the long-knives" episode in June 1934—when Hitler had some of his main opponents killed—and had to be persuaded not to give up hope for Germany's future.[50] He was also disturbed by Himmler's behavior during their appointment at the time of the Olympics. At the meeting the SS leader made a propagandistic statement about Nazism and left before Buchman or his friends had a chance to speak. Buchman apparently said afterward, "Here are devilish forces at work. We can't do anything here." Moreover, prior to the meeting, he told a Danish journalist that Germany had come under the influence of a "terrible, demoniac force" and that an urgent challenge to it was needed; he mentioned in particular the need for an "anti-demoniac counter-action" in the countries surrounding Germany.[51] The details of the interview were reported twenty-six years later, so whether the wording was accurate is hard to know.[52] However, it is true that some people in the OG understood their strategy in the 1930s as trying, through their campaigns in countries bordering on Germany, to present an alternative to national socialism.[53] Buchman was also concerned about Nazi militarism and the mobilization of Germany in the 1930s. For example, watching Hitler open an autobahn in 1933, he declared, "It smells of war," and in 1938 he told von Cramon, "War is coming, and we won't see each other for a very long time." On the other hand, much of his activity of the late 1930s was based on the idea that an alternative to war could be found, and he was stunned when the news of war was actually announced.[54]

Buchman, then, seems to have taken some years to comprehend fully the sinister nature of the Nazi regime—although accusations of him being pro-Nazi were clearly wrong. His actions and remarks suggest that in the mid-1930s he still believed that the Nazi regime could change course, but that he was aware of the evil elements within it. The Nazis themselves were certainly wary of the OG. It became difficult to hold large national house parties from 1934 onward. Permission to import OG literature into the country was refused in 1936, and *Rising Tide* was banned by the propaganda ministry. The Gestapo described the OG as a "dangerous opponent" in November 1936 and as a "Christian opponent" of the national state in a lengthy report of 1939. The German Army, in 1942, forbade officers from having anything to do with the OG.[55] Belden attributed the Nazis' suspicion of the movement to its Christian and international character and to what they saw as its possible use by Western intelligence agencies. Such a view is reinforced by the fact that the Nazi invasion plan for Britain in 1940 described the OG as an "instrument of British imperial political power."[56]

Speaking in Caux a couple of years after the end of the war, Buchman said, "We suffered martyrdom in Germany," noting that the "blood of the martyrs" was the "seed of the Church." He suggested in particular that during the war certain people had, because of their association with the OG, been put in battalions where they were likely to get killed.[57] He probably had specific people in mind, but he did not illustrate his point with examples, so it is also possible that he was referring more generally to experiences of persecution undergone by members of the OG.[58] There were a number of civilians involved with the OG who were put into concentration camps.[59]

Buchman's concerns about communism were already well established by the time the Nazis came to power. He saw the communist doctrine primarily in moral terms. In a letter to Douglas Mackenzie in 1921, he used the phrase "moral Bolshevism" to describe the nature of Soviet propaganda, probably referring to the underlying moral relativism and atheism that he saw in the Soviet ideology.[60] He was still using the same phrase a decade later. During a visit to Lima, Peru, in February 1931, at a time of revolutionary upheaval, he said that communism was rooted in "moral Bolshevism," understanding this to mean materialism and hostility to God and absolute moral standards. "Materialism prepared the soil for Communism," he said.[61] Communism advanced by exploiting people's worst instincts, he also thought. On one occasion in the 1950s, responding to a woman who said that the bad moods and moral compromises that were a feature of her marriage were as bad as communism, he replied, "As bad as Communism? They are Communism."[62] He saw communism more as a certain kind of attitude than a political philosophy. The true alternative to it, he thought, was the kind of revolution engendered by the Holy Spirit. Referring to the challenge of French communism in 1952, he said that the Holy Spirit was the best answer to men such as Jacques Duclos, acting secretary general of the Communist Party in the early 1950s.[63]

Yet Buchman was impressed by the commitment of many communists. In Peru he was struck by the fact that girls in their late teens were propagandists for communism. Elsewhere, news of the ideological commitment of some of the top communists also impressed him. He seems to have had a grudging respect for Lenin. His doctrine "still haunts and stalks the world," he said in Caux in 1947.[64] A year later, comparing Lenin to the czars, he said that Lenin "saw something deeper" and "worked his way into the heart of the Russian people."[65] In China John Roots had known the Soviet agent Michael Borodin, a key figure in winning the Chinese elite to communism. Roots reported to Buchman Borodin's apparent disappointment with the lack of fervor in modern Christians in comparison with the more revolutionary figure of Saint Paul.[66] Communists of that type were a challenge to Christians to live in a more revolutionary way, Buchman believed. Speaking in Caux in 1954, Buchman cited the former Soviet foreign minister, Andrei Vyshinsky, as saying, "We will conquer not with atomic bombs, but with our ideas," to try to strengthen his own supporters' understanding of the ideological battle in the world and the need for an alternative.[67]

Buchman thought that some communist idealism could be redirected. Marxism might be subverted, he thought, in the sense that it could "catch the spirit of Christianity." Indeed, Buchman evidently thought that the Soviet bloc might eventually undergo major changes, for he declared that some of his supporters might work in Moscow one day.[68] The idea of challenging and changing the communist world was to be a key element of MRA's postwar message. It was a recurring theme in Howard's plays, for example. In *The Dictator's Slippers* (1954) Howard explored the possibility of a radical change of direction in a communist state following the death of a dictator, and in *Mr Brown Comes Down the Hill* (1964) the main character praises the commitment to social change of many communists.[69] But Howard's plays also contained warnings about the moral relativism that MRA observers typically associated with communism. In *The Real News* (1954), the newspaper's editor "Mac" Macfarlane is manipulated by a subversive secretary, Simon Slade, a communist who uses people's moral weaknesses to promote his influence.[70]

Much of MRA's postwar literature was directed against communism. A particularly strong expression of this was the pamphlet *Ideology and Co-existence* (1959), which sought to alert people to communist plans for world domination and articulate an alternative philosophy grounded in moral and spiritual values. It was distributed in millions of copies in countries where MRA was influential. Critics suggested that it promoted an exaggerated anticommunism, and subsequently some people in MRA themselves concluded that it had helped to give MRA an overly simplistic anticommunist image.[71] Buchman himself, however, was thoroughly behind it—even though he did not read it before it appeared.[72] The publication of the pamphlet coincided with the widespread use by MRA workers of the slogan "Moral Re-Armament or Communism," also with Buchman's support.[73] Buchman probably took the view that a phrase of this kind pointed to the underlying spiritual struggle he saw going on and that it was the best way of influencing large numbers of people.

Buchman did not see himself as promoting an anticommunist message in a narrow sense. In fact, he was very critical of some of the more shrill anticommunist attitudes then prevalent. It was not enough, he emphasized in Caux in 1951, to be against communism: "We have politicians in America who are frightfully anti-Communist, and they are all wrong! In the way they do it they won't convince anybody." A superior alternative was needed.[74] He was probably thinking of Senator Joseph McCarthy here. MRA leaders clearly did not identify with McCarthyism, because some years later, in 1964, Howard wrote critically of the "sly innuendo about Communism, the private sneer, the public assassination of character of anyone who dares to stand for the rights of the poor," suggesting that McCarthy had proved to be "the Red's best friend."[75] MRA tried hard to counter the charge of anticommunism. For example, the author of an MRA statement in the British *Times* newspaper in March 1961 stressed that communists as well as noncommunists had a part to play in the movement's work, declaring, "Anti-communism is an attitude of hate towards people. Absolute love is one of the standards of Moral Re-Armament. It hates nobody. It does carry one hate: the hate of evil."[76] It was an expression of the traditional Christian idea that a love for sinners could be combined with a hatred of sin.

MRA's worldwide activities and efforts to present itself as an ideological alternative to communism did not go unnoticed in the USSR. Soviet commentators were keen to present MRA as representing American foreign policy and interests. For example, an article in the main party newspaper, *Pravda*, in January 1953, probably written in response to MRA's campaign in India at that time, attacked the movement for being a form of imperialist propaganda, backed by American political leaders, businessmen, clergy, and working-class dissidents, that was dedicated to ending class war.[77] This was far-fetched. MRA never aligned itself with American or Western foreign policy in any formal sense. If it had done so, it would have been unable to appeal to people of a determinedly socialist outlook—for example, Irène Laure and some of the German communists who became involved in MRA—as well as many people with a reform-minded social conscience.

On the other hand, MRA's concerns about communism were shared by many people in Washington. Moreover, its stress on ideology and the battle for hearts and minds was replicated in the American government's growing interest, in the late 1940s and early 1950s, in promoting the cultural side of the Cold War. In 1952 the Psychological Strategy Board, set up under Harry Truman to strengthen the ideological dimension of the struggle with communism, briefly considered trying to harness MRA activities as part of its own efforts. The board decided, however, that MRA's track record in converting communists was not as great as it claimed and concluded that it would be impractical to try to work more closely with it.[78]

Buchman did not come to identify good and evil with West and East in a Manichean kind of way.[79] If he was concerned about the communist threat, he did not see the West as a good role model either, and he was often critical of Western values. The United States, in particular, was often a target of his criticism. Speaking in 1939 at Oglethorpe University in Georgia—after being awarded an honorary doctorate of law there—he suggested that one of the results of the country's materialism was that it wanted everything in "tabloid form." He believed the country could give a "whole new pattern to civilisation" but declared that this could come about only if people started to listen to God. If that happened, the country could give a "worldwide message with a national voice."[80] "A nation's thinking is in ruins before a nation is in ruins," he declared in his "War of Ideas" speech, citing America's dishonesty and impurity as part of the problem. Here he warned of the realities of graft and the underground market, suggesting that some people had been dishonest in gaining war contracts. He also suggested that sexual immorality was laying the basis for revolution in the country in the form of broken homes and the decay of culture and that impurity had become a weapon in the hands of subversive groups. Only America's Christian heritage—which he described as its "rightful ideology"—would be an adequate answer in the battle against materialism.[81] A year later, again in Mackinac, he declared that the country had no ideology.[82] He had similar concerns in the mid-1950s. Washington seemed "so defeated" and "out of tune," he observed in 1956.[83]

MRA's critique of the United States, and the West generally, did not sit easily with some commentators and politicians. Howard's play *The Vanishing Island*, which depicted the democratic process itself as open to corruption, was a case in point. Some American policy makers thought its message ran counter to American interests, and there were rumors in Washington that MRA was somehow procommunist and anti-American.[84] Even some of the MRA's most well-placed friends in Washington, like H. Alexander Smith and the rear admiral Richard E. Byrd—an aviator and explorer who had first met Buchman in 1936—were uncomfortable with it.[85]

Buchman was also concerned about the state of Britain. For example, he was worried by what he saw as British imperial arrogance.[86] The British could be "sticky" and "difficult," he once said.[87] MRA's message on decolonization was that all sides, including the old imperial powers, needed to change, and the presentation of this in MRA film, theater, and personal testimony prompted some concerns in places like Kenya that MRA was anti-imperial.[88] This was an exaggeration, but Buchman and his colleagues did expect the British, as well as African, nationalists to change. In 1956 Buchman compared Britain to a lake with "pure, spring water" in the middle but "dead wood" around the edge. The country needed a "drastic farmyard cleanup," he suggested, adding that God was giving it a "last chance to choose the right road." He said in 1956, "If Britain and America were to defeat Communism today, the world would be in a worse state than it is. Because the other man is wrong doesn't make me right."[89]

In Buchman's mind the central challenge was to find a way of bringing spiritual inspiration into the political world so that people could start to tap into God's creative thinking for humanity. His main method of doing this was to try to bring the power of guidance into play. He thought that divine guidance was the "only practical politics" and that the Holy Spirit had the answer to "every problem."[90] Listening to God could create a dynamic that would have an outcome at the national level, he said at the launch of MRA in 1938: "When man listens, God speaks; when man obeys, God acts; when men change, nations change."[91] More specifically, Buchman suggested that guidance could help bring an answer to war. "We must listen to guidance or we shall listen to guns," he said in September 1938; a few months later, on Armistice Day, he suggested that "silence" could be the "regulator" of men and nations.[92] He also thought that guidance offered an alternative to tyranny. He was fond of citing the Quaker statesman, William Penn, founder of Pennsylvania: "Men must choose to be governed by God, or they will condemn themselves to be ruled by tyrants."[93] The point seems to have been that guidance arose from a source of authority beyond the state. In his BBC broadcast of November 1938, he called for the "dictatorship of the Holy Spirit," implicitly trying to offer an alternative to the Nazi concept of leadership.[94] One of his favorite phrases in the 1930s was "God-control"—which he understood to mean "asking for guidance"—a phrase that also pointed to the idea of God's authority.[95] Whole nations could be guided by

God, Buchman thought. On the last day of his life, in August 1961, he stated that he wanted both Britain and the world to be governed by men governed by God. "Why not let God run the whole world?" he said.[96]

Buchman's vision of democracy reflected this emphasis on guidance. At Visby he said that the "popular practice of democracy"—which he described as people doing whatever they liked in the way they liked—was not true democracy at all. A growing number of people were unwilling to acknowledge the "inner authorities" on which democracy depended, he declared. The OG was a better pattern of democracy: "There you have true democracy. You don't do as you please; you do as God guides."[97] In the 1940s he talked of the need for "inspired democracy," a phrase that proved appealing to some of the German leaders who came to Caux after the war.[98] It was a concept that again reflected his desire to bring an element of spiritual inspiration into the political arena. "Theocracy" was another term Buchman seems to have used, if only on one occasion, to describe what he was seeking.[99] But his vision was not theocratic in the sense that he saw a role for the church in state decision making. It was more that he believed in individuals and groups seeking God's wisdom in an informal way. In general, Buchman's conception of democracy was more moral and spiritual than political. He saw it more as an attitude than a set of institutions. For example, he was concerned that too many advocates of democracy reserved the right to be dictators in their own homes.[100] That was the kind of problem he was seeking to address. It was not that he was against representative institutions. It was simply that he thought that no institution could function effectively if the people running it were not living in an unselfish way.[101]

Buchman's belief that international life needed to come under the guidance of God was illustrated by a speech he gave in Zurich shortly after the Italian invasion of Abyssinia in October 1935. "Nationalism," he said, "can unite a country. Supernationalism can unite a world. God-controlled supernationalism is the only foundation for world peace."[102] The concept of "supernationalism" was not in fact Buchman's. Nathan Söderblom had used it as early as 1919, and it was widely used in ecumenical gatherings in the 1930s, partly on the grounds that the concept of "internationalism" was frowned on in Germany.[103] Buchman thought that international conferences needed a spiritual dimension if they were to be effective. Only a "great spiritual experience" in national leaderships would make any world conference or League of Nations effective, he said on the BBC in 1938.[104] Man without God could not make peace, he insisted a year later.[105] The Holy Spirit was "uniting humanity" through men who listened to and obeyed Him, he said in 1952.[106] According to one of his supporters, the

British diplomat Archie Mackenzie, who was present at some of the founding sessions of the UN, Buchman always expressed an interest in developments in the UN Security Council and General Assembly but thought that the organization needed to focus more attention on the "human factor" in politics if it was to be effective.[107] As with his attitude to democracy, Buchman believed that international institutions were not on their own enough to secure the unity of humankind, if the people running them were not living by the right values.

Buchman was interested in formulating a vision for society as well as government. In a prewar manifesto that appeared in *Rising Tide* he stated that a "God-guided public opinion" would be a source of strength to leadership and that this meant the "dictatorship of the living Spirit of God" would give each man the "inner discipline" he needed and the "inner liberty" he desired.[108] He also wanted to mobilize society. Some of his speeches at the end of the 1930s were consciously directed at the "millions." He talked of "reaching the millions" in his Visby speech in 1938, for example.[109] Then in the United States in December 1939 in a series of worldwide broadcasts he tried to mobilize large numbers of people with a vision of "one hundred million people listening."[110] He was still hoping to find a way of heading off war and thought that a spiritual answer might have been arrived at through a lot of people turning to guidance. It was one of the few occasions when Buchman focused on trying to affect large numbers of people in one individual initiative. A similar desire to generate spiritual renewal in society was evident after the war. The key to the formation of a true democracy, he said in Caux in 1948, was that the people's will was a reflection of God's will. It could happen in Germany, he said, that the voice of God would become the will of the people.[111]

Buchman also stressed the importance of God's guidance and wisdom for the world of industry—on the proper functioning of which he and MRA placed great emphasis before, during, and after World War II. MRA was first launched in East Ham town hall, a place associated with the British labor movement. In his speech at the launch, Buchman stated that when labor, management, and capital became "partners under God's guidance," industry would take its true place in national life. Then, a few months later, he declared that "God-control" could bring industrial harmony and efficiency and that capital and labor could work together like "fingers on the hand."[112] Buchman also tried to formulate a vision for the working class specifically. "Labour led by God can lead the world," he declared at the National Trade Union Club in London in 1938.[113] If it was not led by God, he thought, Marxist materialism would take over.[114] He thought that this was a matter of great importance in what he saw as an increasingly left-wing world.[115] Industrialists too had much to contribute. On the eve of World War II, he suggested that some of Europe's leaders of industry were better placed to give leadership than the older elites: "Courageous men in industry give me more hope. They are used to taking major decisions," he said.[116]

Issues relating to social justice and the relief of poverty also featured in some of Buchman's speeches. At the launch of MRA he declared—using a phrase he was often associated with—"There is enough in the world for everyone's need, but not for everyone's greed."[117] A few months later, he said, "We must have justice, whereby each sees not only his difficulties, but the difficulties of others also."[118] Unemployment was an issue he tried to address. Also in 1938 he suggested that in the "divine scheme of things" there was no such thing as unemployment, and he stressed that under God there would be true equality and brotherhood.[119] "Go back to Denmark and answer unemployment" was his challenge to a group of Danes who came to consult him after the OG meeting at Visby.[120] Buchman's criticism of unemployment was not expressed in terms of specific policy solutions but was an implicit challenge to industrialists to do all that they could to avoid making redundancies. In general, it pointed to a more inclusive approach to management, and some employers who were influenced by MRA took this seriously.[121] Buchman was trying to express a social vision that embraced both the material and the spiritual needs of humanity. In Sri Lanka in 1952, he said, "Empty stomachs will be filled with food, empty hands with work, and empty hearts with an idea that really satisfies."[122]

Much of MRA's wartime energy was devoted to fostering good industrial relations in the United States, in the belief that they would contribute to national defense.[123] Indeed, this was one of the reasons why Truman, prior to becoming president, was interested in MRA—although he held the movement at arms length once he was in office.[124] In 1947 Buchman suggested that miners trained at Caux had improved their production of coal.[125] He thought that the class war was being "superseded" by the MRA approach. MRA also devoted a lot of energy to trying to bring better relations between workers and managers in the British docks—Buchman emphasizing that whoever controlled the docks controlled the "lifeline of nations."[126] MRA supporters claimed that their influence in the British docks was considerable, and recently released British intelligence files confirm that MRA's philosophy did have an impact there.[127] In America MRA approaches were also used to try to tackle labor issues, for example, in relation to a dispute at United Airlines in late 1950.[128] Buchman tried to get inspiration about this from his quiet times. He told a Mackinac audience in

1951, "It came to me in guidance . . . that the airlines carried the message for the rejuvenation of business in America."[129]

In Buchman's mind the selling of policy and sustaining morale were often as important as policy itself. Without winning hearts and minds, morale would plummet. That is why he defended so strongly the idea that MRA workers might avoid military service and instead support the war effort through MRA. His approach here was not the product of a principled opposition to people serving in the military. He was never a pacifist, and MRA spokespeople always insisted that moral re-armament and military preparedness should complement each other rather than be mutually exclusive.[130] In March 1942 he wrote to Truman, who was by then a senator, criticizing those who, in distributing manpower, failed to see the value of a program like MRA that could help to create a "united enlightened public opinion." In particular, he highlighted MRA's contribution to labor relations, stressing that it had good links with both management and labor. He saw this as part of a larger agenda to create what he called "total defense" and the building up of people who were "training in morale."[131] Truman was impressed and subsequently headed a group of public figures who wrote to Franklin Roosevelt condemning the idea of MRA workers being assigned to other work. In the end, though, Buchman lost his younger American supporters to the draft. The result was that the show *You Can Defend America* had to be terminated.[132]

A similar linkage of morale and national defense was evident nearly two decades later, in a 1960 letter Buchman wrote to Robert Schuman, in which he suggested that MRA might have a role to play in turning NATO from being "merely an alliance of military defense" into an "ideological force." The idea grew from a suggestion by General Antoine Béthouart, former French high commissioner in Austria, and Buchman evidently thought he should pass it on to Schuman: "I feel that you with your profound knowledge of Europe can do something fundamental and constructive in NATO along these lines."[133] If nothing came of it, it was still an indication of Buchman's belief that in the Cold War the battle for hearts and minds was central.

The OG and MRA also tried to develop their own narrative in relation to racial questions. The possibility that the OG could help to address racial enmities first became evident in the late 1920s, when some OG visits to South Africa led to trust-building initiatives between people from English and Afrikaner backgrounds. MRA later continued the work of trying to foster racial harmony in South Africa, drawing in a number of radical black nationalists, including William Nkomo, the first president of the Youth League of the African National

Fig. 10 Buchman alongside Mary McLeod Bethune, Mackinac conference center, autumn 1954. Also shown are (*front left*) Nigerian member of Parliament Michael Ogon and (*back left*) the Tolon Na from the Gold Coast (Ghana). Photo: Oxford Group Archives.

Congress.[134] More generally, in the context of the challenges of decolonization, MRA stressed the importance of ethnic reconciliation as a key dimension of nation building. Racial harmony was also emphasized in relation to ethnic divisions in the United States. Speaking at Caux in 1955, Buchman heralded the U.S. Supreme Court decision to end segregation in education the year before, welcoming the end of "all the things that make for bitterness." It enabled, he said, the realization of Abraham Lincoln's principle of equality: "That is rebirth. A great revolution. And we are just at the beginning of it, that all men are born free and equal."[135]

Buchman alluded in this speech to Mary McLeod Bethune, an African American educator, born of slave parents, who had visited Mackinac and Caux the previous year. "Just think what that means for Mary McLeod Bethune," he said.[136] Bethune's life story and encounter with MRA were turned into a musical, *The Crowning Experience*, which ran for five months in Atlanta, Georgia, in 1958, and which was much used by MRA in subsequent years in a film version. It was part of a wider attempt to address racial tension in the United States.

Freedom, for example, was shown in Little Rock, Arkansas, following the violence that broke out there in autumn 1957, after the desegregation of schools.[137] It was not "colour" but "character" that was important, Buchman insisted in 1955, and the idea pervaded the MRA approach to racial issues.[138]

Buchman's emphasis on equality, evident in his response to the desegregation law, was reflected elsewhere. He had obviously been trying to express something on this theme before the war, because he said in 1939 that MRA stood for a "prejudice-free way of living" and that it was a common denominator above "party, race, class, creed, point of view or personal advantage."[139] When the trade unionist and MRA supporter John Riffe, for a time executive vice president of the Congress of Industrial Organizations, died in 1958, Buchman responded with the comment, "An age when all men are equal. That is God's gift. John lived it."[140]

Buchman's personalist rather than systemic approach to political change was at the same time reinforced by what he said about race. The answer to the bitterness associated with racial division was "something that is born of Christ," he said in 1955. He also said that the answer to what he called a "dyspeptic constitution" was a "certain type of person." He was talking of countries such as Nigeria, the Gold Coast (Ghana), and South Africa and seems to have meant that it was people who had gone through a process of personal change that were most needed in these places.[141] The fact that Buchman welcomed desegregation so enthusiastically illustrated the fact that he was thoroughly in favor of certain kinds of political change. Yet at the same time he believed that the most important source of social and national renewal in polarized situations were people whose lives were free from hatred.

The idea that people could change was clearly an essential feature of Buchman's political thinking. Indeed, he saw MRA as a "superior" ideology, on the grounds that it was based on this idea.[142] "Apart from changed lives no civilisation can endure," he asserted in 1934.[143] A couple of years later he declared that a revolution in human nature was the "only hope."[144] By a change in human nature he essentially meant a redirection of motive. Selfishness could be conquered. The crisis in the world, he said in 1947, came not just from the emerging "iron curtain" but also from the "steely selfishness" in people that divided them from one another and God. When men learned to listen to God and obey him, the iron and steel would "melt away."[145]

In postwar MRA this vision of a change in human nature was presented as an alternative to the communist program for creating the "new man." Writing in *Remaking Men* (1954), for example, Paul Campbell and Peter Howard observed that the difficulty of creating the "new type of man" was one of the great challenges facing Soviet communism. MRA offered a better alternative, they stressed, in that it brought a higher power into play: "Change in human nature requires the receiving of power from outside the personality. . . . To be silent and to listen is the operative act in transforming a man's character."[146] In other words, the materialist ideology of communism could not change people, whereas a moral and spiritual ideology, drawing on God's inspiration, could. It was essentially a nondogmatic presentation of the Christian message about spiritual regeneration, articulated to try to counter and at the same time attract the communist world. Trying to bring about such a change in people involved a spiritual struggle, MRA leaders thought. "The basic struggle is for the wills of men. That is the ideological struggle," Buchman said in Mackinac in 1952.[147]

In this connection Buchman took the view that the key to better government was "new statesmen."[148] This again reflected his stress on people rather than systems. He wanted to see "inspired statesmen" and "super-statesmen" who would make "God-control" their program.[149] At the same time, he believed that everyone was meant to be a kind of statesman. "Everybody's job is to find the God-arched master-plan," he once said, lamenting the fact that people let politicians do the thinking for them. Every citizen was important.[150] Real statesmanship also involved the capacity to change people. "I do not believe that a man can be an intelligent statesman unless he knows how to change his own son," he said in 1954.[151]

In Buchman's mind the kind of leadership that was needed was well-expressed in the message of the Jewish prophets. Jeremiah's thinking offered a "framework for the building of a nation," he said in Norway in 1935, and a few years later he recommended Isaiah and Amos for similar reasons.[152] Typically, he thought that an essential feature of this kind of prophetic leadership was the practice of guidance. For example, he linked the influence of figures such as George Washington, Benjamin Franklin, and Abraham Lincoln to the fact that they had listened to God at times of national crisis.[153] He also once commended Nicholas von der Flüe, the fifteenth-century Swiss saint who had helped prevent civil war in his country, for his "gift of divine direction," calling him a "model for the United Nations."[154]

In this connection Buchman also emphasized the capacity of individuals or small groups of people to alter the destiny of their countries. "There is tremendous power in a minority guided by God. Think of a person like Joan of Arc. She saved her nation," he said in September 1938.[155] Buchman also emphasized the way in which communism had originated first with Marx and then with a small group.[156] This emphasis on the capacity of small groups or minorities to alter the course of events was later taken up by British historian Robert C. Mowat—active in MRA—who likened it to Arnold Toynbee's idea of the "creative minority" in history and tried to develop a philosophy of history based on it.[157]

Buchman also assumed that the morality of individual leaders would affect their judgment and ability to govern. There was a tradition in the OG and MRA of linking adherence to absolute moral standards to clarity of thinking. In a speech of 1953, calling for a new kind of leadership in the world, Buchman declared, "Confusion comes from compromise, clarity comes from change," saying that absolute moral standards were the "well-spring of inspired statesmanship."[158] This was an area where Buchman stressed the importance of purity. For example, talking in 1955 about the Pasha of Marrakech, El Glaoui, and his family, Buchman said that only the "radical and cleansing factor of absolute purity" could give them the power to give the right kind of leadership.[159] It was a theme that was given much emphasis in MRA culture at that time. For example, on a visit to Caux in 1953 the Australian Labour politician Kim Beazley concluded that if he embraced "absolute purity," he might be able to make a contribution toward the rehabilitation of the Australian aboriginal people. He understood this to mean that there was a conflict between living for self-gratification and "intelligent care for others" and that the capacity for discipline in his personal life would determine the effectiveness of his battle for social change. He later became a reforming minister of education in 1972–75, with a particular interest in aboriginal questions.[160]

If in his earlier evangelistic work Buchman often stressed the link between purity and personal spirituality, in later years he increasingly emphasized the connection between sexual morality and society. As his "War of Ideas" speech in 1943 illustrated, he believed that sexual immorality was a vehicle for the spread of subversive ideas. He made similar points in a speech that he gave a few months before he died, "All the Moral Fences Are Down," which grew out of ideas expressed by Sir Richard Livingstone, a classicist who had been vice-chancellor of Oxford University in the late 1940s. Livingstone, a friend of Buchman who had died the previous year, had warned that whereas previously people had grown up with a sense of right and wrong—even if they did not always stick to it—there were now no longer any moral fences at all. It was the job of Buchman and MRA to rebuild them, Livingstone had said.[161]

Buchman agreed with Livingstone, and in his speech made some remarks about Japan that were very indicative of the way he linked private morality with the political milieu. Already in January 1959 Buchman had challenged a group of Japanese who visited him in Tucson to try to tackle the problem of "corruption and mistresses in high places," which he said were a more serious problem than communism.[162] Then, in the "Moral Fences" speech, Buchman again talked of the way in which corruption, mistresses, and dishonesty had become a way of life in Japan. But he also singled out certain Japanese leaders who had recently tried to apply MRA principles in their lives and country. According to Buchman, it was these MRA-inspired leaders who had held firm in their commitment to the signing of the recent American-Japanese Treaty of Mutual Cooperation and Security (January 1960)—before which there had been a lot of unrest. A statement by Nobusuke Kishi to Buchman was cited to support this: "At the crucial hour men trained in Moral Re-Armament in labour, youth and politics stood up and refused to compromise with evil."[163] It was people like Saburo Chiba, and other high-level Japanese supporters of MRA, that he had in mind.[164] Buchman's support for the treaty was an example of a situation where he clearly identified with American foreign policy.

As the "Moral Fences" speech indicated, Buchman thought that only those leaders who had a strong moral code, including in relation to sexual behavior, had the inner resilience to stand up against the pressure of the Far Left. The assumption seems to have been that people who were privately self-indulgent in some way had a weakness of character that left them open to manipulation. Concerns about the impact of sexual permissiveness were to remain important in MRA after Buchman's death. This was particularly evident in Britain, where Howard and Lean were among a number of authors who tried to articulate an alternative to what they saw as a growing tide of moral relativism.[165]

Buchman's belief that God had a plan for nations probably owed something to Puritan and Calvinist strains of American religion, in which God's unique plan for the United States was frequently emphasized.[166] He certainly stressed and tried to give expression to the distinctiveness of individual national callings. After 1945, for example, he declared that Japan could be "the lighthouse of Asia" and Nigeria a "pilot nation for the world," and he said that Cyprus had a destiny to "demonstrate unity" to divided nations.[167] He would also pray for particular countries or situations. For example, at the end of World War II he prayed that future years would be "undimmed in God's Holy Spirit in Germany" and that the allies would be kept "pure and unsullied" in the Holy Spirit. In 1952, in front of the tomb of Pakistani leader, Mohammed Ali Jinnah, who he had first met in 1924, he said, "May Pakistan rise and live an answer."[168] He also tried to express a vision for regions and continents. For example, in a Christmas message of 1956 he suggested that since wise men from Arabia and Africa had come to acknowledge the "hope of the world" during the first Christmas, so then Arabia and Africa might be the "unexpected source" giving an answer to chaos.[169]

Buchman believed that it was important to take account of the cultural differences between nations when trying to formulate national visions or strategies. During World War II the MRA team in the United States had made much use of a play called *Drugstore Revolution*, aimed at American urban youth. But shortly after arriving in Caux in 1946, Buchman announced that the play would not be suitable for Switzerland. "You sin in another way," he told his Swiss audience, before going on to state that each person should seek God's wisdom for a national strategy: "That is what each of you must get—God's guidance on His plan for Switzerland, Sweden, every country and the world. He will show you, and I am not going to do it for you."[170] Buchman's alertness to differences of national character was also manifest in some comments he made about Japan in 1952 when he said that the Japanese were "stolid," but that when people really got to know them, they revealed a lot about themselves. He added, "They have that fine sense of prudence that I appreciate."[171]

Buchman often tried to express a vision of how patriotism or nationalism could be a positive force. Some of his speeches of the 1930s seem to have been an attempt to inject positive religious content into the idea of nationalism in such a way that it would deflect the fascist dictators down a peaceful road. In Buchman's mind the key to a healthy patriotism was for God's guidance to be central in a country's life. "The true patriot gives his life to bring his nation under God's control," he said in an Easter Day speech in Denmark in 1936, and a few years later in Boston he suggested that in obedience to God nations would find their "true destiny."[172] The wrong kind of nationalism or anticolonialism had to be met with a new kind of attitude, he also thought. For example, in 1954 he said that the real answer to the Mau Mau rebellion that had broken out in Kenya was what he called "liquid love": "That will win the Mau Mau. You love these people. With discipline. . . . That is the answer. Liquid Love. The thing they have not had."[173]

Buchman's general stress on social and national unity was one reason why he was at a certain level impatient with party politics. The tactical side of politics seems to have irritated him, for he said in 1955 that most statesmen played at politics like "little boys with blocks."[174] The very idea of parties competing against one another for power probably ran counter at some level to his belief that people should work together. He also thought that the spiritual conflict taking place in the life of nations was not represented by the divisions between parties and that this would become increasingly evident over time. Of American political life, he once said, "After a while we'll have no party lines in America. The lines will be drawn between Christ and anti-Christ. It's coming already in Britain."[175] It was partly for these reasons that Buchman did not want his message to be defined as either right or left wing. In his "War of Ideas" speech in 1943, he said, "People get confused as to whether it is a question of being Rightist or Leftist. But the one thing we really need is to be guided by God's Holy Spirit." Buchman was talking about the wider ideological forces at work in the world, and in that context stated that the Holy Spirit is "the Force we ought to study."[176] The implication was that the Holy Spirit had a vision that could transcend limited party political thinking.

Buchman clearly believed that the right direction for national life could be found only when people from different sections of society were able to work together. More specifically, he thought that the discernment of God's will for a country depended on the creation of a certain kind of moral and spiritual alliance. This was evident when he said, at the launch of MRA, that it was the "combined moral and spiritual forces of a nation" that could find God's plan.[177] In his mind the same principle applied globally. It was only the combined forces of the world as a whole that would be able to discern and realize God's purposes for humanity. Of course, as Buchman's theological assumptions indicated, these forces did not have to be formally Christian groups or movements—although they might well have been involved. In his work to generate change at national and international levels, Buchman was seeking to build coalitions of people who had a commitment to God's guidance and absolute moral standards, and these people did not all have to be Christians. Common ground might be found with nonbelievers too, where they countered the moral relativism of the age.[178]

In some ways Buchman's thinking about nationhood and the role of religion within it ran parallel to and reflected those forces in the United States that stressed the importance of "one nation under God" and that had brought about the addition of the words "under God" to the Pledge of Allegiance in 1954. For many Americans, Buchman included, the threat of communism demanded a clearer articulation of the link between faith and democracy.[179] His belief that people of different faiths needed to work more closely together was also replicated more widely in the United States, especially in the context of the Cold War. For example, the future Catholic archbishop Fulton Sheen—a figure whom Buchman thought highly of—was keen to bring Protestants, Catholics, and Jews together to strengthen American resolve against communism.[180] Likewise,

Truman thought of creating a grand religious alliance against the communist threat.[181] In addition, Buchman's thinking was informed by the growing internationalist current in American politics, which had been most evident in the ideas of Woodrow Wilson and which had grown stronger as the global role of the United States increased. He wanted to give a spiritual direction to that kind of tendency.[182] Of course, the impetus for his religious internationalism came partly from the American YMCA.

Hunter argues that, for all his focus on personal change, Buchman always had the ultimate goal of achieving a complete transformation of social structures.[183] This may be true, but it is hard to prove definitely. It remains unclear how far he was actually thinking about change in concrete political terms. The focus of his work was more the transformation of motives than structures, although he thought the latter would often occur as a result of the former. His thought was ambitious, but whether or not it was utopian depends largely on how the concept of utopianism is defined. He did not endorse the kind of politically driven, violent projects associated with the twentieth-century totalitarian dictatorships. In addition, there is no sense that he believed that it was possible to create a kind of sinless world in which redemption was no longer needed. In these senses Buchman was not utopian at all. If, however, utopianism is defined simply as involving a tendency to imagine and try to work toward a better world, then most religious groups can be seen as advocating a utopian program. In this context, the term is well suited to describing Buchman's vision.[184]

There was certainly a millennial element in Buchman's ideas in the sense that he believed in the possibility of building the kingdom of God on earth.[185] He once said he wanted to "change the age of gold into the Golden Age" and in his final will talked about bringing the nations into a "long-looked-for Golden Age," enabled by the cross of Christ.[186] "We are heading right out for a brand new world," he announced at an MRA assembly in Washington, D.C., in 1954.[187] He also believed that he was cooperating with a larger divine plan for the world. The miracle of people being led by God was, he said, "the divinely appointed destiny of mankind."[188] In this sense he had a feeling that history was on the side of MRA. There was a great optimism that permeated the MRA team as a whole. Indeed, at the end of the 1950s and the early 1960s, Buchman and his supporters came to believe that MRA was in a good position to try to bring a moral and spiritual answer to some of the world's most pressing problems.

The optimism sometimes appeared exaggerated and simplistic. For example, Buchman announced in 1959 that governments convinced of MRA would "lead the world immediately into a new era of unity, peace and plenty."[189] Such thinking was liable to disappoint people who through MRA came to believe that a transformation of the world was imminent. On the other hand, Buchman was always prone to enthusiastic statements of this kind, and it would probably be missing the point to interpret them as carefully weighed predictions of what was likely to happen. Rather, he was trying to mobilize nations in the same way that he tried to energize individuals: by giving them a challenge. Buchman's idealism, and the vocabulary in which it was expressed, also sometimes reflected a wider mood. For example, when he talked of creating "a new world order"—as he did on a number of occasions—he was talking in terms that were commonly used by politicians after the two world wars.[190] In addition, his optimism was characteristic of the missionary milieu that had helped to shape his outlook. John R. Mott had famously called for the evangelization of the world within one generation.[191] Buchman's vision for changing the world reflected a similar level of ambition.

Buchman clearly wanted to encourage people to be bold in their thinking. But he sometimes expressed his vision in more moderate terms. For example, he once talked with Oliver Corderoy about "remaking the world" in terms of helping people make decisions: he wanted to see the "cure of hate—by decisions." He said in the late 1940s that remaking the world meant being "originative" of relevant alternatives to evil in economics, government policy, and so on.[192] His thinking was also practical in many ways. Whatever MRA achieved in the way of brokering social or national reconciliation would not have happened without careful planning by Buchman and his team. For example, its systematic program of bringing together European and Asian elites at conferences after 1945 and its long-term efforts to foster what it saw as leadership potential in targeted individuals indicated a clear assumption that social change would not happen without hard work over time. There was also a strong current of realism in Buchman's outlook. If he was more optimistic about the possibility of social transformation than proponents of "Christian realism" like Niebuhr, his enduring belief in the reality of sin or evil indicates that he himself was a realist as well as an idealist. Indeed, he may have had more in common with Niebuhr than it first appeared. Hunter, at least, argued that Niebuhr misunderstood Buchman and that the two men were similar in their conviction about the underlying sinfulness of human nature and people's need for redemption.[193]

Mowat interpreted Buchman's concept of "inspired democracy" to mean that the last word in political decision making would be reached not through discussion or a majority vote but "through God's guidance or inspiration."[194] There is much to be said for this. Whatever the structures Buchman wanted people to find ways of listening to God. He thought that the character of any political system or social order would immediately begin to change when people brought the reality of spiritual life into their decision making. There was no blueprint for political action here that could be applied in any given situation. It was up to individual politicians, as they turned to God for inspiration, in unity with others, to decide how to respond to the challenges they faced.

Conclusion

While Buchman was very adaptable, there was a core set of insights that informed his vision and that actually changed little. Writing in the late 1950s, one of his supporters, Basil Yates, suggested that the underlying architecture of his thought consisted of three elements: the moral underpinnings of faith, obedience to the Holy Spirit, and the normality of God working in the human heart. More generally, he argued that Buchman sought to "remould the whole machinery of life under the categories of faith."[1] It was a good summary.

Yet it is not easy to fit Buchman's ideas into a defined theological system. He was clearly happy living with paradoxes. For example, he had no difficulty combining an emphasis on the cross of Christ with an appreciation of other religions. Similarly, he stressed that the OG was not an alternative to the church, while believing that since the Holy Spirit had brought it into being, it carried the spirit of the church within it. There was also a paradoxical dimension to his understanding of morality, in that he challenged people to measure themselves against absolute moral standards while at the same time stressing that they should not live by rules. Traditional assumptions about doctrine and morality were also combined with a desire to be modern and relevant to contemporary culture.

There was in Lutheranism a precedent for living with paradoxes. For example, there was arguably a dualism in Luther's thinking between the "how" and the "what" of conduct: if the Gospel gave people guidelines of what was true, it left them free to decide how to apply them in a non-Christian cultural setting.[2] Buchman's relatively flexible approach to doctrine can certainly be interpreted as an expression of that kind of thinking. With such an outlook behind him, Buchman could in one context stress the atoning power of Christ, for example, while in another work toward good industrial relations. But there is no evidence that Buchman derived his approach from Lutheranism as such. His emphasis on the Holy Spirit, which allowed him that flexibility, did not come from any one theological tradition. It was also probably an outcome of his essentially practical nature as much as the expression of a particular spiritual vision.

One reason why Buchman was eager to avoid pinning MRA down to some clear theological position was that he saw it as something that was in the process of being revealed by God. At the end of his life, he wryly told a friend that he was "learning more about moral re-armament every day."[3] In a similar vein he once said of some colleagues who were trying to avert a crisis at an MRA conference, "It's harder for them than for me, because I don't belong to MRA."[4] He saw his task as trying to discern the Holy Spirit's evolving purposes for the movement rather than provide a clearly defined and final expression of MRA.

The existence of tensions or paradoxes at the heart of Buchman's vision and the relatively unsystematic nature of his ideas were important elements in his success. They meant that MRA could be constantly reinventing its message and that people from different cultures could explain it in different ways. On the other hand, they sometimes made it hard for Buchman's team to define clearly what their work was about. To some degree, they were also responsible for the air of mystery that at times surrounded the work. A movement that was best understood through its stories and interpreted differently in different countries was not easy for outsiders to categorize. It could also make it hard for people within the movement to know just how far the message of MRA could be creatively adapted without losing its essential core. In some ways these problems were the inevitable outcome of Buchman's attempt to create a global network where different spiritual traditions had a part.

In a more recent formulation that also reflected the unsystematic nature of Buchman's vision, the Russian philosopher Grigorii Pomerants—who first visited Caux in 1992—suggested that Buchman's legacy was not an orthodoxy or a set of easily recited principles but a "practice or 'orthopraxy' found in dozens of scattered examples." On the other hand, he also noted that there was a "religious subtext" in Buchman's thought, describing MRA as a "fellowship of the Holy Spirit which blows everywhere."[5] Beneath the unsystematic exterior of MRA's outlook, there remained an underlying emphasis on what Buchman saw as the reality of the Holy Spirit at work in the world.

The word that Buchman himself often used in earlier years to indicate the flexible and adaptable nature of his thinking was "life." Many of the things Buchman said were intended to engender life in, or provoke responses from, people. Life, in his mind, was not something that could be reduced to a creed but was rather the outcome of a living relationship with God. The emphasis on religious experience rather than doctrine in MRA was an outcome of this way of thinking. As Gabriel Marcel once said, MRA was not a theology or philosophy but an "experience."[6]

There was a personalist element in Buchman's thinking here. He thought the Holy Spirit was a kind of person and that he had strategies that worked through people to repair broken relationships and bring social unity. It is surely no accident that thinkers like Marcel or Paul Tournier should have admired Buchman. Their interest in personhood and interpersonal relations was very compatible with his thinking.[7] There was also a kind of existential element in Buchman's approach, reflected in his interest in individuals and his tendency to ask people questions about what they were living for rather than their beliefs. It was surely no coincidence, for example, that the writings of Holocaust survivor and founder of logotherapy, Viktor Frankl, were sometimes cited by MRA writers—particularly after Buchman's death. In *Man's Search for Meaning* (1946), Frankl had suggested that people could find freedom from certain psychological problems when they gained a sense of purpose for their lives.[8]

Strains of pietism and holiness teaching were clearly very much present in Buchman's thought and ways of working. These were first conveyed to him by his Lutheran background, the American YMCA, and the Keswick Convention. There is a case for saying that Buchman simply used or repackaged ideas from these traditions rather than come up with original ideas of his own.[9] This was evident in his approach to guidance, for example. He took the practice of listening to God from F. B. Meyer, built his own life around it, and then suggested that it was something that anyone from any faith, and even without any faith, could try—and that it was as easy and normal as turning on the radio. God himself was thus made familiar and approachable.[10]

Yet Buchman did ultimately expand on the practice of guidance as it was then used by Meyer and other contemporary evangelicals. He tried to foster, through the quiet time, a kind of creative or prophetic thinking that focused on national and international life. Part of his originality as a religious leader lay here. It was not the idea of guidance that was distinctive to him but the context in which he sought to apply the concept and the creative potential he saw in it. In the OG and MRA the quiet time was taken out of its more traditional ecclesiastical setting and used to encourage reflection on social conflict and international relations. Implicit in this was a wish to break down divisions between religious and secular thinking and practices. The deployment by the OG and MRA of other spiritual practices such as restitution, apology, sharing, and the telling of stories in contexts in which social, economic, and political questions were addressed reflected the same tendency.

The expansion in Buchman's concept of guidance was the fruit of an evolving interpretation of what the Holy Spirit was doing in the world. He increasingly thought that it was calling people from across social, religious, and national divides to work together to create a different kind of international community or family. Furthermore, in the face of the ideological battles of the mid-twentieth century he had an almost restless desire to come up with a philosophy and a movement that would reflect this. The Holy Spirit could be a source of strategic thinking about vital issues, he believed. MRA was his expression of what he thought a Holy Spirit–led vision and strategy might look like in the face of the world situation in 1938. The idea was explained in slightly different ways over the years. Its articulation as an ideology in 1943 reflected a desire to offer an alternative to materialist thinking in the context of the war of ideas in the world. Buchman thought that the forces of materialism could be met by the "force" of the Holy Spirit, and he wanted MRA groups—often containing people from different denominations and faiths—to be a vehicle for bringing this force into play wherever they were working.[11]

In specifically theological terms, Buchman's thinking cannot be easily defined as either conservative or liberal. He avoided the fundamentalist-modernist controversy.[12] In spite of his openness to different religious cultures, he never questioned traditional Christian theology, and he used the Bible in a precritical way.[13] In recalling his experience at Keswick, he stressed the way in which his encounter with the cross of Christ and his decision to try to make amends for his bitterness led to a renewed contact with the Holy Spirit. The work of Christ and the movement of the Holy Spirit were thus presented as collaborative in a way that reflected traditional Trinitarian theology. He was not the promoter of natural religion, as some thought, and the atonement always remained central to his thinking.

If some critics saw him as underemphasizing Christ's uniqueness, he himself saw his work as trying to make the rule of Christ a reality in both Christian and non-Christian cultures. His tendency to cite extracts from some of the great evangelical hymns, even in later years, was testimony to the way in which the Christian culture that shaped him always retained a powerful hold on his imagination.

In addition, Buchman was a strong adherent of Christianity's traditional moral teachings, believing them to be an essential component of the life of faith. He believed that people's moral choices determined the way they saw the world. Conviction of sin, and restitution for it where possible, were vital moments in a person's discovery or recovery of faith. Buchman's decision to place "honesty" first in the list of the absolute moral standards was an indication of how important he thought it was. But "purity," especially in relation to sexual behavior, was clearly also stressed strongly by Buchman—for the spiritual creativity that he thought it released in people. At the same time, it should be said that Buchman's moral outlook, demanding though it was, left considerable space for the individual conscience. The quiet time was conceived as a means through which people could come to their own conclusions about what God was saying to them, although there was a corresponding emphasis on accountability to others too.

As his respect for the personal conscience indicated, Buchman's thinking also contained more liberal characteristics, reflected in his nondenominationalism and openness to other faiths. His primary purpose was not to get people to believe in Christian doctrines but to have an experience of Christ or the Holy Spirit. That experience did not always have to be described in Christian vocabulary. Although many people came to Christianity through Buchman's work, especially in the interwar era, he did not encourage people from other faiths to convert, and he seems to have believed that it was possible to have an experience of Christ without naming it as such. If Buchman was searching after a new framework of thought, it was partly in this sphere. Michael Hutchinson wrote after Buchman's death that the church needed an "adequate doctrine of the Holy Spirit," by which he meant the kind of thinking that would take the work of Christ beyond limits set by the human mind, shedding light on the building of trust with people of other faiths, and that would enable a higher wisdom for policy makers.[14]

While MRA did not in any formal sense try to develop a doctrine of how the Spirit of God could operate outside the framework of Christianity as such, there were theologians who were trying to do so. Karl Rahner, of course, was one of them. Others who in the years after Buchman's death tried to explore this question, especially in relation to the non-Christian religions, included the future Anglican bishop of Winchester, John V. Taylor, and the Spanish Catholic professor of comparative religion, Raimundo Panikkar.[15] Buchman's work can be seen as a practical, as opposed to intellectual, exploration of this theme.

In some ways MRA had the characteristics of a religious order or community. Indeed, Alan Thornhill suggested that MRA was comparable to the Jesuits—although it was mixed in terms of gender. Similarly, Morris Martin suggested that if MRA had grown from Catholic roots, it might have turned into a lay order.[16] Certainly Buchman had sought to create a fellowship-based network that was arguably more like a kind of far-flung and diverse monastic community than a formal organization. Indeed, there was something Franciscan in the loose theological and organizational structures that characterized MRA. Perhaps significantly, Buchman was always an admirer of Saint Francis of Assisi and was in Assisi for the celebration of the seven-hundredth anniversary of the saint's death in 1926.[17] From the twentieth century, the devotional rather than dogmatic focus of MRA culture also had something in common with monastic groups like the Taizé community in western France, founded by Brother Roger Schutz. It was not surprising that in the years after Buchman's death, there were a number of MRA workers who had connections with Taizé.[18] Where Buchman differed from these groups, of course, was in his collaboration with people from the non-Christian world.

The mixture of conservative and liberal features present in Buchman's theology was also evident in his political thinking. At a certain level Buchman believed that any political system could be made to work, as long as its leadership turned to God for answers. Democracy itself would be preserved not so much by institutions as by individuals living good lives. The personal was the key to the national, or the "intimate" to the "global," as Marcel put it in trying to describe the essence of the Caux conferences.[19] This view reflected a conservative tendency to stress personal morality rather than institutions as the key to good government—although Buchman never denied the importance of institutions or political change. There was also a strong emphasis on national vocation and national unity in Buchman's thought, although there was a corresponding internationalist element too. At the same time, Buchman was liberal, if not radical, in his belief that anybody could get wisdom from God or their conscience and that change and the creation of a new world order were genuinely possible. His vision of industry, for example, implied that workers and management could cooperate together in a real way, and in this sense his thinking was subversive of overly top-down models.

Buchman clearly recognized that some political systems were more adapted to the modern age than others, and he instinctively took the side of the West in certain situations. At the same time, he seems to have had doubts about the combative nature of multiparty politics, and he took the view that beyond left and right divisions there were often deeper spiritual issues at stake. He also thought that at a personal level the leaders of the democracies and the dictatorships were subject to the same moral and spiritual temptations, and thus the former were not morally superior to the latter. His approach to trying to change the totalitarian regimes obviously did not involve direct confrontation. Instead, he wanted, though the agency of changed individuals, to try to redirect their energy into constructive channels. Of all the explanations, that is the one that best explains his desire to meet Nazi leaders in the 1930s and MRA's attempts to appeal to communists after 1945. No one was beyond the reach of God's grace, Buchman thought, however evil they might appear. Some thought his approach naive, and judgment flawed, especially in relation to national socialism. Others, however, were ready to credit him for his attempt to change even the worst of dictators.

In some ways MRA's postwar philosophy was a response to war and conflict. The message it forged after 1945 was grounded in an underlying narrative about the possibility of reconciliation that was shaped by World War II, the Cold War, industrial unrest, and the hatred engendered by colonialism. The adaptability of the philosophy was rooted in the fact that it sought to wrestle with human motivation and intrapersonal relations rather than adopt particular stances on issues. This was another area where MRA was distinctive. At the same time, Buchman was not alone in stressing the relevance of what is sometimes called "track II" diplomacy to international affairs and also in seeing a connection between spirituality and public issues. There were other religious organizations and actors in the twentieth century who tried to use nonofficial channels to promote conflict resolution, thereby complementing more political forms of dialogue.[20]

Buchman's vision cannot, of course, be separated from his personality. Yet his character is hard to describe. As with his view of the world, there were some contrasting elements in his makeup and mentality. In his leadership style he could be strong, even authoritarian, yet also unobtrusive and self-effacing. He was a sensitive person who was good at making friends, yet he also had the ability to stand back and approach people in an unemotional, even clinical, way. He had an enormous amount of energy—especially before his stroke—yet regularly insisted that he did nothing and God did everything. He was not, according to Signe Strong, a mystic, yet he had a "natural inwardness."[21]

"No one can guess which way the live cat on the hearthrug will jump"—as opposed to the dead one on the mantelpiece—Buchman once observed. He might accurately have said the same about himself. He could be unpredictable, although according to Corderoy, this was due more to mischief than caprice.[22] The question remains as to whether this unpredictable quality was the mark of a man close to God. Those who worked with him believed that the latter was part of it. Bunny Austin, for example, thought that his words and actions were full of the "unexpectedness of the Holy Spirit."[23]

NOTES

Abbreviations

AOG-UK   Archives of the Oxford Group and Moral Re-Armament, Dial House, Whitbourne, Worcestershire, United Kingdom
FB-HTS   Papers of Frank Buchman, Archives, Hartford Theological Seminary
MRA-ACV   Papers of Moral Re-Armament, Archives Cantonales Vaudoises, Switzerland
MRA-LOC   Records of Moral Re-Armament, Manuscript Division, Library of Congress, Washington D.C.

Introduction

1. Buchman, "Chaos Against God," 74–78. Buchman was contributing to a series of talks on the Validity of Religious Experience.

2. See, for example, Hamilton, *MRA*.

3. This statistic, which comes from *Time and Tide*, September 2–8, 1965, 1, includes both people who devoted their lives to full-time work with MRA and those who took time off from their jobs to join campaigns.

4. G. Williamson, *Inside Buchmanism*, 195.

5. Franz König, Cardinal Archbishop of Vienna, cited in Lean, *Frank Buchman*, 2; statement by Cardinal König, November 15, 1984, file 3, Lean references, AOG-UK.

6. Buchman received the Cross of the Chevalier of the Legion of Honour from France (1950); the Grand Cross of the German Order of Merit (1952); the Japanese Order of the Rising Sun, second class (1956); and the Legion of Honour with Gold Medal of the Philippines (1956). For details of others given to Buchman, see file 3.500.24, AOG-UK. See also Lean, *Frank Buchman*, 374, 392, 491.

7. Luttwak, "Franco-German Reconciliation," 55. The Schuman Plan (1950) was a proposal to unite the iron and coal industries of France and West Germany under one authority. It became the basis for the European Coal and Steel Community (1952), which in turn laid the foundation for the European Economic Community (1958).

8. On the OG-AA connection, see B. [Burns], *Oxford Group*, and Mercadante, *Victims and Sinners*, chaps. 4, 5. On Faith at Work, see I. Harris, *Breeze of the Spirit*. For Buchman's influence on Abram Vereide, founder of the Prayer Breakfast, see Grubb, *Modern Viking*, 51.

9. For example, Buchman is presented as an eccentric fascist sympathizer in Miller, *Truman*, esp. 364–68; Sharlet, *Family*, 127; and Ball, *Guardsmen*, 198–99. See also the depiction of Buchman in Denise Giardina's novel about Dietrich Bonhoeffer, *Saints and Villains*, 213–14.

10. Peter Howard to his wife, Doë, February 12, 1946, cited in Wolrige Gordon, *Peter Howard*, 199; Begbie, *Life Changers*, 24.

11. See Raven, "Theologian's Appreciation," in Spencer, *Meaning of the Groups*, 14.

12. Julian Thornton-Duesbery, cited in T. Spoerri, *Dynamic out of Silence*, 108.
13. Kraybill, "Transition," 224; Jarlert, *Oxford Group*, 51.
14. T. Spoerri, *Dynamic out of Silence*, 136. For many years Spoerri was a professor of European literature at Zurich University.
15. Van Dusen, "Apostle," 4; D. Belden, "Origins and Development," 30–35.
16. Keene, "Doctrine of Guidance," 120–21.
17. Hunter, *World Changing*, 2–3, 91–94; Lean, *Frank Buchman*, 532.
18. Lean, *Frank Buchman*, 1.
19. Jarlert, *Oxford Group*, 41.
20. R. Niebuhr, *Christianity and Power Politics*, 159–65; Driberg, *MRA*, 16. For a rebuttal of Driberg's *MRA*, see Thornton-Duesbery, *Open Secret of MRA*. Driberg also argued that MRA was anti-Christian and antidemocratic. *Mystery of Moral Re-Armament*, 304–5.
21. Sack uses the term "bricolage" to describe Buchman's method, arguing that he created his system from whatever ideas were at hand, in response to particular needs. *Moral Re-Armament*, 3; Randall, "Life-Changing," 37.
22. Kuling was a summer colony for foreigners in the hills above Kiukiang. The main records of this conference, which are in file 3.500.2, AOG-UK, consist of thirty-one transcripts of meetings or sessions, most of them featuring Buchman. An edited, but unpublished, version of these talks, titled "Where Personal Work Begins," was produced in 1984 by Lawson Wood. file 3.500.2, AOG-UK. The main conference ran from August 5 to 14, 1918, while there were also preliminary meetings from August 1 to 3. Morris Martin, "Chronological Outline," file 3, Lean references, AOG-UK.
23. Buchman, *Remaking the World*.
24. Buchman collaborated with others in constructing his speeches until 1938, but nevertheless worked on every word. Thereafter, he increasingly relied on others to compose the speeches. Martin began drafting Buchman's letters in 1939, although not always the most personal ones. Morris Martin, e-mails to author, April 4, 2005, and August 2, 2005.
25. "Transcript," Putney Heath House Party, 1922, file 3500.4, AOG-UK; Lawson Wood, "Verbatim Notes from Meetings," 1937, file 3.500.9, AOG-UK; W.L.M.C., *Builder*; Frank Buchman, "Sayings," Caux, 1948, and "Guidance," 1941–55, file 6.0785, AOG-UK; Morris Martin, "Day-Book for 1940," "Year-Book for 1945," "Brown file/Travels from 1948," "Year-Book for 1951," file 6.1197, AOG-UK. These notebooks were all edited by Robert C. Mowat. Martin wrote his biography of Buchman—used by Lean as the basis for his biography—at a time when he was closely involved with MRA. Morris Martin, Manuscript Biography, file 6.0876, AOG-UK. His subsequent memoir, *Always a Little Further*, was written from more of a distance.
26. Austin, *Frank Buchman*; Purdy, *My Friend, Frank Buchman*; Signe Strong, "Recollections," 2006–7, file 6.0248, AOG-UK. Strong's text is a transcript of answers to questions by Ailsa Hamilton about working with Buchman from 1938 to 1961.

Chapter 1

1. Biographical details are from Lean, *Frank Buchman*, 3–5.
2. Driberg, *Mystery of Moral Re-Armament*, 21.
3. Hunter, *World Changing*, 103.
4. Sherry and Hellerich, "Formative Years," 240–51.
5. Keene, "Doctrine of Guidance," 36.
6. Frank Buchman, "Spiritual Diagnosis," sec. 2, August 8, 1918, Kuling, file 3.500.2, AOG-UK, 11.

7. Lawson Wood, "Verbatim Notes from Meetings," 1937, file 3.500.9, AOG-UK, 13.

8. D. S. Cairns to Miss Talbot, November 11, 1929, MS 3384/1/3 (1914–44), Special Collections, Aberdeen University Library, United Kingdom. For German pietist writings, see Erb, *Pietists*, and Arndt, *True Christianity*. See also Stoeffler, *Rise of Evangelical Pietism*, 180–246.

9. Chesnut, *Changed by Grace*, 5; Clark, *Oxford Group*, 118–19.

10. Wood, "Verbatim Notes from Meetings," AOG-UK, 13.

11. Van Dusen, "Apostle," 4.

12. Lean, *Frank Buchman*, 17.

13. Ibid., 10–11.

14. See Sherry and Hellerich, "Formative Years," 252.

15. T. Spoerri, *Dynamic out of Silence*, 20.

16. Lean, *Frank Buchman*, 20–28. See also Frank Buchman, October 1, 1956, 7:30 A.M., Mackinac, container 145, MRA-LOC. The live recording of this talk, titled "My Experience with the Cross," can be found in file 3.500.0, AOG-UK. For Buchman's vision for the hospice, see his twenty-page handwritten letter to the trustees, probably 1907, container 143, MRA-LOC.

17. Lean, *Frank Buchman*, 29.

18. On the Keswick tradition, see Price and Randall, *Transforming Keswick*.

19. For some different accounts, see D. Belden, "Origins and Development," 102–5.

20. Account in Laun, *Unter Gottes Führung*, 189–92, cited in Keene, "Doctrine of Guidance," 42.

21. Buchman, Mackinac, MRA-LOC.

22. Laun, *Unter Gottes Führung*, 189–92, cited in Keene, "Doctrine of Guidance," 42; Lean, *Frank Buchman*, 31.

23. Lean, *Frank Buchman*, 512.

24. This account is in Russell, *For Sinners Only*, 58. For more on Penn-Lewis's spirituality, see Penn-Lewis, *Centrality of the Cross*.

25. Buchman, undated sermon, starting from "The Joy at Easter," container 152, MRA-LOC.

26. Frank Buchman, untitled, August 2, 1918, Kuling, file 3.500.2, AOG-UK, 12–13.

27. Lean, *Frank Buchman*, 32.

28. Frank Buchman, "Transcript," 1922, Putney Heath House Party, file 3500.4, AOG-UK, 70.

29. Hambrick-Stowe, *Charles G. Finney*, 11–14. For more on conversion narratives, see Hindmarsh, *Evangelical Conversion Narrative*.

30. Lean, *Frank Buchman*, 92.

31. See Hunter, *World Changing*, 169.

32. Price and Randall, *Transforming Keswick*, 121; Randall, *Evangelical Experiences*, 248.

33. Frank Buchman, "Personalizing Your Job," August 6, 1918, Kuling, file 3.500.2, AOG-UK, 1.

34. Crowley, "Miracle on the Mall," 64, 70. For similar, if slightly different, statistics, see Lean, *Frank Buchman*, 35.

35. Stewart, *Henry B. Wright*, 76.

36. Lean, *Frank Buchman*, chap. 5; Guldseth, *Streams*, 90.

37. Hopkins, *John Mott*, 150.

38. Guldseth, *Streams*, 83.

39. Lean, *Frank Buchman*, 35–36; Randall, "Arresting People for Christ," 3–4; Clark, *Oxford Group*, 42.

40. Crowley, "Miracle on the Mall," 70.

41. Buchman, "Making of a Miracle," in Campbell, *Art of Remaking Men*; Lean, *Frank Buchman*, 37. According to Martin, Buchman also focused on a fourth person, the college football coach; Morris Martin, Manuscript Biography, file 6.0876, AOG-UK, chap. 5, p. 6. Pickle's full name was William Gilliland.
42. Guldseth, *Streams*, 92.
43. Lean, *Frank Buchman*, 45–46.
44. Denning, *Listening to God*, 2–3.
45. Frank Buchman to Parents, November 6, 1915, container 2, MRA-LOC.
46. Denning, *Listening to God*, 3.
47. Lean, *Frank Buchman*, 46.
48. D. Belden, "Origins and Development," 254.
49. Lean, *Frank Buchman*, 60.
50. Walter spent three months working with Buchman in Asia in 1917. *Soul Surgery*, 105.
51. Clark, *Oxford Group*, 46–47.
52. The wealthy supporter was the industrialist and one-time president of the YMCA, Cleveland H. Dodge; Frank Buchman, "The 1912–13 Report of the Pennsylvania College Young Men's Christian Association," container 150, MRA-LOC, 1–2.
53. Frank Buchman, June 10, 1948, 5:00 P.M., Riverside, container 401, MRA-LOC.
54. Frank Buchman to Douglas Mackenzie, December 31, 1917, container 139, MRA-LOC; Frank Buchman to Dean M. W. Jacobus, ca. 1917, written from Shanghai, container 139, MRA-LOC.
55. Lean, *Frank Buchman*, 67, 85, 96. For more on Logan Roots's spiritual outlook, see Huthwaite, *From China with Love*.
56. Stewart, *Henry B. Wright*, 221–22.
57. Keene, "Doctrine of Guidance," 33; Clark, *Oxford Group*, 129. See also Dinger, *Moral Re-Armament*, 109–15; and Macintosh, *Personal Religion*, 378–95.
58. Buchman, "Personal Work," *United Church Herald*, 463.
59. D. Belden, "Origins and Development," 14, 54–55, 169.
60. Wright, *Will of God*, 5–12, 72, 93.
61. Guldseth, *Streams*, 87.
62. Keene, "Doctrine of Guidance," 28.
63. Lean, *Frank Buchman*, 74–78.
64. Frank Buchman, Saturday afternoon meeting, August 3, 1918, Kuling, file 3.500.2, AOG-UK, 1; Buchman, August 2, 1918, AOG-UK, 1.
65. Wolrige Gordon, *Peter Howard*, 187.
66. Statement by A. M. Mann, 1922, *Friends of Westminster College: Bulletin*, April 1969, Archives of Westminster College, Cambridge.
67. Guldseth, *Streams*, 106.
68. Frank Buchman, first meeting, August 1, 1918, Kuling, file 3.500.2, AOG-UK, 4; Keene, "Doctrine of Guidance," 55n. Drummond first gave this address in the mid-1880s. For an early edition that also contains some of Drummond's other devotional works, see *Greatest Thing*.
69. Keene, "Doctrine of Guidance," 63.
70. Chesnut, *Changed by Grace*, 61; Cairns to Talbot, November 11, 1929, Aberdeen University Library.
71. Buchman read *The Secret of Inspiration* in 1916–17. Hunter, *World Changing*, 127. Frank Buchman to Sam Shoemaker, April 26, 1920, file 3.500.3, AOG-UK.
72. Clark, *Oxford Group*, 47; Buchman, first meeting, AOG-UK, 7. For a version of this, see Lawrence, *Practice*.
73. Frank Buchman, "Victory in Christ," August 8, 1918, Kuling, file 3.500.2, AOG-UK; Jowett, *School of Calvary*, chap. 5.

74. Buchman, "Spiritual Diagnosis," August 8, 1918, AOG-UK, 3.
75. Randall, "Arresting People for Christ," 5–6; Jarlert, *Oxford Group*, 60.
76. See Randall, *"Entire Devotion to God."*
77. See Buchman's positive reference to the Wesleys at Putney Heath. "Transcript," AOG-UK, 91. See Lean, *John Wesley, Anglican*, for an expression of the wider MRA interest in John Wesley.
78. Chesnut, *Changed by Grace*, xii.
79. Frank Buchman, Tuesday morning, August 9, 1918, Kuling, file 3.500.2, AOG-UK, 1; *Victory in Christ*, 1.
80. Buchman to Trumbull, May 31, 1918, and October 1, 1918, container 93, MRA-LOC.
81. Lean, *Frank Buchman*, 11–12. For a version of Butler's work, see *Analogy of Religion*.
82. Speer, *Marks of a Man*; Buchman, "Spiritual Diagnosis," August 8, 1918, AOG-UK, 4. Some years later Buchman sent this book to Michael, then prince and later king of Romania. Frank Buchman to Princess Helen, April 30, 1937, file 3.1828, AOG-UK.
83. Speer, *Principles of Jesus*, 33–36; *Victory in Christ*, 209–18.
84. Wright, *Will of God*, 169–217, 169.
85. Howard, *Frank Buchman's Secret*, 26.
86. This phrase, Buchman noted, was also a favorite of Gandhi's. Buchman, afternoon meeting, July 18, 1954, Caux, PP 746, 4.4.3.1/9, MRA-ACV. The exact Moffat translation is "consecrated with the fire of the discipline."
87. Buchman, August 2, 1918, AOG-UK, 2.
88. Frank Buchman, August 14, 1947, 11:00 A.M., Caux, PP 746, 4.4.3.1/2, MRA-ACV.
89. Chesnut, *Changed by Grace*, 83, 107, 135.
90. Wright, *Will of God*, 167–217.
91. Buchman, "Spiritual Diagnosis," August 10, 1918, AOG-UK, 6.
92. Lean, *Frank Buchman*, 77.
93. Wood, "Verbatim Notes from Meetings," AOG-UK, 11.
94. Sack, *Moral Re-Armament*, 42.
95. Ekman, *Experiment with God*, 58.
96. Lean, *Frank Buchman*, 130.
97. Frank Buchman, June 9, 1948, 5:30 P.M., Riverside, container 401, MRA-LOC.
98. Jim Baynard-Smith, "Talk on Buchman," October 2005, file 6.0105, AOG-UK, 4.
99. Youniss, "G. Stanley Hall," 225.
100. Frank Buchman, "Spiritual Diagnosis," sec. 2, August 8, 1918, Kuling, file 3.500.2, AOG-UK, 9; Buchman, "Spiritual Diagnosis," August 10, 1918, AOG-UK, 1.
101. Thompson, *Drink and Be Sober*, 27.
102. Stewart suggested that "on top" phrases were an extension of an idea originating with the English neurologist John Hughlings Jackson (1835–1911), in which it was said that narcotics initially attacked the higher planes of the mentality. *Henry B. Wright*, 222–23.
103. Buchman, August 2, 1918, AOG-UK, 3.
104. Lean, *Frank Buchman*, 396.
105. Wright, *Will of God*, 191.
106. Buchman, "Spiritual Diagnosis," August 10, 1918, AOG-UK, 5.
107. Wright, *Will of God*, xi.
108. Buchman, "Personalizing Your Job," AOG-UK, 2–3.
109. Frank Buchman, untitled, August 13, 1918, Kuling, file 3.500.2, AOG-UK, 2.
110. Buchman, Saturday afternoon meeting, AOG-UK, 4.
111. Buchman, August 2, 1918, AOG-UK, 5.
112. Walter, *Soul Surgery*, 21, 61; Buchman, August 2, 1918, AOG-UK, 2.
113. Wright, *Will of God*, 167–217.

114. Buchman, cited by Howard in a summary of his guidance, January 6, 1965, Howard to Purdy, January 7, 1965, container 196, MRA-LOC.

115. Cited in a letter from Geoffrey Pugh to author, July 1, 2009. In 1951 Buchman used the "thud" metaphor to describe the effect of sin more generally: "Sin leaves us with a dull, heavy thud. 'The blood of Jesus Christ cleanseth us from all sin.' . . . That is the answer." "Turn on the Light," 195.

116. Wright, *Will of God*, 179; Bushnell, "Lost Purity Restored," in *New Life*, 176.

117. Austin, *Frank Buchman*, 81; *Crossroad*; Seeley, *Ecce Homo*, 14. Whether Buchman knew that this line came from Seeley's book is not clear.

118. See, for example, the comment by Alan Thornhill in Lean, *Frank Buchman*, 292.

119. Hunter, *World Changing*, 98. The hymn in question was "Jesus, Lover of My Soul." See *Hymnary*, accessed October 26, 2012, http://www.hymnary.org/text/jesus_lover_of_my_soul_let_me_to_thy_bos.

120. Clark, *Oxford Group*, 68; Lean, *Frank Buchman*, 104.

121. See D. Belden, "Origins and Development," 181.

122. Buchman, Saturday afternoon meeting, AOG-UK, 8, 9.

123. The two men apparently got angry and left, only to return the following day to acknowledge the pertinence of Buchman's question and commit themselves to the Christian life. Clark, *Oxford Group*, 105–6.

124. Lennox, *Henry Drummond*, 34.

125. See Hall, *Adolescence*, 432.

126. Sack, *Moral Re-Armament*, 14. In Caux in 1953 Buchman said that the blood of Jesus Christ was the answer to "all sorts of impurity," citing in particular "sodomy" and "lesbianism." July 12, 1953, 11:00 A.M., PP 746, 4.4.3.1/8, MRA-ACV.

127. Wood, "Verbatim Notes from Meetings," AOG-UK, 13.

128. Hunter, *World Changing*, 98–102. See also D. Belden, "Origins and Development," 176–79.

129. Wood, "Verbatim Notes from Meetings," AOG-UK, 10. The line is taken from Tennyson's poem "Locksley Hall." See Tennyson, *Tennyson's Poetry*, 116.

130. See Clark, *Oxford Group*, 107.

131. Lean, *Frank Buchman*, 79–81.

132. Wood, "Verbatim Notes from Meetings," AOG-UK, 11.

133. This was probably in the postwar era. Martin, *Always a Little Further*, 191–93.

134. Hunter, *World Changing*, 100. For Lean's views on this, see Hunter, *World Changing*, 100.

135. Buchman, August 2, 1918, AOG-UK, 8.

136. Buchman, Saturday afternoon meeting, AOG-UK, 3.

137. Thornton-Duesbery, *Sharing*, 4.

138. Wesley, cited in Chesnut, *Changed by Grace*, 27.

139. Buchman, Saturday afternoon meeting, AOG-UK, 4–5.

140. This point is made by Sack, *Moral Re-Armament*, 5, 12.

141. "Personal Work," *Time*, October 18, 1926, 28–29. A decade later, on April 20, 1936, *Time* magazine put a picture of Buchman on its front cover, subtitled "Cultist Buchman."

142. For more on the Princeton episode, see Lean, *Frank Buchman*, chap. 12; Purdy, *My Friend, Frank Buchman*, chap. 3; Sack, *Moral Re-Armament*, chap. 2; and Sack, "Men Want Something Real." See also See Clark, *Oxford Group*, 72–73.

143. Chesnut, *Changed by Grace*, 27–29.

144. Falby, "Modern Confessional," 256–59; Tournier, cited in Lean, *Frank Buchman*, 153.

145. Boobbyer, "B. H. Streeter," 558. See also Layman, *Oxford Group*, 27; and Sack, "Up-and-Outers," 51–52.

146. Brown, "Physician's Criticism," in Spencer, *Meaning of the Groups*, 66, 71. See also Henson, *Group Movement*, 53–60; Gwyer, "Comments of an Educationalist," 67.

147. Van Dusen, "Apostle," 9.

148. Lean, *Frank Buchman*, 85.

149. Frank Buchman to David Yui, August 21, 1918, file "Kuling conference," container 133, MRA-LOC.

150. Campbell, *Art of Remaking Men*, 78.

151. Buchman also thought that forty-five was an important age for older people. Buchman, "Spiritual Diagnosis," August 9, 1918, AOG-UK, 8.

152. Layman, *Oxford Group*, 41–51.

153. Drummond, *Ideal Life*, 305–14; Drummond, in "Dealing with Doubt," *Addresses*, 265; Keene, "Doctrine of Guidance," 14.

154. Buchman, Saturday afternoon meeting, AOG-UK, 7; Buchman, first meeting, AOG-UK, 8.

155. Austin, *Frank Buchman*, 81; Hunter, *World Changing*, 99–101.

156. Cited in *Crossroad*.

157. For a summary of Buchman's early methods from the Penn State Christian Association archives, see Clark, *Oxford Group*, 44–45.

158. Martin, Manuscript Biography, AOG-UK, chap. 3, p. 8; Buchman to Dean M. W. Jacobus, May 30, 1917, folder 349, box 27, FB-HTS.

159. Lean, *Frank Buchman*, 43.

160. Buchman, *Remaking the World* (1941), 3.

Chapter 2

1. See Frank Buchman to Henry B. Wright, September 20, 1918, in Stewart, *Henry B. Wright*, 222.

2. Clark, *Oxford Group*, 125.

3. Buchman had in mind the then dean of the Los Angeles Bible Institute, R. A. Torrey, although exactly what he quarreled with in Torrey's methods is not clear. Frank Buchman to Sam Shoemaker, April 26, 1920, file 3.500.3, AOG-UK.

4. Frank Buchman, August 14, 1947, 11:00 A.M., Caux, PP 746, 4.4.3.1/2, MRA-ACV.

5. "Editorial Notes," 138.

6. Frank Buchman, August 13, 1947, 11:00 A.M., Caux, PP 746, 4.4.3.1/2, MRA-ACV.

7. Buchman, "Electronics of the Spirit," 225.

8. Frank Buchman, August 10, 1944, 11:00 A.M., Mackinac, container 144, MRA-LOC, 9.

9. Denning, *Listening to God*, 5–6; Frank Buchman, "Transcript," 1922, Putney Heath House Party, file 3500.4, AOG-UK, 91.

10. Hunter, *World Changing*, 130.

11. W.L.M.C., *Builder*, 17.

12. Denning, *Listening to God*, 5–6.

13. Frank Buchman, August 9, 1918, "Victory in Christ," Kuling, file 3.500.2, AOG-UK (2), 5.

14. T. Spoerri, *Dynamic out of Silence*, 187.

15. Clark, *Oxford Group*, 99.

16. Lean, *Frank Buchman*, 36.

17. Buchman, Pocket Diary 1921–22, file 3.500.1, AOG-UK, 71; Hunter, *World Changing*, 113.

18. Campbell never regretted his decision. *Dose*, 33–34.

19. Stewart, *Henry B. Wright*, 51. See also Guldseth, *Streams*, 90.
20. Buchman, first meeting, August 1, 1918, Kuling, file 3.500.2, AOG-UK, 7.
21. Lean, *Frank Buchman*, 75, 252; Collis, *Silver Fleece*, 106.
22. Buchman, Mackinac, June 2, 1952, 11:00 A.M., MRA-LOC, container 396.
23. W.L.M.C., *Builder*, 3, 14, 15.
24. Buchman, first meeting, AOG-UK, 7. In his talk Buchman wrongly attributed the lines to the Quaker poet John Greenleaf Whittier. He also slightly misquoted the poem. The original lines read, "A grace of being, finer than himself / That beckons and is gone." Buchman used the term "one's self" instead of "himself." For the original, see Lowell, *Complete Poetical Works*, 413.
25. Frank Buchman, "Spiritual Diagnosis," August 8, 1918, Kuling, file 3.500.2, AOG-UK (1), 6.
26. Buchman, "Revolution," 40.
27. Denning, *Listening to God*, 5-6.
28. Lean, *Frank Buchman*, 37.
29. Begbie, *Life Changers*, 142.
30. Lean, *Frank Buchman*, 498-99.
31. Ibid., 119. See also Frank Buchman, September 15, 1952, 11:00 A.M., Caux, PP 746, 4.4.3.1/7, MRA-ACV.
32. Buchman, "Turn on the Light," 190-91; Lean, *Frank Buchman*, 107.
33. Purdy, *My Friend, Frank Buchman*, 18, 16.
34. Howard, *Frank Buchman's Secret*, 26; Lean, *Frank Buchman*, 93.
35. Sherry and Hellerich, "Formative Years," 260.
36. Pope Pius XI, *Atheistic Communism*, 49. In a later translation by G. D. Smith, this appeal was translated as a "call for spiritual re-armament." See Smith, *Atheistic Communism*, 54. See also T. Spoerri, *Dynamic out of Silence*, 122.
37. Lean, *Frank Buchman*, 262. The Group publication that Blomberg was working on was the Swedish version of the OG pictorial, *Rising Tide*. Jarlert downplays the influence of Blomberg in the origins of the term "moral re-armament"; see *Oxford Group*, 46-47.
38. Lean, *Frank Buchman*, 262; Frank Buchman, August 11, 1947, 11:00 A.M., Caux, PP 746, 4.4.3.1/2, MRA-ACV.
39. Lean, *Frank Buchman*, 134.
40. Buchman, "God Calling the World," 12.
41. Lawson Wood, "Verbatim Notes from Meetings," 1937, file 3.500.9, AOG-UK, 5.
42. Buchman, "Electronics of the Spirit," 220.
43. Austin, *Frank Buchman*, 57.
44. Buchman, "God Calling the World," 12.
45. W.L.M.C., *Builder*, 17.
46. Lean, *Frank Buchman*, 531.
47. Campbell, *Art of Remaking Men*, 79.
48. He said this line in response to a question by British Conservative member of Parliament, Patrick Wolrige Gordon. Anne Wolrige Gordon to author, January 13, 2012.
49. Buchman to Shoemaker, April 26, 1920, AOG-UK.
50. W.L.M.C., *Builder*, 8.
51. Frank Buchman, June 9, 1948, 5:30 P.M., Riverside, container 401, MRA-LOC. The phrase, as published in *Remaking the World*, was slightly different: "Union is the grace of rebirth." See "Answer to Any 'Ism,'" 166. Theophil Spoerri used the same phrase at the beginning of "Moral Re-Armament," in stating that "rebirth" was another name for "renaissance," 53.
52. Buchman, August 10, 1944, MRA-LOC.
53. Ibid.

54. Buchman, June 2, 1952, MRA-LOC.
55. Buchman, August 19, 1946, Caux, 11:15 A.M., PP 746, 4.4.3.1/1, MRA-ACV.
56. Henson, *Group Movement*, 64. For more on Henson's hostility to Buchman, see Morris Martin, Manuscript Biography, file 6.0876, AOG-UK, chap. 17, p. 5; and Boobbyer, "B. H. Streeter," 549.
57. Van Dusen, "Oxford Group Movement," 248–50. For other critics of the OG approach to guidance, see Harrison, *Saints Run Mad*, 53–68; Raven, "Theologian's Appreciation," in Spencer, *Meaning of the Groups*, 28–31; Lunn, *Enigma*, 181; and Driberg, *Mystery of Moral Re-Armament*, 192–99.
58. D. S. Cairns to Frank Buchman, June 23, 1929, container 18, MRA-LOC. Cairns chaired Commission IV at the World Missionary Conference in Edinburgh in 1910, which focused on the Christian message in relation to non-Christian religions. He was later principal of the United Free Church College in Aberdeen from 1929 to 1937. Frank Buchman, "1912–13 Report of the Pennsylvania State College YMCA," container 150, MRA-LOC, 1; D. S. Cairns to Frank Buchman, December 16, 1913, container 18, MRA-LOC.
59. Buchman to Shoemaker, April 26, 1920, AOG-UK.
60. Allen, *He That Cometh*, 135, cited in Keene, "Doctrine of Guidance," 125; Martin, Manuscript Biography, AOG-UK, chap. 11, p. 6.
61. Wood, "Verbatim Notes from Meetings," AOG-UK, 5.
62. Frank Buchman to Philippe Mottu, March 4, 1939, PP 746, 7.4.2/15, MRA-ACV.
63. Buchman, September 23, 1947, 11:00 A.M., Caux, PP 746, 4.4.3.1/2, MRA-ACV, 2.
64. Buchman, first meeting, AOG-UK, 7.
65. Basil Yates, cited in Jarlert, *Oxford Group*, 55.
66. Buchman, "Hurricane of Common Sense," 260, 269.
67. Buchman, "Moral Re-Armament," 48.
68. Buchman, "Framework," 73.
69. Gundersen, *Incorrigibly Independent*, 91.
70. Grubb, *Modern Viking*, 51.
71. Raven, "Theologian's Appreciation," in Spencer, *Meaning of the Groups*, 22–24.
72. Buchman to Shoemaker, April 26, 1920, AOG-UK.
73. Buchman, "Framework," 72.
74. Frank Buchman to Garth Lean, December 11, 1936, container 54, MRA-LOC.
75. Frank Buchman to John Roots, March 7, 1942, container 76, MRA-LOC.
76. Russell, *For Sinners Only*, 112. Buchman nevertheless believed that there might be occasions when it did matter whether or not he had a second helping. Keene, "Doctrine of Guidance," 124.
77. Van Dusen, "Apostle," 15.
78. Buchman, first meeting, AOG-UK, 9.
79. Frank Buchman, guidance book, November 1938, Geneva, file 6.0296, AOG-UK; "How Did Buchman Become the Man He Was?," file 6.0785, AOG-UK.
80. Lean, *Frank Buchman*, 405. See also Buchman, August 13, 1947, MRA-ACV.
81. Cited in Roland Wilson to Graham Turner, July 11, 1976, file 3, Lean references, AOG-UK.
82. Hunter, *World Changing*, 174; Morris Martin, "Day-Book for 1940," file 6.1197, AOG-UK, 2.
83. Oliver Corderoy, April 28, 1982, file 3, Lean references, AOG-UK. Corderoy worked with Buchman from 1948 to 1951 and for a time after 1956.
84. Ailsa Hamilton, "A Spiritual History of MRA," 1995, file 6.0248, AOG-UK, 4.
85. Oliver Corderoy to Garth and Margot Lean, April 1982, file 3, Lean references, AOG-UK; Lean, *Good God, It Works*, 69.

86. Eister, *Drawing Room Conversion*, 165. "Reason, Evidence, Luminous Thinking" was a phrase originally used by Russell in *For Sinners Only*, 240.
87. Drummond, "How to Know the Will of God," in *Ideal Life*, 313.
88. Streeter, *God Who Speaks*, 182–88, 191. See also Boobbyer, "B. H. Streeter," 561.
89. Father Trösch, cited in Lunn, *Enigma*, 181.
90. Buchman to Shoemaker, April 26, 1920, AOG-UK.
91. See "With Woldemichael," file 6.0785, AOG-UK; W.L.M.C., *Builder*, 3.
92. Herbert Grevenius, cited in Ekman, *Experiment with God*, 21.
93. Jim Baynard-Smith, "Notes of Times with Buchman, 1952–53," file 6.0105, AOG-UK, 3.
94. Frank Buchman, Saturday afternoon meeting, August 3, 1918, Kuling, file 3.500.2, AOG-UK, 6–7.
95. Frank Buchman, August 3, 1946, 5:15 P.M., Caux, PP 746, 4.4.3.1/1, MRA-ACV; Buchman, September 23, 1947, MRA-ACV.
96. Signe Strong, "Recollections," 2006–7, file 6.0248, AOG-UK, tape 4.
97. Frank Buchman, September 7, 1955, 11:00 A.M., Caux, PP 746, 4.4.3.1/10, MRA-ACV.
98. W.L.M.C., *Builder*, 17.
99. Keene, "Doctrine of Guidance," 79, 192, 305–24, quote on 313. Keene was specifically countering the view expressed by Erdman Harris ("Three Contemporary Approaches") that OG spirituality was characterized by a sort of "dualistic, evangelical, phenomenal supernaturalism." See also Jarlert, *Oxford Group*, 70.
100. See Kelly (1893–1941), *Testament of Devotion*, and Laubach (1884–1970), *Letters*. Interestingly, Laubach, like Buchman, was an alumnus of Perkiomen Seminary (studying there from 1904 to 1905); Sherry and Hellerich, "Formative Years," 240.
101. Martin, Manuscript Biography, AOG-UK, chap. 7, p. 9. For a full account, see Lean, *Frank Buchman*, 57–58.
102. Frank Buchman, "Guidance," June 7 and 8, 1951, file 6.0785, AOG-UK.
103. Ole Bjørn Kraft, the foreign minister of Denmark, was an admirer of MRA; Eduard von Steiger was president of the Swiss Confederation in 1951; and Achille Marazza was a prominent Italian Christian Democrat. Lean, *Frank Buchman*, 443; McLean, *Whatever Next*, 118.
104. Baynard-Smith, "Buchman, 1952–53," AOG-UK, 2, 5.
105. Lean, *Frank Buchman*, 416, 424. On Nehru's tea with Buchman at Jaipur House, see Henderson, *Ice in Every Carriage*, 113–15.
106. Michael Barrett, cited in Lean, *Frank Buchman*, 423.
107. Inboden, *Religion*, 195, 211, 224.
108. Howard J. Rose, *The Quiet Time*, ca. 1920s, file 6.1014, AOG-UK, 1. For the same list, see Russell, *For Sinners Only*, 94.
109. Keene, "Doctrine of Guidance," 155–76. Keene used the word "telepathic" in a metaphoric rather than a literal sense (161).
110. Streeter, *God Who Speaks*, 167.
111. On AA, see Rudy and Greil, "Alcoholics Anonymous," 43–44. See also Chesnut, *Changed by Grace*, 9.
112. For a study of different accounts of the OG's impact on people, both positive and negative, see Clark, *Oxford Group*, 136–234.
113. Buchman to Shoemaker, April 26, 1920, as summarized by Lean, *Frank Buchman*, 76. See also Buchman, "How to Listen," 36.
114. Buchman, "How to Listen," 36.
115. Buchman, "Framework," 72.
116. "FNDB and How He Dealt with People," file 6.0785, AOG-UK.
117. Cited by Geoffrey Pugh in conversation with author, November 13, 2009.

118. Frank Buchman to Sam Shoemaker, ca. January 1924, container 83, MRA-LOC.
119. Frank Buchman to Ray Purdy, January 28, 1930, container 231, MRA-LOC.
120. Buchman, MRA National Assembly in the USA, July 30, 1939, cited in Sack, *Moral Re-Armament*, 114.
121. See Jarlert, *Oxford Group*, 144, 437. See also D. Belden, "Origins and Development," 383–86.
122. See, for example, Mottu, *Pile and Face*, 133.
123. L. W. Grensted, cited in Jarlert, *Oxford Group*, 68.
124. Hamilton, "Spiritual History of MRA," AOG-UK, 5. See also Mottu, *Pile and Face*, 133.
125. Wright addressed this theme during his visits to Penn State to help Buchman in 1910. Stewart, *Henry B. Wright*, 75.
126. Ekman, *Experiment with God*, 52.
127. Buchman, September 23, 1947, MRA-ACV.
128. Driberg argues this point, on evidence derived from Henson, in *Mystery of Moral Re-Armament*, 198. According to Thornton-Duesbery, Driberg based his argument on a source that was known to be unreliable. *Open Secret of MRA*, 32.
129. Lean, for example, thought Buchman was "more sensitive to God's direction" than anyone else he had met. *Good God, It Works*, 63.
130. Hunter, *World Changing*, 27.
131. William Jaeger, cited in Lean, *Frank Buchman*, 188.
132. W.L.M.C., *Builder*, 5.
133. Buchman to Purdy, May 29, 1930, MRA-LOC.
134. Henderson, *Ice in Every Carriage*, 180.
135. Baynard-Smith, "Buchman, 1952–53," AOG-UK, 3. See also Buchman, "Guidance or Guns?," 63.
136. Keene, "Doctrine of Guidance," 185.
137. Lean, *Good God, It Works*, 75. See also Howard, *Frank Buchman's Secret*, 95.
138. See Strong, "Recollections," AOG-UK, tape 1.
139. Howell, *Escape to Live*.
140. Boobbyer, "B. H. Streeter," 560.
141. Rose, *When Man Listens*.
142. Winslow, *When I Awake*.
143. Waddy, *Skills of Discernment*.
144. Marcel, "Letter of Personal Reassurance," in *Fresh Hope*, 2, 9.
145. See chapter 8, on Papua New Guinean teacher, Alice Wedega, in Henderson, *All Her Paths*, esp. 87. See also Cecil Abel, "The Kunika Story," in file 124, AOG-UK.

Chapter 3

1. Buchman cited these verses without any reference to their titles. Carmichael, *Mountain Breezes*, 198, 251. Campbell, *Art of Remaking Men*, 81, 106; Frank Buchman, August 27, 1944, 11:00 A.M., Mackinac; June 10, 1948, Riverside; Miami, January 21, 1952, 10:30 A.M., container 399, MRA-LOC.
2. Frank Buchman, "Spiritual Diagnosis," August 8, 1918, Kuling, file 3.500.2, AOG-UK(1), 3–4.
3. Frank Buchman, "The College Hero," ca. 1895, cited in Sack, *Moral Re-Armament*, 8.
4. Lean, *Frank Buchman*, 17.
5. Frank Buchman, "Personal Work," *Muhlenberg*, 1. See also Sherry and Hellerich, "Formative Years," 250–52.
6. Ober and Mott, *Personal Work*; Trumbull, *Individual Work for Individuals*.

7. Walter, *Soul Surgery*, 9–18.

8. Buchman, "Personal Work," *United Church Herald*, 463.

9. Buchman, "Personal Evangelism," *Bulletin*, file 3.500.1, AOG-UK, 2–5. The passages cited were Mark 8:22–26 and John 4:1–30.

10. Frank Buchman, third meeting, August 3, 1918, Kuling, file 3.500.2, AOG-UK, 2; Frank Buchman, Saturday afternoon meeting, August 3, 1918, Kuling file 3.500.2, AOG-UK, 10.

11. Van Dusen, "Apostle," 2.

12. Hunter, *World Changing*, 109.

13. Frank Buchman, Monday morning meeting, August 5, 1918, Kuling, file 3.500.2, AOG-UK, 2; Buchman, Saturday afternoon meeting, AOG-UK, 10.

14. Frank Buchman, untitled, August 12, 1918, Kuling, file 3.500.2, AOG-UK, 6. At the same time Buchman seems to have doubted that Beecher was an ideal role model. Years later, in 1955, he said of him, "Henry, oh how he preached. Henry certainly brought hell up to its proper place. And his family had to live with him." Buchman, September 7, 1955, 11:00 A.M., Caux, PP 746, 4.4.3.1/1–2, MRA-ACV. These comments may have partly been in reference to the notorious adultery trial of 1875, in which Beecher was accused of having an affair with a married woman.

15. Frank Buchman to Dean M. W. Jacobus, letter outlining a "Temporary Program for a Conference of Theological Seminaries," n.d., container 139, MRA-LOC.

16. Frank Buchman to Murray Webb-Peploe, August 24, 1921, container 100, MRA-LOC.

17. Frank Buchman, July 29, 1954, 5:15 P.M., Caux, PP 746, 4.4.3.1/9, MRA-ACV.

18. Buchman, Monday afternoon, August 4, 1918, Kuling, file 3.500.2, AOG-UK, 2; Buchman, first meeting, August 1, 1918, Kuling, file 3.500.2, AOG-UK, 3.

19. Buchman, Monday afternoon, August 5, 1918, AOG-UK, 1. The idea of having ten-day conferences seems to have originated with Moody. Guldseth, *Streams*, 97.

20. Buchman, third meeting, AOG-UK, 4; Buchman, Monday morning meeting, AOG-UK, 3–4.

21. Frank Buchman to Douglas Mackenzie, July 16, 1921, folder 349, box 27, FB-HTS.

22. Frank Buchman to Sam Shoemaker, October 23, 1923, container 83, MRA-LOC.

23. Lean, *Frank Buchman*, 159, 248, 257.

24. Mowat, *Message of Frank Buchman*, 56.

25. Buchman, July 29, 1954, MRA-ACV.

26. Buchman, first meeting, AOG-UK, 6.

27. Lean, *Frank Buchman*, 534.

28. Cited in document starting "In 1927 . . . ," file 3.500 3/4, AOG-UK.

29. Lean, *Frank Buchman*, 171.

30. Howard, *Frank Buchman's Secret*, 100.

31. Buchman said that this postcard, which accompanied an invitation he received to attend the Disarmament Conference in Washington, D.C., "revolutionized" his life. Frank Buchman, August 5, 1950, 11:00 A.M., Caux, PP 746, 4.4.3.1/5, MRA-ACV.

32. Frank Buchman, Tuesday morning, August 6, 1918, Kuling, file 3.500.2, AOG-UK, 8–9.

33. For Wright on the "point of contact," see Stewart and Wright, *Practice of Friendship*, 55–57. See also Buchman, Monday morning meeting, AOG-UK, 2.

34. Buchman, Monday morning meeting, AOG-UK, 2; Buchman, Saturday afternoon meeting, AOG-UK, 10.

35. The other suggestions were diagnosing the other person's difficulty; making the moral test (discovering what particular problem was impeding a person's spiritual development); avoiding argument; conducting interviews oneself; adapting truth to the hearer's need;

bringing people face to face with Christ; showing people the way out of their particular difficulties; bringing people to decisive action; and giving specific advice about such things as Bible study, prayer, and overcoming temptation. Walter, *Soul Surgery*, 43–44.

36. T. Spoerri, *Dynamic out of Silence*, 181.
37. See ibid., 188.
38. See Walter, *Soul Surgery*. "Conservation" was soon replaced with "continuance," in OG summaries of these principles; see Roots, "Apostle to Youth," 810.
39. Buchman, "Spiritual Diagnosis," August 9, 1918, AOG-UK, 9–10.
40. See Drummond, "Spiritual Diagnosis," in *New Evangelism*, 198. Buchman said that reading "Spiritual Diagnosis" after his second visit to China in 1918 had confirmed what he had been doing. Buchman to "Zab," April, 1924, file 3.500.5, AOG-UK. It seems more likely, however, that he read the essay for the first time in the course of the second Chinese trip rather than after it.
41. Walter, *Soul Surgery*, 9.
42. Lean, *Frank Buchman*, 74.
43. Stewart, *Henry B. Wright*, 222.
44. Clark, *Oxford Group*, 47.
45. Buchman, first meeting, AOG-UK, 3.
46. Frank Buchman, "Transcript," 1922, Putney Heath House Party, file 3500.4, AOG-UK, 69. See also Sack, *Moral Re-Armament*, 17.
47. Lean, *Good God, It Works*, 10.
48. Charles Finney, cited in McLoughlin, *Revivals*, 125–27.
49. Stanley, *World Missionary Conference*, 3–5.
50. James's book was cited in the bibliography in Wright, *Will of God*, xi.
51. Frank Buchman, "Personalizing Your Job," August 9, 1918, Kuling, file 3.500.2, AOG-UK, 1.
52. Austin, *Frank Buchman*, 71.
53. Thornton-Duesbery, *Sharing*, 7.
54. F. B. Meyer, cited in Walter, *Soul Surgery*, 31–32; Randall, "Arresting People for Christ," 5.
55. Drummond, "New Evangelism," in *New Evangelism*, 20, 28.
56. Howard, *Frank Buchman's Secret*, 91.
57. For a postwar example of using Pickle's story, from a speech in California in 1948, see "Making of a Miracle," in Campbell, *Art of Remaking Men*.
58. As recounted by Rev. Principal A. G. MacLeod to Dr. Elston Hill, May 15, 1970, Archives of Westminster College, Cambridge.
59. Buchman, "Miracles in the North," 20.
60. Hamilton, *MRA*, 5–6.
61. Lean, *Frank Buchman*, 101.
62. Chesnut, *Changed by Grace*, 21.
63. Buchman, Saturday afternoon meeting, AOG-UK, 9.
64. See Sack, *Moral Re-Armament*, 37.
65. Hamilton, *MRA*, 5.
66. Roots, "Apostle to Youth," 808.
67. Sack, "Men Want Something Real," 263–65.
68. Turner, "Religion," in *University of Oxford*, 295; Hamilton, *MRA*, 4.
69. Lean, *Frank Buchman*, 171.
70. Van Dusen, "Apostle," 8.
71. See Drummond, "Spiritual Diagnosis," in *New Evangelism*, 191–210; Walter, *Soul Surgery*, 31.

72. Buchman, "Spiritual Diagnosis," August 8, 1918, AOG-UK (2), 3–6.
73. Thornhill, *Best of Friends*, 64; Russell, *For Sinners Only*, 39.
74. Lean, *Frank Buchman*, 469.
75. Begbie, *Life Changers*, cited by Sack, *Moral Re-Armament*, 44.
76. Austin, *Frank Buchman*, 68.
77. Buchman, "Spiritual Diagnosis," August 9, 1918, AOG-UK, 4; Buchman, "Spiritual Diagnosis," August 10, 1918, AOG-UK, 4.
78. Austin, *Frank Buchman*, 81.
79. Lawson Wood, "Verbatim Notes from Meetings," 1937, file 3.500.9, AOG-UK, 18.
80. Wimber, *Power Healing*, 192.
81. Ibid., 192, 204. See 1 Corinthians 12.8 (King James Version).
82. Sack, *Moral Re-Armament*, 193.
83. Jarlert, *Oxford Group*, 35.
84. See Randall, *Evangelical Experiences*, 258–60; Bebbington, *Evangelicalism*, 240–42.
85. Gates, *Any Hope, Doctor?*, and Swaim, *Arthritis*.
86. Lean, *Frank Buchman*, 311–15. For Gates's involvement in looking after Buchman, see ibid., 312, 470.
87. Signe Strong, "Recollections," 2006–7, file 6.0248, AOG-UK, tape 5.
88. Lean, *Frank Buchman*, 341.
89. Piguet, *Love of Tomorrow*, 9.
90. Lean's account of the episode differs slightly from Piguet's. *Buchman*, 352–53.
91. Montville, "Psychoanalytic Enlightenment," 306. See the stories cited by Henderson in *No Enemy to Conquer*, 81, 137–41. For MRA's impact on a German war veteran, see Gareis, *Stepping Stones*, chaps. 4–7.
92. Morris Martin, "Day-Book for 1940," file 6.1197, AOG-UK, 9.
93. Wood, "Verbatim Notes from Meetings," AOG-UK, 19.
94. Frank Buchman to Edwin Sparks, n.d., written from Canton Christian College, container 150, MRA-LOC. Sparks was president of Penn State from 1908 to 1920.
95. Cato [Michael Foot, Peter Howard, and Frank Owen], *Guilty Men*.
96. Howard's books on MRA included *Innocent Men*, *Ideas Have Legs*, and *World Rebuilt*.
97. Howard, *Frank Buchman's Secret*, 92–96.
98. Hunter was much influenced by two books that Buchman was then recommending: Smith's *Christian's Secret*, and *Live the Victorious Life*, by An Unknown Christian. See also Hunter, *World Changing*, 169–70.
99. Michael Sentis, interview with the author, Prissé, France, August 2011.
100. Peter Howard, cited in Guldseth, *Streams*, 123.
101. Roger Hicks, "Something for Everybody: A Story of Moral Re-Armament," file, 6.0751, AOG-UK, chaps. 3, 4.
102. Peter Howard to Ray Purdy, February 13, 1963, container 196, MRA-LOC.
103. Collis, *Silver Fleece*, 117.
104. Mottu, *Pile and Face*, 101–2, 136–37, 159.
105. Frank Buchman to Philippe Mottu, January 1961, PP 746, 7.4.2/15, MRA-ACV. At the time Mottu seems to have concurred with Buchman, for he wrote to him six months later confessing to a number of character failings and moral lapses. Mottu to Buchman, July 1961, PP 746, 7.4.2/15, MRA-ACV.
106. Blanton Belk, cited in Guldseth, *Streams*, 123; Lean, *Frank Buchman*, 470.
107. Lean, *Frank Buchman*, chap. 39.
108. Wolrige Gordon, *Peter Howard*, 295.
109. Strong, "Recollections," AOG-UK, tape 1.
110. John Wood, telephone interview with the author, June 18, 2012; Mackenzie, *Faith in Diplomacy*, 55.

111. Martin, "Day-Book for 1940," AOG-UK, 2.
112. T. Spoerri, *Dynamic out of Silence*, 183.
113. Lean, *Frank Buchman*, 403.
114. Frank Buchman, August 10, 1944, Mackinac, container 144, MRA-LOC.
115. Strong says that Buchman prayed daily for an enhanced sense of humor for either one or two years. "Recollections," AOG-UK, tape 5.
116. Lean, *Good God, It Works*, 66.
117. Campbell, *Dose*, 42.
118. Lean, *Frank Buchman*, 367; Lean, *Good God, It Works*, 73.
119. *Frank Buchman Eighty*, 117–18.
120. W.L.M.C., *Builder*, 12.
121. T. Spoerri, *Dynamic out of Silence*, 34.
122. Frank Buchman to George Stewart, May 12, 1921, container 87, MRA-LOC.
123. Thornhill, *Best of Friends*, 126.
124. Lean, *Frank Buchman*, 400.
125. Ibid., 158.
126. Frank Buchman, August 2, 1918, Kuling, file 3.500.2, AOG-UK, 1–2.
127. W.L.M.C., *Builder*, 6, 9, 10, 12.
128. Lean, *Frank Buchman*, 179.
129. Frank Buchman, "My Experience with the Cross," recording, October 1, 1956, 7:30 A.M., Mackinac, file 3.500.0, AOG-UK.
130. W.L.M.C., *Builder*, 8.
131. Thornhill, *Best of Friends*, 69.
132. Frank Buchman to B. H. Streeter, April 6, 1935, file 3.2154, AOG-UK; Boobbyer, "B. H. Streeter," 553.
133. Lean, *Good God, It Works*, 67–68. For details of the hymn, see *Hymnary*, accessed October 24, 2012, http://www.hymnary.org/text/Jesus_I_my_cross_have_taken_all_to_le.
134. T. Spoerri, *Dynamic out of Silence*, 70; Buchman, "How to Listen," 36.
135. Clark, *Oxford Group*, 110.
136. See Van Dusen, "Oxford Group Movement," 245.
137. Buchman to Mottu, November, 18, 1937, MRA-ACV.
138. R. Murray, *Group Movements*, 16. See also pages 287–372 for a succinct overview of OG spirituality. Murray was canon of Worcester at the time of writing. For a skeptical Catholic view, linking MRA with heresies associating themselves with the Holy Spirit, see Suenens, *Right View*, 36–37.
139. Clark, *Oxford Group*, 42.
140. D. Belden, "Origins and Development," 254.
141. Lean, *Frank Buchman*, 92, 115.
142. Frank Buchman to Mrs. Tjader, January 11, 1925, cited in Lean, *Frank Buchman*, 116. Carmichael's work as a missionary took place under the auspices of the Keswick Convention. Price and Randall, *Transforming Keswick*, 110; Randall, *Evangelical Experiences*, 240.
143. Lean, *Frank Buchman*, 115.
144. T. Spoerri, *Dynamic out of Silence*, 70.
145. Lean, *Frank Buchman*, 295.
146. Ibid., 137.
147. Frank Buchman, cited by Howard in summary of guidance, January 6, 1965, sent to Purdy on January 7, 1965, container 196, MRA-LOC.
148. Lean, *Frank Buchman*, 533.
149. Wolrige Gordon, *Peter Howard*, 285.
150. Buchman, third meeting, AOG-UK, 8.

151. Lean, *Frank Buchman*, 65; Martin, *Always a Little Further*, 191; Sack, *Moral Re-Armament*, 22.
152. Austin, *Frank Buchman*, 81.
153. Strong, "Recollections," AOG-UK, tapes 5, 6.
154. Wood, "Verbatim Notes from Meetings," AOG-UK, 11.
155. Buchman, August 2, 1918, AOG-UK, 8.
156. Lean, *Frank Buchman*, 470.
157. Howard, *Frank Buchman's Secret*, 118.
158. Wood, "Verbatim Notes from Meetings," AOG-UK, 10.
159. Frank Buchman, July 13, 1950, 11:00 A.M., Caux, PP 746, 4.4.3.1/5, MRA-ACV.
160. Lean, *Frank Buchman*, 511.
161. Austin, *Frank Buchman*, 80.
162. Lean, *Frank Buchman*, 68.
163. Austin, *Frank Buchman*, 87.
164. Mrs. Allways, cited in Howard, *Through the Garden Wall*, 73.
165. Evans, *Freewoman*.
166. Wood, "Verbatim Notes from Meetings," AOG-UK, 11.
167. Forde, *Guidance*.
168. Lean, *Frank Buchman*, 166, 352–53. For stories of women in MRA, particularly in relation to peace making, including Laure, see Henderson, *Her Paths Are Peace*.
169. Buchman, "Spiritual Diagnosis," August 8, 1918, AOG-UK (2), 4.
170. Frank Buchman, July 12, 1953, 11:00 A.M., Caux, PP 746, 4.4.3.1/8, MRA-ACV.
171. Russell, *For Sinners Only*, 275–76. See also Campbell, *Dose*, 67–69.
172. Buchman, "Chaos Against God," "Birthday Talk," 79, 77, 50.
173. Buchman, August 10, 1944, MRA-LOC, 5, 9.
174. Campbell, *Dose*, 70–71.
175. Randall, *Evangelical Experiences*, 245–48.
176. P. Spoerri, *No End*, 11; T. Spoerri, "Moral Re-Armament," 58.
177. Tournier, *Listening Ear*, 107. On Tournier's debt to Buchman, see also Hunter, *World Changing*, 78–80.
178. Lean and Peters, *Stories*. See also Jaeger, *Lose My Vision*, 122.
179. A point made by Sentis, interview, August 2011.
180. Lean and Peters, *Stories*, 58.
181. Buchman, "Experience with the Cross," AOG-UK.
182. Strong, "Recollections," AOG-UK, tape 4.
183. Wood, "Verbatim Notes from Meetings," AOG-UK, 15. See also D. Belden, "Origins and Development," 181.
184. Strong, "Recollections," AOG-UK, tape 4.
185. Hunter, *World Changing*, 99. For more on Gandhi and the principle of "brahmacharya," see Gandhi, *Autobiography*, 171–79.
186. Twitchell, *Strength of a Nation*, 9–10; Lean, *Frank Buchman*, 473.
187. Strong, "Recollections," AOG-UK, tape 11.
188. Lean, *Frank Buchman*, 473–76.
189. Arnold Lunn, *Tablet*, September 18, 1954, cited in Mowat, *Report on Moral Re-Armament*, 45.
190. Lean, *Frank Buchman*, 309.
191. Hunter, *World Changing*, 99.
192. Austin, *Frank Buchman*, 84–85.
193. Lean, *Frank Buchman*, 8, 173.

Chapter 4

1. F. B. Meyer, cited in Randall, *Spirituality and Social Change*, 35.
2. Sack, *Moral Re-Armament*, 21.
3. Frank Buchman, third meeting, August 3, 1918, Kuling, file 3.500.2, AOG-UK, 1.
4. Frank Buchman, "Transcript," 1922, Putney Heath House Party, file 3500.4, AOG-UK, 49.
5. Morris Martin, Manuscript Biography, file 6.0876, AOG-UK, chap. 11, p. 1.
6. See Harry Addison, "The Contribution of Moral Re-Armament to Christian Theology," unpublished draft, 21 pp., file 6.0785, AOG-UK, 4.
7. Frank Buchman to Garth Lean and Morris Martin, November 26, 1936, container 54, MRA-LOC.
8. Clark, *Oxford Group*, 47–48.
9. Martin, Manuscript Biography, AOG-UK, chap. 11, p. 6. At Putney Heath Buchman said he believed in knowing Plato, but that people had to know the Bible too. Buchman, "Transcript," AOG-UK, 72. See also Hunter, *World Changing*, 95.
10. Lean, *Frank Buchman*, 198; Van Dusen, "Oxford Group Movement," 248.
11. Isaiah 50:4, 5; Amos 8:11; Habakkuk 2:1–2; Frank Buchman, August 12, 1947, 11:00 A.M.; August 21, 1947, 11:00 A.M., Caux, PP 746, 4.4.3.1/2, MRA-ACV. See also Buchman's references to Psalm 46:10, Isaiah 40:31, and John 3:8 on August 3, 1946, 11:00 A.M. and August 19, 1946, Caux, 11:15 A.M., PP 746, 4.4.3.1/1, MRA-ACV.
12. Buchman, "World Crisis," 112.
13. H. D. A. Major, "Modern Churchman's Commendation," 124–26; Boobbyer, "B. H. Streeter," 557–58.
14. Buchman, "War of Ideas," 144. See also "Is There an Answer?," ibid., 176.
15. For example, he said in 1951, "'The Blood of Jesus Christ God's Son cleanseth us from all sin.' I don't know how it happens, but it works." Morris Martin, "Year-Book for 1951," file 6.1197, AOG-UK, 3. See also Bockmühl, *Frank Buchmans Botschaft*. References to this book are to a translation by Manfred W. Fleischmann, titled "Frank Buchman's Message and Its Significance for the Protestant Churches," 27, in possession of the author. Bockmuehl was enthusiastic about Buchman's approach to guidance. Bockmuehl, *Listening to the God*, 5–9. The meeting in Caux is mentioned in a letter from Logan Kirk to author, March 14, 2003.
16. Buchman, "Revolution Under the Cross," 148.
17. Thornhill, *Best of Friends*, 134–35.
18. Signe Strong, "Recollections," 2006–7, file 6.0248, AOG-UK, tape 7. For Miles's hymn, see *Hymnary*, accessed October 24, 2012, http://www.hymnary.org/text/I_come_to_the_garden_alone.
19. Lean, *Frank Buchman*, 313.
20. W.L.M.C., *Builder*, 8.
21. Martin, "Year-Book for 1951," AOG-UK, 3. The hymns can be found at *Hymnary*, accessed October 26, 2012, http://www.hymnary.org/text/rock_of_ages_cleft_for_me_let_me_hide and http://www.hymnary.org/text/Jesus_lover_of_my_soul_let_me_to_thy_bos.
22. Buchman, October 1, 1956, 7:30 A.M., Mackinac, container 145, MRA-LOC, 4.
23. Buchman, "War of Ideas," 144.
24. Bockmuehl, "Frank Buchman's Message," 17.
25. Buchman, "Chaos Against God," 76.
26. Frank Buchman, July 7, 1937, file 3.500.8, AOG-UK.
27. Buchman, "MRA," 85.
28. Buchman, "New Statesmanship," 211.
29. See "Request for a Grant from the Ford Foundation," May 1959, file USA 116, AOG-UK, 3.

30. Gundersen, *Incorrigibly Independent*, 127.
31. Buchman, "Answer to Any 'Ism,'" 166.
32. Francis Goulding, "Muslim Lands Today," November 8, 1949, file CofGR 40, AOG-UK, 1.
33. Buchman's first link with Gandhi came through Henry Whitehead, Anglican bishop of Madras. "Outline of Buchman's visits to Asia, 1915–1919," file 3, Lean references, AOG-UK. See also Martin, Manuscript Biography, AOG-UK, chap. 6, p. 3; Frank Buchman, July 30, 1953, 11:00 A.M., Caux, PP 746, 4.4.3.1/8, MRA-ACV.
34. Frank Buchman, August 13, 1950, 11:00 A.M., Caux, PP 746, 4.4.3.1/5, MRA-ACV.
35. Lean, *Frank Buchman*, 120.
36. Frank Buchman, July 28, 1955, 11:00 A.M., Caux, PP 746, 4.4.3.1/10, MRA-ACV.
37. Peter Howard, September 26, 1956, 5:15 P.M., Caux, PP 746, 4.4.3.1/11, MRA-ACV.
38. Buchman, July 30, 1953, MRA-ACV.
39. Frank Buchman, July 17, 1954, 5:15 P.M., Caux, PP 746, 4.4.3.1/9, MRA-ACV.
40. Henderson, *Ice in Every Carriage*, 97, 156.
41. Buchman, "Answer to Any 'Ism'" and "Electronics of the Spirit," 167, 223.
42. Frank Buchman to King Mohammed V, November 9, 1959, container 63, MRA-LOC. See also Almond, *American*, 106–7, for details of a letter by Buchman to King Sa'ud of Saudi Arabia, February 28, 1954.
43. See "Shah of Iran Decorates Dr Buchman," press release, 2, container 141, MRA-LOC. Buchman mistakenly suggested in the letter that the translation was in German. Lean, *Frank Buchman*, 4.
44. Buchman, "Answer to Any 'Ism,'" 167.
45. *Frank Buchman Eighty*, 113–14. See also Hannon, "Seeds of Change," 100–103.
46. Henderson, *Ice in Every Carriage*, 188.
47. Rajmohan Gandhi, letter, July 27, 2006, copy in possession of the author.
48. See Boobbyer, "Moral Re-Armament," 230.
49. Lean, *Frank Buchman*, 201; MacEwan, *Tatanga Mani*, 84–88.
50. Henderson, *Ice in Every Carriage*, 34.
51. Lean, *Frank Buchman*, 526.
52. Sentis, "France," 63.
53. *Frank Buchman Eighty*, 117. It should be added, however, that the following year Buchman sent Kurowski a Christmas message that contained a verse from the hymn, "O Little Town of Bethlehem," beginning with the lines, "O Holy Child of Bethlehem, descend to us, we pray." Frank Buchman to Paul Kurowski, December 23, 1959, container 52, MRA-LOC. This may have been connected with the fact that in a letter to Buchman the previous day Howard had mentioned that Kurowski was drinking regularly and that there were rumors that there was more than one woman in his life; Peter Howard to Frank Buchman, December 22, 1959, container 47, MRA-LOC.
54. Frank Buchman to Murray Webb-Peploe, August 24, 1921, container 100, MRA-LOC.
55. Buchman, August 13, 1950, MRA-ACV.
56. See Walter, *Soul Surgery*, 104; Stanley, *World Missionary Conference*, 2.
57. Latourette, *World Service*, 432.
58. See Wuthnow, *Restructuring of American Religion*, chap. 6.
59. D. Belden, "Origins and Development," 272–73.
60. Jarlert, *Oxford Group*, 40, 274; Lean, *Frank Buchman*, 121, 179, 416; D. Belden, "Origins and Development," 259.
61. Frank Buchman to Mrs. L. M. Parker, September 23, 1920, container 152, MRA-LOC. Streeter was also an admirer of Sadhu Sundar Singh; see Streeter and Appasamy, *Sadhu*.
62. Frank Buchman to Nathan Söderblom, January 7, 1931, file 3.1993, AOG-UK.

63. See D. Belden, "Origins and Development," chap. 12.
64. Henderson, *Ice in Every Carriage*, 55, 25; Wolrige Gordon, *Peter Howard*, 257.
65. Bebbington, *Evangelicalism*, 235.
66. Frank Buchman to Douglas Mackenzie, November 25, 1918, container 139, MRA-LOC.
67. Buchman continued in the same letter, "Organic, however, means only that which is in living communion with the living Christ, and so the Group really is the church awakened, on the march, fighting and conquering"; Buchman to Lean and Martin, November 26, 1936, MRA-LOC.
68. Lean, *Good God, It Works*, 72.
69. Garrett Stearly, "Some Reflections on Moral Re-Armament," n.d, in possession of the author; see also Lean, *Frank Buchman*, 269.
70. Bebbington, "Oxford Group Movement," 501; "Moral Re-Armament and the Biblical View," *Christianity Today*, September 29, 1958, 23, cited in Inboden, *Religion*, 194. Randall notes that the OG generally appealed to liberal rather than conservative evangelicals in the interwar period. *Evangelical Experiences*, chap. 8.
71. Hastings, *History of English Christianity*, 201. See also Bockmuehl, "Frank Buchman's Message," 2.
72. Alan Thornhill to Michael Henderson, May 17, 1972, file 6.0737, AOG-UK.
73. Lean, *Frank Buchman*, 30-31, 111, 266, 388, 421, 449.
74. D. Belden, "Origins and Development," 18.
75. Buchman, "Wrong Way," 257. See also Lean, *Frank Buchman*, 226; and D. Belden, "Origins and Development," 109.
76. Lean, *Frank Buchman*, 226.
77. T. Spoerri, *Dynamic out of Silence*, 181.
78. Lean, *Frank Buchman*, 513.
79. Michael Hutchinson, "Focus on the Holy Spirit: A Personal View of Moral Re-Armament," file 6.1176, AOG-UK, 4.
80. Lean, *Frank Buchman*, 513, 406-7.
81. Rahner, "Anonymous Christians," in *Theological Investigations*, 390-98, 403.
82. See Stanley, *World Missionary Conference*, chap. 8.
83. D. Belden, "Origins and Development," 154, 257.
84. Clark, *Oxford Group*, 113.
85. Lean, *Frank Buchman*, 184; Russell, *For Sinners Only*, 24.
86. Martin, Manuscript Biography, AOG-UK, chap. 15, p. 17.
87. Frank Buchman, August 12, 1952, 5:15 P.M., Caux, PP 746, 4.4.3.1/7, MRA-ACV.
88. Statement by Cardinal König, November 15, 1984, file 3, Lean references, AOG-UK.
89. See *Moral Re-Armament*. The chapter on MRA's theology was drafted by Dennis Nineham, the then professor of biblical and historical theology at King's College, London; the chapter on psychology by Geoffrey Allen, then principal of Ripon Hall, Oxford (and involved in the OG in the early 1930s); and the section on MRA's social outreach by Canon E. R. Wickham; Lean, *Frank Buchman*, 435-41.
90. Lean, *Frank Buchman*, 444-45, 517-18. See Suenens, *Right View*, and Dinger, *Moral Re-Armament*.
91. Adam, "Christianity in the West," 374-77, and Schöllgen, "Modern Man," in Buchman, *Remaking the World*, 378-82; For some of Scott's correspondence with Buchman, see container 81, MRA-LOC.
92. See "Quiet Times, Guidance of God and Sharing," translated from French, file "Miscellaneous: Undated," container 128, MRA-LOC.
93. Frank Buchman to Francis Woodlock, October 23, 1933, cited in Lean, *Frank Buchman*, 441.

94. Personal memoirs of Lady Mary Rennell, ca. 1950, in possession of the author.
95. Frank Buchman, "Sayings," 1948, Caux, file 6.0785, AOG-UK.
96. Strong, "Recollections," AOG-UK, tape 1. This was probably in 1940 at the Lake Tahoe retreat.
97. Sentis, "France," 63.
98. Sentis, *L'Avenir*, 58.
99. Bockmuehl, "Frank Buchman's Message," 13.
100. Morris Martin, "Day-Book for 1940," file 6.1197, AOG-UK, 4.
101. Buchman, "War of Ideas," 144.
102. Frank Buchman, August 18, 1947, 11:00 A.M., Caux, PP 746, 4.4.3.1/2, MRA-ACV.
103. See, for example, Streeter, "Professor Barth," 146, and the comments by Adam and Schöllgen in Buchman, *Remaking the World*, 375, 378, 383. Gabriel Marcel stated that there was no attempt at conversion since MRA was not a religion or a sect. "Letter of Personal Reassurance," in *Fresh Hope*, 7.
104. Lawson Wood, "Verbatim Notes from Meetings," 1937, file 3.500.9, AOG-UK, 13, 4.
105. Jarlert, *Oxford Group*, 104–7.
106. D. Belden, "Origins and Development," chap. 14.
107. Lean, *Frank Buchman*, 304.
108. Barth, "Church or Group Movement?" For Barth on the OG, see also Barth, *Karl Barth–Emil Brunner*, 213–16, 237–40, 249, 263, 292. Similarly to Barth, Dietrich Bonhoeffer thought that the OG replaced the witness of the Gospel with the witness of personal change; Bethge, *Dietrich Bonhoeffer*, 470.
109. Streeter, "Professor Barth," 145.
110. Hunter, *World Changing*, 136.
111. Thornton-Duesbery, *Expository Times*, May 1932, cited in McConnachie, *Barthian Theology*, 172.
112. Frank Buchman to Emil Brunner, August 31, 1934, file 3.0282, AOG-UK.
113. Drummond, "Problem of Foreign Missions," in *New Evangelism*, 121–22, 130.
114. W.L.M.C., *Builder*, 16.
115. Robert Schuman cited in Buchman, *Remaking the World*, 348.
116. Jarlert, *Oxford Group*, 326. This talk was distinctive among Buchman's speeches in that it was spontaneous. It was taken down in shorthand by Martin's future wife, Enid. Morris Martin, e-mail to author, April 8, 2005.
117. Buchman, "Revival," 54–56.
118. Lean, *Frank Buchman*, 254.
119. Eddy, *Revolutionary Christianity*. See D. Belden, "Origins and Development," 252–54.
120. D. Belden, "Origins and Development," 279. See also Jarlert, *Oxford Group*, 223, 303–12.
121. Buchman, "Revival," 56.
122. T. Spoerri, *Dynamic out of Silence*, 97.
123. Frank Buchman, June 9, 1948, 5:30 P.M., Riverside, container 401, MRA-LOC.
124. Buchman, August 13, 1950, MRA-ACV.
125. Recollections of Oliver Corderoy (yellow paper), file 3, Lean references, AOG-UK.
126. Layman, *Oxford Group*, 130.
127. T. Spoerri, *Dynamic out of Silence*, 181.
128. Lean, *Frank Buchman*, 406.
129. T. Spoerri, *Dynamic out of Silence*, 104.
130. Notes attached to letter from Frank Buchman to Gilbert Beaver, March 29, 1915, box 2, Gilbert Beaver Papers, Kautz Family YMCA Archives, University of Minnesota Libraries, Minneapolis.
131. Frank Buchman, July 29, 1954, 5:15 P.M., Caux, PP 746, 4.4.3.1/9, MRA-ACV.

132. Jim Baynard-Smith, e-mail to author, December 3, 2010.
133. Frank Buchman to Sam Shoemaker, November 24, 1922, container 83, MRA-LOC.
134. Frank Buchman to Theophil Spoerri, February 13, 1934, file 3.2012, AOG-UK.
135. Frank Buchman to H. Alexander Smith, July 30, 1927, container 84, MRA-LOC.
136. Frank Buchman to Emil Brunner, October 14, 1932, cited in Jarlert, *Oxford Group*, 73.
137. Buchman to Brunner, August 31, 1934, AOG-UK.
138. Brunner, *Church*, 48.
139. For Bonhoeffer's criticism of the Hossenfelder visit, see *Dietrich Bonhoeffer Works*, 32.
140. Lean, *Frank Buchman*, 212–13.
141. Kenaston Twitchell, "Oxford," 8–9, file UK 4.3.1, AOG-UK,
142. Frank Buchman to Theophil Spoerri, December 11, 1936, file 3.2012, AOG-UK.
143. T. Spoerri, *Dynamic out of Silence*, 181–82, 193, 183.
144. Streeter, *God Who Speaks*, 2.
145. For details, see Boobbyer, "Streeter," 566–67.
146. Grensted, *Person of Christ*, 246, 4.
147. Raven, "Theologian's Appreciation," in Spencer, *Meaning of the Groups*, 29.
148. Hunter, *World Changing*, 92.
149. Buchman to T. Spoerri, December 11, 1936, AOG-UK.

Chapter 5

1. Lean, *Frank Buchman*, 244.
2. Frank Buchman to Garth Lean and Morris Martin, November 26, 1936, container 54, MRA-LOC.
3. Lawson Wood, "Verbatim Notes from Meetings," 1937, file 3.500.9, AOG-UK, 19.
4. Buchman, "Revival," 54.
5. Van Dusen, "Apostle," 1.
6. Buchman, "Revolution," 40.
7. T. Spoerri, *Dynamic out of Silence*, 175.
8. Buchman, "Humanity at the Crossroads," 66.
9. Jarlert, *Oxford Group*, 437.
10. T. Willard Hunter to Michael Henderson, June 25, 2000, file 6.0737, AOG-UK.
11. Buchman, "Answer to Crisis," 160–61.
12. Buchman, "National Defence," 129.
13. Frank Buchman, August 11, 1947, 11:00 A.M., Caux, PP 746, 4.4.3.1/2, MRA-ACV.
14. Frank Buchman, August 13, 1947, 11:00 A.M., Caux, PP 746, 4.4.3.1/2, MRA-ACV.
15. Pierre Spoerri, August 13, 2012, Caux, file 6.1209, AOG-UK. This hymn regularly appeared in American hymn books between the years 1928 and 1964; see *Hymnary*, accessed October 18, 2012, http://www.hymnary.org/text/all_the_past_we_leave_behind.
16. Morris Martin, "Day-Book for 1940," file 6.1197, AOG-UK, 11.
17. John Wood, telephone interview with author, June 18, 2012.
18. Buchman, "Revival," 53.
19. Buchman, "MRA," 86; Martin, "Day-Book for 1940," AOG-UK, 11, 1.
20. W.L.M.C., *Builder*, 1.
21. Hunter, *World Changing*, 24.
22. W.L.M.C., *Builder*, 7.
23. Sack, *Moral Re-Armament*, 54.
24. Martin, *Always a Little Further*, 91–95. For a photographic and documentary account of Buchman's wartime work in the United States, see Strong, *Preview*.
25. Buchman, "National Defence."

26. Lean, *Frank Buchman*, 36, 510; Campbell, *Art of Remaking Men*, 88–106.
27. Frank Buchman to Alexander Smith, January 26, 1928, container 84, MRA-LOC.
28. Buchman, "Chaos Against God," 80.
29. Jarlert, *Oxford Group*, 39, 44.
30. W.L.M.C., *Builder*, 5, 16, 13.
31. D. Belden, "Origins and Development," 260.
32. Morris Martin, "Brown File/Travels from 1948," file 6.1197, AOG-UK, 3.
33. Frank Buchman to Henry Ford, June 20, 1936, file 3.0718, AOG-UK. On Ford's encounters with the OG and MRA, see also Hunter, *World Changing*, 69–71, 148–49, 182–83.
34. "Notes on Interview with Prime Minister Baldwin," December 19, 1936, file 3.500.5, AOG-UK. On Baldwin's links with the OG, see P. Williamson, "Christian Conservatives," 619.
35. Morris Martin, "Day-Book for 1940," AOG-UK, 6.
36. Frank Buchman to Nnamdi Azikiwe, telex, November 11, 1960, file 3.0083, AOG-UK.
37. Peter Hannon, "An Ordinary Person," file 6.0741, AOG-UK, 7. For Azikiwe's speeches about MRA, see Azikiwe, *Zik*, 254–61.
38. Frank Buchman, July 17, 1954, 5:15 P.M., Caux, PP 746, 4.4.3.1/9, MRA-ACV.
39. John Roots, in particular, was responsible for drafting a memorandum that was circulated among American policy makers in the early months of 1949. See Inboden, *Religion*, 206; and "Memo on China Policy," folder 5, box 497, MC 120, H. Alexander Smith Papers, Princeton University Library, Princeton, N.J. See also Roots to Frank Buchman, January 8, 29; March 21; May 11, 1949, file 3.1815, AOG-UK; Private Memorandum on China Policy to Frank Pace, Minister of the Budget, May 5, 1949, file 3.1815, AOG-UK.
40. Buchman, "Good Road," 152; Ho Ying-chin, "Guiding Forth," *New World News*, February 1947, 6; Allen and Smyth, *People, Pagodas, and Pyramids*, 178.
41. The decoration was the Grand Cordon of the Order of the Brilliant Star of the Republic of China. Statement by Taipei, May 3, 1956, file 3.500.24, AOG-UK.
42. Frank Buchman to Chiang Kai-shek, May 3, 1956, file 3.0422, AOG-UK. See also Buchman, "Brave Men Choose," 306.
43. Austin, *Frank Buchman*, 84.
44. Alan Thornhill, "Statesmanship Home-Made," container 349, MRA-LOC, 2. Thornhill was fellow and chaplain of Hertford College, Oxford, 1931–36. See also Lean, *Frank Buchman*, 322–23, 505, 508.
45. Harriman, *Matched Pair*, 217.
46. Willard Hunter, "The Story of Mission Point," accessed May 3, 2011, http://www.iofc.org/mackinac-island-history-hunter-eriksson.
47. Thornhill, *Significance*, 13.
48. Howard, *Frank Buchman's Secret*, 38.
49. Saburo Chiba to Frank Buchman, January 5, 1961, file 3.0423, AOG-UK; Frank Buchman to Konrad Adenauer, January 3, 1961, file 3.0010, AOG-UK.
50. *Asia Center Odawara*, 5.
51. D. Belden, "Origins and Development," 259.
52. Buchman, "War of Ideas," 144. He said in 1947 that the league had been a "colossal failure." Frank Buchman, August 12, 1947, 11:00 A.M., Caux, PP 746, 4.4.3.1/2, MRA-ACV.
53. For details of the dinner, including lists of attendees and speakers, see file "League of Nations," container 325, and file "Switzerland, 1934–71," container 346, MRA-LOC.
54. Lean, *Frank Buchman*, 274–75. For Patijn's speech, see file "Geneva, 1938," container 244, MRA-LOC.
55. McGee, *Song for the World*, 57.
56. Martin, "Day-Book for 1940," AOG-UK, 5.
57. Frank Buchman, May 31, 1952, 11:30 A.M., Mackinac, container 396, MRA-LOC.

58. Lean, *Frank Buchman*, 306. The ideas in *You Can Defend America* first appeared in a short handbook; see *You Can Defend America*.
59. Boobbyer, "Cold War." *The Vanishing Island* was co-written with MRA musician Cecil Broadhurst.
60. Michael Henderson to author, January 5, 2011; *Moral Re-Armament Information Service*, 4, no. 12 (November 18, 1955): 1.
61. On U Nu's links with Buchman, see Lean, *Frank Buchman*, 491–92, 507.
62. Lean, *Frank Buchman*, 173; D. Belden, "Origins and Development," 266–67.
63. Frank Buchman, September 7, 1955, 11:00 A.M., Caux, PP 746, 4.4.3.1/10, MRA-ACV.
64. See Stowe, *Uncle Tom's Cabin*, 57.
65. Buchman said that he saw *Uncle Tom's Cabin* at Odd Fellows Hall. This may have been in Allentown. Frank Buchman, July 28, 1955, 11:00 A.M., and September 7, 1955, 11:00 A.M., Caux, PP 746, 4.4.3.1/10, MRA-ACV. Buchman also cited Louisa M. Alcott's books *Little Men* and *Little Women* with approval in his speech of July 28, 1955.
66. The authors of *Freedom* were Mannaseh Moerane, vice president of the African Teachers of South Africa; John Amata, a Nigerian student leader; and Dr. Abayifaa Karbo, a Ghanaian member of Parliament. Boobbyer, "Moral Re-Armament," 221–23.
67. Boobbyer, "Moral Re-Armament," 227–30.
68. Buchman, "Revival," 56; Guldseth, *Streams*, 111.
69. Buchman, "Answer to Crisis," 156.
70. Driberg, *Mystery of Moral Re-Armament*, chap. 15.
71. Frank Buchman to Alan Thornhill, referring to Aage Falk Hansen, May 13, 1935, file 3.2214, AOG-UK.
72. See, for example, Buchman's comments about the Congo and about Asian Reconciliation in "All the Moral Fences," "Solid Rock," and "Brave Men Choose," 281, 290, 306; and Lean, *Frank Buchman*, 306.
73. Buchman, "Answer to Any 'Ism,'" 162.
74. D. Belden, "Origins and Development," 310–16.
75. Piguet, *Love of Tomorrow*, 43–47; Montville, "Psychoanalytic Enlightenment," 306–7.
76. Lean, *Frank Buchman*, 354.
77. Frank Buchman, September 23, 1947, 11:00 A.M., Caux, PP 746, 4.4.3.1/2, MRA-ACV.
78. Wood and Wood, *Have Ocean, Will Travel*, 49.
79. See Luttwak, "Franco-German Reconciliation," 37–63; and Lean, *Frank Buchman*, chaps. 32, 33.
80. Konrad Adenauer to Frank Buchman, April 28, 1950, file 3.0010, AOG-UK; Lean, *Frank Buchman*, 356.
81. Frank Buchman to Konrad Adenauer, cited in Austin and Konstam, *Mixed Double*, 178.
82. Luttwak, "Franco-German Reconciliation," 49–55. See also Twitchell, *Regeneration in the Ruhr*.
83. Basil Entwistle to Garth Lean, file 3, Lean references, AOG-UK.
84. Buchman, "Ideas Are God's Weapons," 235; Buchman, May 31, 1952, MRA-LOC, 3. Buchman was in Japan from August 5 to 17, 1916. Morris Martin, "Chronological Outline," file 3, Lean References, AOG-UK.
85. W.L.M.C., *Builder*, 8.
86. Entwistle, *Japan's Decisive Decade*, 159; Lean, *Frank Buchman*, 295.
87. Frank Buchman "Guidance," April 21, 1951, file 6.0785, AOG-UK.
88. Van Dusen, "Apostle," 13.
89. Frank Buchman, August 5, 1946, Caux, PP 746, 4.4.3.1/1, MRA-ACV, 5.
90. Lean, *Frank Buchman*, 328; Mackenzie, *Faith in Diplomacy*, 49–55; Archie Mackenzie, July 20, 2008, Caux, file 6.0862, AOG-UK.

91. Jim Baynard-Smith, "Notes of Times with Buchman, 1955–56," file 6.0105, AOG-UK, 1.

92. Wolrige Gordon, *Peter Howard*, 242.

93. Morris Martin, "Day-book for 1951," file 6.1197, AOG-UK, 2.

94. See Lean, *Frank Buchman*, 490–91, for details on the awarding of this decoration, including the opposition of the American ambassador in Japan to Buchman receiving the Order of the Rising Sun, first class.

95. Driberg, *Mystery of Moral Re-Armament*, 42, 181.

96. Buchman, "MRA," 86.

97. The woman in question was Elizabeth Whyte, widow of the famous Scottish preacher. Lean, *Frank Buchman*, 215–16.

98. Lean, *Frank Buchman*, quote on 57; Howard, *Frank Buchman's Secret*, 32.

99. Jim Baynard-Smith, "Talk on Buchman," October 2005, file 6.0105, AOG-UK, 5; Baynard-Smith, "Buchman, 1952–53" and "Buchman, 1955–56," AOG-UK, 6, 5.

100. Baynard-Smith, "Buchman, 1952–53," AOG-UK, 6.

101. Frank Buchman, Monday morning meeting, August 5, 1918; August 2, 1918, Kuling, file 3.500.2, AOG-UK, 2, 8.

102. Frank Buchman, "Personalizing Your Job," August 6, 1918, Kuling, file 3.500.2, AOG-UK, 1.

103. Frank Buchman to Sherwood Day, April 22, 1919, container 139, MRA-LOC.

104. Guldseth, *Streams*, 99–100; Lennox, *Henry Drummond*, chap. 18.

105. Wood, "Verbatim Notes from Meetings," AOG-UK, 16.

106. Thornhill, *Best of Friends*, 74; Lean, *Frank Buchman*, 434. See also Frank Buchman to Sam Shoemaker, December 22, 1923, cited in Sack, *Moral Re-Armament*, 48.

107. Lean, *Frank Buchman*, 298–304. See also Howard, *Innocent Men*.

108. Jim Baynard-Smith, "Notes on Times with Buchman," Morocco, file 6.0105, AOG-UK, 2–3. Many in MRA assumed that Driberg was in some way affiliated to the Far Left, a fact that seems to have been borne out by evidence that he was recruited by the KGB in 1956. Andrew and Mitrokhin, *Mitrokhin Archive*, 523.

109. Frank Buchman, June 2, 1952, 11:00 A.M., Mackinac, container 396, MRA-LOC.

110. Buchman, "Answer to Any 'Ism,'" 168–69.

111. Frank Buchman to Fredrik Ramm, March 22, 1936, file 3.1740, AOG-UK.

112. Frank Buchman, August 27, 1944, 11:00 A.M., Mackinac, container 144, MRA-LOC, 7.

113. Austin, *Frank Buchman*, 68.

114. Lean, *Frank Buchman*, 472.

115. Howard, *Frank Buchman's Secret*, 12–13.

116. Henderson, *Ice in Every Carriage*, 31.

117. Lean, *Frank Buchman*, 202.

118. Boobbyer, "Moral Re-Armament," 230–32.

119. Lean, *Frank Buchman*, 21, 97–98, 530–51. In 1952 Buchman stated that he received fifty dollars a month from an insurance company. August 12, 1952, 5:15 P.M., Caux, PP 746, 4.4.3.1/7, MRA-ACV.

120. Lunn, *Enigma*, 24.

121. The man was Roger Hicks, who went on to work with MRA full-time. Lean, *Frank Buchman*, 197.

122. Frank Buchman to Gilbert Harris, December 15, 1955, container 41, MRA-LOC. Also, on finance, see Lean, *Frank Buchman*, 341, 425.

123. I am indebted to Ian Randall for this insight. See also Price and Randall, *Transforming Keswick*, 106.

124. Clark, *Oxford Group*, 44–45; Sack, *Moral Re-Armament*, 58–61, 132–33.

125. Lean, *Frank Buchman*, 249.
126. Frank Buchman, October 7, 1951, 11:00 A.M., Caux, PP 746, 4.4.3.1/6, MRA-ACV.
127. Buchman, August 12, 1952, MRA-ACV.
128. T. Spoerri, *Dynamic out of Silence*, 104.
129. Buchman, "Revolution," 37; Frank Buchman, August 12, 1954, 5:15 P.M., Caux, PP 746, 4.4.3.1/9, MRA-ACV.
130. Frank Buchman, August 24, 1952, 11:00 A.M., Caux, PP 746, 4/4/3/1/7, MRA-ACV.
131. Buchman, August 12, 1952, MRA-ACV.
132. Frank Buchman, July 13, 1950, 11:00 A.M., Caux, PP 746, 4.4.3.1/5, MRA-ACV.
133. Gabriel Marcel, June 2, 1959, Mackinac, PP 746, 5.2.3/73, MRA-ACV; "Eminent French Philosopher at Caux," press release, September 12, 1958, PP 746, 5.2.3/73, MRA-ACV. See also Marcel's "Et Spiritum Sanctum," *MRA Information Service*, September 15, 1956, 4.
134. W.L.M.C., *Builder*.
135. Frank Buchman, August 21, 1947, 11:00 A.M., Caux, PP 746, 4.4.3.1/2, MRA-ACV.
136. Buchman, *Korea Mission Field*, March 1919, cited in D. Belden, "Origins and Development," 255–56.
137. Purdy, *My Friend, Frank Buchman*, chap. 4; Lean, *Frank Buchman*, 87. See also Harvey, "John D. Rockefeller Jr.," 198–209.
138. See Lean, *Frank Buchman*, 313.
139. Martin, *Always a Little Further*, 103, 164.
140. Mottu, *Pile and Face*, 71.
141. Lean, *Frank Buchman*, 502–4; Campbell, *Dose*, 64.
142. Paul Campbell, letter to his wife, Annejet, February 16, 1959, in *Dose*, 86.
143. Hunter, *World Changing*, 191; Lean, *Frank Buchman*, 527.
144. Stearly, cited in Lean, *Frank Buchman*, 526.
145. Jaeger, *Lose My Vision*, 116; Martin, *Always a Little Further*, 188.
146. Henderson, *Forgiveness Factor*, 273.
147. MRA's campaign in Congo in 1960 was an example of its ability to act quickly. See Boobbyer, "Moral Re-Armament," 227–30.
148. Martin, *Always a Little Further*, 189–90.
149. Lean, *Frank Buchman*, 533.
150. The full story of this split remains to be written. Some perspectives on it can be found in Henderson, *Forgiveness Factor*, 273–77; Jaeger, *Lose My Vision*, chap. 9; Martin, *Always a Little Further*, chap. 19; P. Spoerri, *No End*, chap. 7; and Sack, *Moral Re-Armament*, chap. 7.
151. See statement by Moral Re-Armament, Inc., June 1976, New York, file 6.0296, AOG-UK.

Chapter 6

1. See Martin, *Always a Little Further*, 110.
2. Morris Martin, Manuscript Biography, file 6.0876, AOG-UK, chap. 20, p. 10.
3. Buchman, "Moral Re-Armament."
4. Buchman, "World Crisis," 107, 146.
5. Lean, *Frank Buchman*, 320; Buchman, "War of Ideas."
6. Buchman, "War of Ideas," 141.
7. Buchman, "World Philosophy," 146.
8. Harry Addison, "Moral Re-Armament as an Ideology," 1990, file 6.0008, AOG-UK, 2.
9. Buchman, "Good Road," 155.
10. Frank Buchman, July 13, 1954, 11:00 A.M., Caux, PP 746, 4.4.3.1/9, MRA-ACV.

11. Yates, "Buchman's Contribution," 62.
12. Buchman, "War of Ideas," 142.
13. Buchman, "World Philosophy," 146; W.L.M.C., *Builder*, 4.
14. See also Martin, *Always a Little Further*, 108–10.
15. Buchman, "National Defence," 126.
16. Henderson, *Ice in Every Carriage*, 74. See also Howard, *Ideas Have Legs*, 78–82.
17. Howard, *Ideas Have Legs*, 81–82.
18. See Monsignor George Leonard to Gordon D. Wise, May 20, 1991, file 6.0008, AOG-UK.
19. W.L.M.C., memo, October 15, 1988, file 6.1176, AOG-UK.
20. Martin, *Always a Little Further*, 103. AA formally broke away from the OG in 1937.
21. Frank Buchman, August 18, 1947, 11:00 A.M., Caux, PP 746, 4.4.3.1/2, MRA-ACV.
22. Buchman, "Pattern for Statesmanship," 60.
23. See Clark, *Oxford Group*, 98.
24. Buchman, "Trained Force," "National Defence," 133, 132.
25. A point made by Sack, *Moral Re-Armament*, 89.
26. Eister, *Drawing Room Conversion*, 13; Lean, *Frank Buchman*, 269.
27. Frank Buchman to Emil Brunner, December 23, 1933, cited in P. Spoerri, "Reconciliation Comes from Change," in Mackenzie and Young, *Worldwide Legacy*, 305.
28. Frank Buchman, July 26, 1953, Caux, PP 746, 7.4.4.3.1/8, MRA-ACV.
29. Lean, *Frank Buchman*, 254.
30. Buchman, "War of Ideas," 139.
31. Victor Kitchen, "Recollections of Frank Buchman," file 3.1216, AOG-UK.
32. See Bennett, *Social Salvation*, 53–59; David Belden, "Why Didn't Frank Buchman Deal Well With Power?," *Forum on MRA*, no. 3, November 1990, file 6.0120, AOG-UK.
33. See D. Belden, "Origins and Development," 275; and Lean, *Frank Buchman*, 239.
34. Frank Buchman to Margaret Tjader, October 6, 1926, file 3.2229, AOG-UK. For the particular speech in Perugia on October 5, 1926, see Mussolini, *Opera Omnia*, 227–30.
35. Lean, *Frank Buchman*, 122.
36. Frank Buchman to Gerhard Heine, December 14, 1921, cited in Jarlert, *Oxford Group*, 45.
37. Cited in an unpublished draft manuscript by Pierre Spoerri (son of Theophil Spoerri), "Frank Buchman and the Germans," chap. 3, in possession of the author.
38. Buchman took some of his colleagues to the Nuremberg rallies. B. H. Streeter accompanied him to the second of them, and both men were struck by the increased mobilization of Germany that it represented. The meeting during the Olympics was arranged after Buchman met Himmler at a lunch party. Lean, *Frank Buchman*, 236–38.
39. Von Cramon was employed by the SS for eighteen months from November 1935, although it seems that in practice she worked for only five months. For details of these and related matters, see Lean, *Frank Buchman*, 203–6, 233–38; Rosemarie Haver (daughter of von Cramon), interview by Graham Turner, n.d., file 3, Lean references, AOG-UK; and Haver to Garth Lean, September 30, 1984, file 3, Lean references, AOG-UK. See also Padfield, *Himmler*, 202–3.
40. Frank Buchman, interview by William Birnie, *New York–World Telegram*, August 26, 1936, 1, 8; Driberg, *Mystery of Moral Re-Armament*, 68; Hunter, *World Changing*, 51–52.
41. Driberg, *Mystery of Moral Re-Armament*, chap. 4; George Seldes, ed., *In Fact*, September 4, 1944, 1. See also *In Fact*, June 10, 1941; January 18, 1943; May 29, 1944; March 26, 1945; and Seldes, articles in *Witness to a Century*, 387–88. For Seldes's communist links, see Haynes et al., *Spies*, 168–70.
42. Martin, Manuscript Biography, AOG-UK, chap. 19, p. 30.

43. Hunter argues that Buchman's aim was not appeasement but "genuine change on both sides." *World Changing*, 45, 59, 117.
44. Lean, *Frank Buchman*, 251; Buchman, interview by Birnie, *New York–World Telegram*, 1. See also Wise, *Great Aim in Life*, 162.
45. See Sack, *Moral Re-Armament*, 94.
46. Bonhoeffer, *Dietrich Bonhoeffer Works*, 218.
47. R. Niebuhr, *Christianity and Power Politics*, chap. 12.
48. Morris Martin, "Day-Book for 1940," file 6.1197, AOG-UK, 4.
49. Churchill, *Great Contemporaries*, 210.
50. Buchman's reaction was reported by von Cramon to Hans Stroh, one of the OG leaders in Germany. Lean, *Frank Buchman*, 234.
51. Ibid., 238. The journalist was Jakob Kronika, correspondent of the daily *Flensborg Avis*.
52. D. Belden, "Origins and Development," 277.
53. K. Belden, *Hour of the Helicopter*, 41.
54. Lean, *Frank Buchman*, 208, 241, 287.
55. Thornton-Duesbery, *Open Secret of MRA*, 63; Lean, *Frank Buchman*, 242.
56. D. Belden, "Origins and Development," 272–74; Schellenberg, *Invasion 1940*, 51.
57. Frank Buchman, August 11, 1947, 11:00 A.M., Caux, PP 746, 4.4.3.1/2, MRA-ACV.
58. Pierre Spoerri suggests that at the end of the 1930s and during the war years German members of the OG divided into four identifiable groups: those who tried to work for change within the regime, those who focused on renewal within the churches, those who became involved in the resistance, and those who made the survival of their families a priority. "Frank Buchman," chap. 6.
59. Lean, *Frank Buchman*, 242.
60. Frank Buchman to Douglas Mackenzie, July 16, 1921, folder 349, box 27, FB-HTS.
61. Lean, *Frank Buchman*, 147–48.
62. Peter Howard, "Buchman, Eisenhower, Khrushchev," *Gazette de Lausanne*, late 1950s, special supplement, file 6.0770, AOG-UK.
63. Frank Buchman, June 2, 1952, 11:00 A.M., Mackinac, container 396, MRA-LOC.
64. Frank Buchman, August 12, 1947, 11:00 A.M., Caux, PP 746, 4.4.3.1/2, MRA-ACV.
65. Frank Buchman, September 6, 1948, 11:00 A.M., Caux, PP 746, 4/4/3/1/3, MRA-ACV.
66. John Roots, cited in Lean, *Frank Buchman*, 71, 147.
67. Frank Buchman, August 12, 1954, 11:00 A.M., Caux, PP 746, 4.4.3.1/9, MRA-ACV.
68. Buchman, August 18, 1947, MRA-ACV.
69. Howard, *Dictator's Slippers*; Howard, *Mr. Brown*, 81.
70. Boobbyer, "Cold War," 213.
71. See, for example, Driberg, *Mystery of Moral Re-Armament*, 151.
72. Peter Howard to Philippe Mottu, April 20, 1964, PP 746, 7.4.2/15, MRA-ACV; Lean, *Frank Buchman*, 515–16.
73. See, for example, Buchman, "Ideas Are God's Weapons," "Hurricane of Common Sense," "Brave Men Choose," 235, 259, 301–2.
74. Frank Buchman, October 7, 1951, 11:00 A.M., Caux, PP 746, 4.4.3.1/6, MRA-ACV.
75. Boobbyer, "Cold War," 208.
76. "Moral Re-Armament," *Times*, March 30, 1961, 5. See also "Warner Theatre," *Times*, February 16, 1961, 7.
77. "Ideologicheskaia diversiia soedinennykh shtat," *Pravda*, January 8, 1953, 1.
78. These details come from Inboden, *Religion*, 218.
79. See also Boobbyer, "Cold War," 205.
80. Buchman, "Illumined America." Buchman was also awarded an honorary doctorate of divinity by Muhlenberg College in 1926. Lean, *Frank Buchman*, 121.

81. Buchman, "War of Ideas," 143–45.
82. Frank Buchman, August 10, 1944, 11:00 A.M., Mackinac, container 144, MRA-LOC.
83. Frank Buchman, "My Experience with the Cross," recording, October 1, 1956, 7:30 A.M., Mackinac, file 3.500.0, AOG-UK.
84. Lean, *Frank Buchman*, 480–81.
85. Inboden, *Religion*, 220–21.
86. Lean, *Frank Buchman*, 251.
87. Frank Buchman, June 4, 1952, 11:00 A.M., Mackinac, container 396, MRA-LOC.
88. See Boobbyer, "Moral Re-Armament," 226.
89. Jim Baynard-Smith, "Notes on Times with Buchman, 1955–56," file 6.0105, AOG-UK, 5.
90. Buchman, "One Heart," "God Calling the World," 18, 12.
91. Buchman, "Moral Re-Armament," 46.
92. Buchman, "Guidance or Guns?," "Framework," 62, 73.
93. William Penn, cited in Buchman, "Ideas Are God's Weapons," 241.
94. Buchman, "Chaos Against God," 78; D. Belden, "Origins and Development," 268.
95. Buchman, "Guidance or Guns?," 63. See also "We Must Forge," ibid., 100.
96. Lean, *Frank Buchman*, 529.
97. Buchman, "Revival," 56.
98. Frank Buchman, September 24, 1947, Caux, PP 746, 4.4.3.1/9, MRA-ACV; Lean, *Frank Buchman*, 351–52.
99. There were no references to theocracy in *Remaking the World*, but Buchman was cited as talking of theocracy in his interview with Birnie, *New York World-Telegram*, 8.
100. Buchman, "Chaos Against God," 79; Ekman, *Experiment with God*, 47–48.
101. See Martin, *Always a Little Further*, 108–10.
102. Buchman, "One Heart," 18.
103. Jarlert, *Oxford Group*, 40.
104. Buchman, "Chaos Against God," 78.
105. Buchman, "World Crisis," 110.
106. Buchman, "What We Need," 202.
107. Mackenzie, introduction to Mackenzie and Young, *Worldwide Legacy*, 10.
108. Buchman, "Destiny of Nations."
109. Buchman, "Revival," 56.
110. Buchman, "Listening Millions."
111. Frank Buchman, August 21, 1948, Caux, PP 746, 4.4.3.1/3, MRA-ACV.
112. Buchman, "Moral Re-Armament," "Humanity at the Crossroads," 47, 65. Whether or not Buchman was aware of it, the "fingers on the hand" image had echoes of a sentence used by African American educator Booker T. Washington in a speech on the possibility of racial cooperation in 1895: "In all things that are purely social we can be as separate as the fingers, yet one as the hand in all things essential to mutual progress." Thornbrough, *Booker T. Washington*, 35.
113. Buchman, "Labour's Spiritual Heritage," 84.
114. Frank Buchman, "Guidance," March 1946, file 6.0785, AOG-UK.
115. Frank Buchman, September 2, 1945, Mackinac, container 393, MRA-LOC.
116. T. Spoerri, *Dynamic out of Silence*, 107.
117. Buchman, "Moral Re-Armament," 46. This phrase originated with an engineer, Bill Sinclair, who was active in the OG. Statement by Michael Smith, July 21, 2008, file 6.1060, AOG-UK.
118. Buchman, "Pattern for Statesmanship," 59.
119. Buchman, "Chaos Against God," 77.

120. Martin, Manuscript Biography, AOG-UK, chap. 22, p. 7. See also Jørgensen, *Denmark*, 13–21.
121. See Vickers, *Spin a Good Yarn*, 77–83.
122. Henderson, *Ice in Every Carriage*, 50.
123. Buchman, "National Defence," 129.
124. Lean, *Frank Buchman*, 324.
125. Buchman, "Answer to Crisis," 158.
126. Buchman, "Destiny of East and West," 177, 183.
127. Intelligence reports, KV 5/67, 1950–52, item 329a, British National Archives, Kew, London; Day, "M15 Cold War Secrets," 9; Boobbyer, "Tabloid News Story?," 6–7.
128. Lean, *Frank Buchman*, 426–27.
129. Frank Buchman, June 7, 1951, Mackinac, container 144, MRA-LOC.
130. Howard, *Innocent Men*, 131–32. See also Lean, *Frank Buchman*, 289.
131. Frank Buchman to Harry Truman, March 5, 1942, file 3.2252, AOG-UK.
132. Lean, *Frank Buchman*, 310, 316–17.
133. Frank Buchman to Robert Schuman, January 19, 1960, file 3.1905, AOG-UK.
134. Lean, *Frank Buchman*, 140–45, 458–59.
135. Frank Buchman, July 28, 1955, 11:00 A.M., Caux, PP 746, 4.4.3.1/10, MRA-ACV.
136. Ibid. Mary McLeod Bethune was the founder in 1904 of the Daytona Industrial and Educational Training School for Negro Girls, Florida, which after merging with the Cookman Institute in Jacksonville in 1923, became Bethune-Cookman College (now University).
137. Lean, *Frank Buchman*, 500.
138. Frank Buchman, September 7, 1955, 11:00 A.M., Caux, PP 746, 4.4.3.1/10, MRA-ACV.
139. Buchman, "MRA," 85.
140. Grogan, *John Riffe*, 202.
141. Buchman, July 28, 1955, MRA-ACV.
142. Buchman, "Nations," 227.
143. Buchman, "New Illumination," 5.
144. Buchman, "Revolution," 37.
145. Buchman, "Answer to Crisis," 156.
146. Campbell and Howard, *Remaking Men*, 8, 43–44.
147. Buchman, "What We Need," 202.
148. Buchman, "New Statesmanship," 211.
149. Buchman, "Pattern for Statesmanship," "One Thing," 61, 69.
150. Buchman, "War of Ideas," "National Defence," 144–45, 128.
151. Frank Buchman, July 29, 1954, 5:15 P.M., Caux, PP 746, 4.4.3.1/9, MRA-ACV.
152. Buchman, "Norway Ablaze," "World Crisis," 8, 112.
153. Buchman, "Listening Millions," 121.
154. Buchman, "Good Road," 154–55.
155. Buchman, "Guidance or Guns?," 63.
156. Buchman, "War of Ideas," 139.
157. Mowat, *Message of Frank Buchman*, 45. See also Mowat, *Climax of History*, and Mowat, *Decline and Renewal*.
158. Buchman, "New Statesmanship," 211.
159. Jim Baynard-Smith, "Notes on Times with Buchman," Morocco, file 6.0105, AOG-UK, 4.
160. *Father of the House*, 82, 206.
161. Buchman, "All the Moral Fences," 272–73. See also Livingstone, *Education*.
162. The play *Shaft of Light* was subsequently written by the group from Japan to address these issues. Lean, *Frank Buchman*, 508.

163. Buchman, "All the Moral Fences," 272. Kishi's full statement, dated January 22, 1961, can be found in file 3.1214, AOG-UK.

164. A small group met in July 1960 to plan the expansion of MRA in Japan, including Sogo Shinji, president of the National Railways; Yamagiwa Masamichi, governor of the Bank of Japan; and Keizo Shibusawa, former finance minister. Masa Shibusawa to Frank Buchman, July 14, 1960, file 3.1946, AOG-UK.

165. See, for example, Howard, *Britain and the Beast*; and Cook and Lean, *Black and White Book*. Lean also co-authored books on the moral situation in Britain with Arnold Lunn; see, for example, Lunn and Lean, *New Morality*.

166. Jarlert, *Oxford Group*, 41–42.

167. Buchman, "Electronics of the Spirit," "Message to Nigeria," "Message to Cyprus," 223, 271, 270.

168. Lean, *Frank Buchman*, 331, 422.

169. Buchman, "Unexpected Source," 233.

170. Frank Buchman, August 5, 1946, Caux, PP 746, 4.4.3.1/1, MRA-ACV.

171. Frank Buchman, May 29, 1952, 11:00 A.M., Mackinac, container 396, MRA-LOC.

172. Buchman, "Place to Start," "Forgotten Factor," 25, 105.

173. Frank Buchman, July 15, 1954, 11:00 A.M., Caux, PP 746, 4.4.3.1/9, MRA-ACV.

174. Frank Buchman, August 6, 1955, 11:00 A.M., Caux, PP 746, 4.4.3.1/10, MRA-ACV.

175. Frank Buchman, "Sayings," 1948, Caux, file 6.075, AOG-UK.

176. Buchman, "War of Ideas," 145.

177. Buchman, "Moral Re-Armament," 48.

178. Buchman's thinking here was similar to that of the Russian philosopher Semyon Frank (1877–1950), who in the early Cold War argued that the underlying ideological battle in the world was not between Left and Right but between those committed to absolute moral principles and the sanctify of life on the one hand and the defenders of materialism and relativism on the other. Boobbyer, "Faith," 270–72, 283.

179. See Canipe, "Under God."

180. Sherwood, *Preaching*, 55–58. Buchman called Sheen a "great Catholic leader." "Answer to Any 'Ism,'" 166. Sheen was also generously quoted in an anthology of readings inspired by MRA: Prescott, *New Day*.

181. Kirby, "Harry Truman's Religious Legacy," 79, 94; Truman, *Mr. Citizen*, 119.

182. For a discussion of the Wilsonian and internationalist elements in Alexander Smith's vision, see Inboden, *Religion*, 198, 216.

183. Hunter, *World Changing*, 91.

184. Winter, *Dreams*, 1–10. See also Jarlert, *Oxford Group*, 41, 44.

185. Sack, *Moral Re-Armament*, 145.

186. Buchman, "National Press Club," 87; Lean, *Frank Buchman*, 531.

187. Frank Buchman, December 31, 1954, 11:00 A.M., Washington, D.C., container 402, MRA-LOC.

188. Buchman, "World Crisis," 111.

189. Buchman, "God Is the Answer," 248.

190. Buchman, "One Heart," 18; Martin, "Day-Book for 1940," AOG-UK, 11; Frank Buchman, August 16, 1947, Caux, PP 746, 4.4.3.1/2, MRA-ACV.

191. Mott, *Evangelization of the World*.

192. Cited in Oliver Corderoy, April 28, 1982, file 3, Lean references, AOG-UK; Lean, *Frank Buchman*, 407.

193. R. Niebuhr, *Christian Realism*; Hunter, *World Changing*, 143.

194. Mowat, *Message of Frank Buchman*, 13.

Conclusion

1. Yates, "Buchman's Contribution," 56, 58–61.
2. H. R. Niebuhr, "Christ and Culture in Paradox," in *Christ and Culture*, 178.
3. Lean, *Frank Buchman*, 406.
4. Ailsa Hamilton, "A Spiritual History of MRA," 1995, file 6.0248, AOG-UK, 1.
5. Pomerants, *Spiritual Movement*, 37, 23.
6. Marcel, "Letter of Personal Reassurance," in *Fresh Hope*, 6.
7. Tournier, *Listening Ear*, 107.
8. Frankl, *Search for Meaning*, 98. For MRA authors citing Frankl, see Evans, *Freewoman*, 22; Wilhelmsen, *Man and Structures*, 14; and Lester and Spoerri, *Rediscovering Freedom*, 20.
9. Morris Martin, Manuscript Biography, file 6.0876, AOG-UK, chap. 11A, 3.
10. See Lean, *Frank Buchman*, 171.
11. See Buchman, "War of Ideas," 141, 145.
12. D. Belden, "Origins and Development," 13.
13. Kenaston Twitchell, "Oxford," file 4.3.1, AOG-UK, 8–9.
14. Michael Hutchinson to Gordon Wise, March 24, 1990, file 6.1176, AOG-UK.
15. Rahner, "Anonymous Christians," in *Theological Investigations*, 390–98, 403; Taylor, *Go-Between God*; Panikkar, *Unknown Christ of Hinduism*. See also Israel, *Smouldering Fire*.
16. Recollections of Alan Thornhill (yellow paper), July 1976, file 3, Lean references, AOG-UK, 14; Martin, *Always a Little Further*, 189.
17. Buchman to Tjader, October 6, 1926, AOG-UK.
18. Michel Sentis, for example, was friendly with Brother Roger. Sentis, interview with author, Prissé, France, August 2011. Brother Roger himself spoke favorably of Buchman. Lean, *Frank Buchman*, 531.
19. Marcel, cited in T. Spoerri, *Dynamic out of Silence*, 163.
20. See Johnston and Sampson, *Religion*, for some examples. See also Johnston's introduction to ibid., 4; and Montville, "Psychoanalytic Enlightenment," 309.
21. Signe Strong, "Recollections," 2006–7, file 6.0248, AOG-UK, tapes 1, 11.
22. Oliver Corderoy, cited in Lean, *Frank Buchman*, 179.
23. Austin, *Frank Buchman*, 60.

BIBLIOGRAPHY

Published Works by Frank Buchman

Speeches

Buchman's main speeches, broadcasts, and statements were published in the collection *Remaking the World*. The first edition appeared in 1947, and revised editions came out in 1953, 1958, and 1961. This publication grew out of an anthology of extracts from speeches selected by A. H. Baker and Julian P. Thornton-Duesbery (London: Heinemann, 1941). Some of Buchman's speeches were subsequently reprinted in *The Revolutionary Path: Moral Re-Armament in the Thinking of Frank Buchman* (London: Grosvenor Books, 1975). The following are speeches from the revised edition of *Remaking the World* (London: Blandford Press, 1961).

"All the Moral Fences Are Down." Caux. April 1961, 272–83.
"America Awake!" Stockbridge, Mass. June 4, 1936, 26–29.
"The Answer to Any 'Ism'—Even Materialism." Riverside. June 2, 1948, 162–69.
"The Answer to Crisis." Caux. July 15, 1947, 156–61.
"Backbone of the Real America." Washington, D.C. June 4, 1939, 91–92.
"A Birthday Talk to East London Families." East Ham. May 29, 1938, 49–50.
"Brave Men Choose." Caux. June 4, 1961, 295–307.
"Bread, Peace, Hope." New Delhi. January 1953, 205.
"Chaos Against God." London. November 27, 1938, 74–80.
"The Destiny of East and West." Gelsenkirchen. May 28, 1950, 177–84.
"The Destiny of Nations." A manifesto from *Rising Tide*. November 1937, 42.
"The Electronics of the Spirit." Mackinac. May 1955, 219–25.
"For All Men Everywhere." Written in Morocco. 1954, 212–18.
"The Forgotten Factor." Boston. August 27, 1939, 103–5.
"Framework of a Mighty Answer." London. November 11, 1938, 71–73.
"God Calling the World." Denmark. June 9, 1935, 10–12.
"God Is the Answer to the Modern Confusion That Dogs Us." Mackinac. June 1959, 242–49.
"The Good Road." Caux. June 4, 1947, 149–55.
"Guidance or Guns?" Interlaken. September 6, 1938, 62–64.
"How to Listen." Birmingham, England. July 26, 1936, 35–36.
"Humanity at the Crossroads." Interlaken. September 10, 1938, 65–67.
"A Hurricane of Common Sense." Mackinac. June 1960, 259–69.
"Ideas Are God's Weapons for a New World." Mackinac. June 1957, 234–41.
"An Illumined America." Oglethorpe University. June 1939, 93–94.
"Is There an Answer? There Is." Caux. June 4, 1949, 170–76.
"Labour's Spiritual Heritage." London. November 1938, 81–84.
"Listening Millions." New York. December 2, 1939, 116–21.

"A Message to Cyprus." N.p. August 16, 1960, 270.
"A Message to Greece." London. June 4, 1938, 51–52.
"A Message to Nigeria." N.p. September 30, 1960, 271.
"Miracles in the North." New York. November 20, 1935, 19–23.
"Moral Re-Armament." East Ham. May 29, 1938, 45–48.
"Moral Re-Armament and National Defence." San Francisco. June 4, 1940, 124–32.
"MRA: A National Necessity." London. January 1939, 85–86.
"Nations That Will Not Think." London. June 4, 1956, 226–32.
"A New Illumination." Oxford. July 1934, 4–5.
"The New Statesmanship to End Confusion." London. June 4, 1953, 206–11.
"Norway Ablaze." Oslo. March 1935, 6–9.
"One Heart, One Will, One Goal." Zurich. October 6, 1935, 17–18.
"The One Sure Hope." San Francisco. August 28, 1939, 101–2.
"One Thing Can Swing the Balance." Geneva. September 15, 1938, 68–70.
"Our Primary Need." Geneva. January 1932, 3.
"Pattern for Statesmanship." Interlaken. September 2, 1938, 59–61.
"The Place to Start." Denmark. April 12, 1936, 24–25.
"Preview of a New World." Hollywood Bowl. July 19, 1939, 95–96.
"Remakers of the World." N.p. A Christmas message. [1940], 135.
"Report to the National Press Club." Washington, D.C. May 8, 1939, 87–90.
"Revival, Revolution, and Renaissance." Visby. August 16, 1938, 53–58.
"A Revolution to Cure a Revolution." London. August 9, 1936, 37–41.
"A Revolution Under the Cross." New York. April 23, 1946, 147–48.
"The Rise of a New Spirit." N.p. January 1940, 122–23.
"Solid Rock or Sinking Sand." Caux. May 1961, 284–94.
"Spearhead of a World Answer." Oxford. July 28, 1935, 13–16.
"A Trained Force." Philadelphia. June 4, 1941, 133–34.
"Turn on the Light." Mackinac. June 1951, 189–95.
"The Unexpected Source." N.p. December 1956, 233.
"The War of Ideas." Mackinac. July 1943, 139–45.
"We Must Forge New Weapons." Monterey Peninsula, California. July 22, 1939, 99–100.
"What Are You Living For?" Gelsenkirchen. June 4, 1950, 185–88.
"What We Need Is Something Electric." Mackinac. June 1952, 196–202.
"Will God Control America?" Philadelphia. June 19, 1936, 30–34.
"The World Philosophy." San Francisco. June 4, 1945, 146.
"A World Philosophy Adequate for World Crisis." Broadcasts from San Francisco and Boston. October 29, 1939, 106–15.
"The Wrong Way and the Right Way." Mackinac. June 4, 1959, 250–58.

Selected Other Works by Frank Buchman

"The Making of a Miracle." In *The Art of Remaking Men*, edited by Paul Campbell, 88–106. Bombay: Himmat Publications Trust, 1970.
"Personal Evangelism." China Continuation Committee. *Bulletin*, no. 11 (1918): 2–12.
"Personal Work." *Muhlenberg*, November 1902, 1–3.
"Personal Work." *United Church Herald* 7, no. 11 (1916): 461–64.
"Where Personal Work Begins." Edited by Lawson Wood. Unpublished manuscript, 1984.

Other Sources

Adam, Karl. "Moral Re-Armament and Christianity in the West." In Buchman, *Remaking the World* (1961), 374–77.
Allen, Geoffrey. *He That Cometh*. London: Maclehose, 1932.
Allen, Leonard Bliss, and Kathleen Smyth. *People, Pagodas, and Pyramids*. N.p.: privately printed, 1985.
Almond, Harry J. *An American in the Middle East*. Caux: Caux Books, 2009.
Andrew, Christopher, and Vasili Mitrokhin. *The Mitrokhin Archive*. London: Lane / Penguin Press, 1998.
Arndt, Johann. *True Christianity*. London: Society for Promoting Christian Knowledge, 1979.
Asia Center Odawara: Postwar Japan and the Work of Moral Re-Armament. Tokyo: MRA House, 2008.
Austin, H. W. "Bunny." *Frank Buchman as I Knew Him*. London: Grosvenor Books, 1975.
Austin, H. W. "Bunny," and Phyllis Konstam. *A Mixed Double*. London: Chatto and Windus, 1969.
Azikiwe, Nnamdi. *Zik: A Selection from the Speeches of Nnamdi Azikiwe*. Cambridge: Cambridge University Press, 1961.
B. [Burns], Dick. *The Oxford Group and Alcoholics Anonymous: An A.A.-Good Book Connection*. Seattle: Glen Abbey Books, 1992.
Ball, Simon. *The Guardsmen: Harold Macmillan, Three Friends, and the World They Made*. London: HarperCollins, 2004.
Barth, Karl. "Church or Group Movement?" *London Quarterly and Holborn Review*, January 1937, 1–9.
———. *Karl Barth–Emil Brunner: Briefwechsel; 1916–1966*. Zurich: Theologischer Verlag, 2000.
Beazley, Kim E. *Father of the House: The Memoirs of Kim E. Beazley*. Fremantle: Fremantle Press, 2009.
Bebbington, David. *Evangelicalism in Modern Britain*. London: Routledge, 1989.
———. "The Oxford Group Movement Between the Wars." In *Voluntary Religion*, edited by William J. Sheils and Diana Wood, 495–507. Studies in Church History 23. Oxford: Basil Blackwell, 1986.
Beecher, Henry Ward. *Yale Lectures on Preaching*. New York: Ford, 1872.
Begbie, Harold. *Life Changers*. London: Mills and Boon, 1923. Published in the United States as *More Twice Born Men* (New York: Putnam, 1923).
Belden, David. "The Origins and Development of the Oxford Group Movement (Moral Re-Armament)." PhD diss., Oxford University, 1976.
Belden, Ken D. *The Hour of the Helicopter*. Yeovil, UK: Linden Hall, 1992.
Bennett, John C. *Social Salvation*. New York: Scribner's Sons, 1935.
Bethge, Eberhard. *Dietrich Bonhoeffer: A Biography*. Rev. ed. Minneapolis: Fortress Press, 2000.
Bockmühl [Bockmuehl], Klaus. *Frank Buchmans Botschaft und ihre Bedeutung für die protestantischen Kirchen*. Bern: Haupt, 1963.
———. "Frank Buchman's Message and Its Significance for Protestant Churches." Translated by Manfred W. Fleischmann. Unpublished manuscript translation of *Frank Buchmans Botschaft*.
———. *Listening to the God Who Speaks*. Colorado Springs: Helmers and Howard, 1990.
Bonhoeffer, Dietrich. *Dietrich Bonhoeffer Works*. Vol. 13, *London, 1933–1935*, edited by Hans Goedeking, Martin Heimbucher, and Hans-Walter Schleicher. Minneapolis: Fortress Press, 2007.

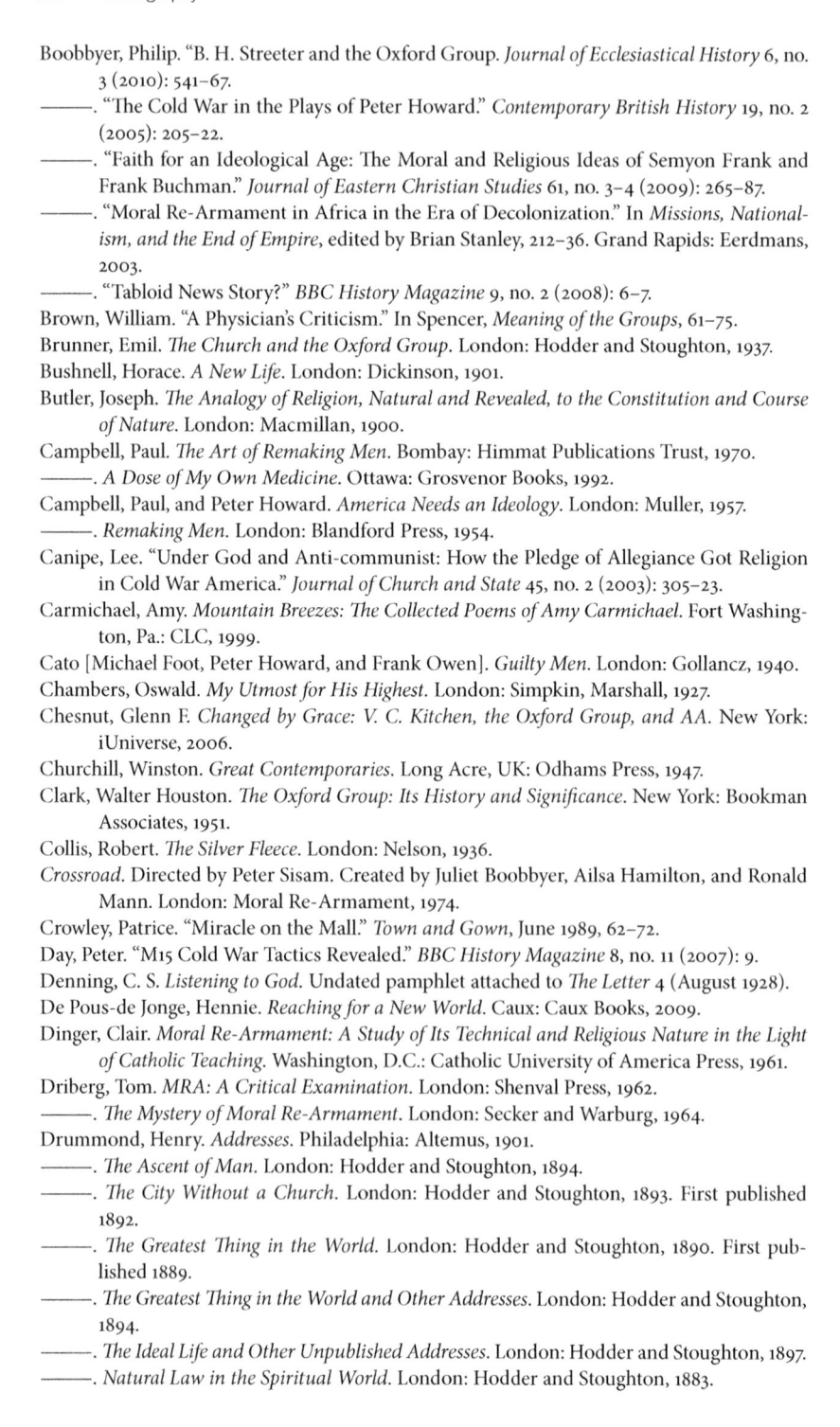

Boobbyer, Philip. "B. H. Streeter and the Oxford Group. *Journal of Ecclesiastical History* 6, no. 3 (2010): 541–67.
———. "The Cold War in the Plays of Peter Howard." *Contemporary British History* 19, no. 2 (2005): 205–22.
———. "Faith for an Ideological Age: The Moral and Religious Ideas of Semyon Frank and Frank Buchman." *Journal of Eastern Christian Studies* 61, no. 3–4 (2009): 265–87.
———. "Moral Re-Armament in Africa in the Era of Decolonization." In *Missions, Nationalism, and the End of Empire*, edited by Brian Stanley, 212–36. Grand Rapids: Eerdmans, 2003.
———. "Tabloid News Story?" *BBC History Magazine* 9, no. 2 (2008): 6–7.
Brown, William. "A Physician's Criticism." In Spencer, *Meaning of the Groups*, 61–75.
Brunner, Emil. *The Church and the Oxford Group*. London: Hodder and Stoughton, 1937.
Bushnell, Horace. *A New Life*. London: Dickinson, 1901.
Butler, Joseph. *The Analogy of Religion, Natural and Revealed, to the Constitution and Course of Nature*. London: Macmillan, 1900.
Campbell, Paul. *The Art of Remaking Men*. Bombay: Himmat Publications Trust, 1970.
———. *A Dose of My Own Medicine*. Ottawa: Grosvenor Books, 1992.
Campbell, Paul, and Peter Howard. *America Needs an Ideology*. London: Muller, 1957.
———. *Remaking Men*. London: Blandford Press, 1954.
Canipe, Lee. "Under God and Anti-communist: How the Pledge of Allegiance Got Religion in Cold War America." *Journal of Church and State* 45, no. 2 (2003): 305–23.
Carmichael, Amy. *Mountain Breezes: The Collected Poems of Amy Carmichael*. Fort Washington, Pa.: CLC, 1999.
Cato [Michael Foot, Peter Howard, and Frank Owen]. *Guilty Men*. London: Gollancz, 1940.
Chambers, Oswald. *My Utmost for His Highest*. London: Simpkin, Marshall, 1927.
Chesnut, Glenn F. *Changed by Grace: V. C. Kitchen, the Oxford Group, and AA*. New York: iUniverse, 2006.
Churchill, Winston. *Great Contemporaries*. Long Acre, UK: Odhams Press, 1947.
Clark, Walter Houston. *The Oxford Group: Its History and Significance*. New York: Bookman Associates, 1951.
Collis, Robert. *The Silver Fleece*. London: Nelson, 1936.
Crossroad. Directed by Peter Sisam. Created by Juliet Boobbyer, Ailsa Hamilton, and Ronald Mann. London: Moral Re-Armament, 1974.
Crowley, Patrice. "Miracle on the Mall." *Town and Gown*, June 1989, 62–72.
Day, Peter. "M15 Cold War Tactics Revealed." *BBC History Magazine* 8, no. 11 (2007): 9.
Denning, C. S. *Listening to God*. Undated pamphlet attached to *The Letter* 4 (August 1928).
De Pous-de Jonge, Hennie. *Reaching for a New World*. Caux: Caux Books, 2009.
Dinger, Clair. *Moral Re-Armament: A Study of Its Technical and Religious Nature in the Light of Catholic Teaching*. Washington, D.C.: Catholic University of America Press, 1961.
Driberg, Tom. *MRA: A Critical Examination*. London: Shenval Press, 1962.
———. *The Mystery of Moral Re-Armament*. London: Secker and Warburg, 1964.
Drummond, Henry. *Addresses*. Philadelphia: Altemus, 1901.
———. *The Ascent of Man*. London: Hodder and Stoughton, 1894.
———. *The City Without a Church*. London: Hodder and Stoughton, 1893. First published 1892.
———. *The Greatest Thing in the World*. London: Hodder and Stoughton, 1890. First published 1889.
———. *The Greatest Thing in the World and Other Addresses*. London: Hodder and Stoughton, 1894.
———. *The Ideal Life and Other Unpublished Addresses*. London: Hodder and Stoughton, 1897.
———. *Natural Law in the Spiritual World*. London: Hodder and Stoughton, 1883.

---. "The New Evangelism and Its Relation to Cardinal Doctrines." In Drummond, *New Evangelism*, 3–43.
---. *The New Evangelism and Other Papers*. London: Hodder and Stoughton, 1899.
---. "Spiritual Diagnosis." In Drummond, *New Evangelism*, 191–210.
Eddy, Sherwood. *Revolutionary Christianity*. Chicago: Willett, Clark, 1939.
"Editorial Notes." *Korea Mission Field* 14, no. 7 (July 1918).
Eister, A. W. *Drawing Room Conversion*. Durham: Duke University Press, 1950.
Ekman, Gösta. *Experiment with God: Frank Buchman Reconsidered*. London: Hodder and Stoughton, 1972.
Entwistle, Basil. *Japan's Decisive Decade*. London: Grosvenor Books, 1985.
Erb, Peter C., ed. *Pietists: Selected Writings*. London: Society for Promoting Christian Knowledge, 1983.
Evans, Claire. *Freewoman*. London: Grosvenor Books, 1979. Originally published as *Le Défi féminin* (Caux: Editions de Caux, 1977).
Falby, Alison. "The Modern Confessional: Anglo-American Religious Groups and the Emergence of Lay Psychotherapy." In *Journal of the History of the Behavioral Sciences* 39, no. 3 (2003): 251–67.
Forde, Eleanor Napier. *Guidance: What It Is and How to Get It*. New Haven, 1927.
Frank Buchman Eighty. London: Blandford Press, 1958.
Frankl, Viktor E. *Man's Search for Meaning*. London: Hodder and Stoughton, 1964. First published in 1946.
Gandhi, Mohandas Karamchand. *An Autobiography: The Story of My Experiments with Truth*. London: Cape, 1949.
Gareis, Hansjörg. *Stepping Stones: A German Biography*. N.p.: Xlibris Corp, 2001.
Gates, Irene. *Any Hope, Doctor?* London: Blandford Press, 1964.
Giardina, Denise. *Saints and Villains*. New York: Norton, 1998.
Gordon, S. D. *Quiet Talks on Power*. New York: Revell, 1901.
Grensted, L. W. *The Person of Christ*. London: Nisbet, 1932.
Grogan, William. *John Riffe of the Steelworkers*. New York: Coward-McCann, 1959.
Grubb, Norman. *Modern Viking*. Grand Rapids: Zondervan, 1961.
Guldseth, Mark. *Streams*. [Homer?], Alaska, 1982.
Gundersen, Paul. *Incorrigibly Independent*. Caux: Caux Books, 1995.
Gwyer, Barbara. "Comments of an Educationalist." In *Oxford and the Groups*, edited by Richard H. S. Crossman, 63–71. Oxford: Blackwell, 1934.
Hall, G. Stanley. *Adolescence: Its Psychology and Relations to Physiology, Anthropology, Sociology, Sex, Crime, Religion, and Education*. 2 vols. New York: Appleton, 1921. First published 1904.
Hambrick-Stowe, Charles E. *Charles G. Finney and the Spirit of American Evangelicalism*. Grand Rapids: Eerdmans, 1996.
Hamilton, Loudon. *MRA: How It All Began*. London: Moral Re-Armament, 1968.
Hannon, Peter, Suzan Burrell, Amina Dikedi-Ajakaiye, and Ray Purdy. "Seeds of Change for Africa." In Mackenzie and Young, *Worldwide Legacy*, 98–119.
Harriman, Jarvis. *Matched Pair: The Elys of Embassy Row*. Tucson: Pooh Stix Press, 1999.
Harris, Erdman. "A Study of Three Contemporary Approaches to the Problem of Divine Guidance." PhD diss., Union Theological Seminary, New York, 1934.
Harris, Irving. *Breeze of the Spirit: Sam Shoemaker and the Story of Faith at Work*. New York: Seabury Press, 1978.
Harris, James Rendel. *The Guiding Hand of God*. London: National Council of Evangelical Free Churches, 1905.
Harrison, Marjorie. *Saints Run Mad: A Criticism of the "Oxford" Group Movement*. London: Lane, 1934.

Harvey, Charles E. "John D. Rockefeller Jr. and the Interchurch World Movement of 1919–1920: A Different Angle on the Ecumenical Movement." *Church History* 51, no. 2 (1982): 198–209.
Hastings, Adrian. *A History of English Christianity, 1920–1985*. London: Collins, 1986.
Haynes, John Earl, Harvey Klehr, and Alexander Vassiliev, eds. *Spies: The Rise and Fall of the KGB in America*. New Haven: Yale University Press, 2009.
Henderson, Michael. *All Her Paths Are Peace*. West Hartford: Kumarian Press, 1994.
———. *The Forgiveness Factor*. Salem, Ore.: Grosvenor Books, 1996.
———. *Ice in Every Carriage*. Caux: Caux Books, 2010.
———. *No Enemy to Conquer: Forgiveness in an Unforgiving World*. Waco: Baylor University Press, 2009.
Henson, Herbert Hensley. *The Group Movement*. London: Oxford University Press, 1933.
Hindmarsh, D. Bruce. *The Evangelical Conversion Narrative: Spiritual Autobiography in Early Modern England*. Oxford: Oxford University Press, 2005.
Hopkins, C. Howard. *John Mott, 1865–1955: A Biography*. Grand Rapids: Eerdmans, 1979.
Howard, Peter. *Britain and the Beast*. London: Heinemann, 1963.
———. *The Dictator's Slippers*. London: Blandford Press, 1964.
———. *Frank Buchman's Secret*. London: Heinemann, 1961.
———. *Ideas Have Legs*. London: Muller, 1945.
———. *Innocent Men*. London: Heinemann, 1941.
———. *Mr. Brown Comes Down the Hill*. London: Blandford Press, 1964.
———. *The Real News*. London: Blandford Press, 1954.
———. *That Man Frank Buchman*. London: Blandford Press, 1946.
———. *Through the Garden Wall*. London: Blandford Press, 1963.
———. *The World Rebuilt*. London: Blandford Press, 1951.
Howard, Peter, and Cecil Broadhurst. *The Vanishing Island*. London, 1955.
Howell, Edward. *Escape to Live*. London: Longmans, Green, 1947.
Hunter, T. Willard. *World Changing Through Life Changing: The Frank Buchman Revolution*. Claremont: Regina Press, 2009.
Huthwaite, Motokoto, ed. *From China with Love: The Personal Letters of Bishop and Mrs. Logan Roots*. Norwalk: Eastbridge, 2010.
Ideology and Co-existence. Pamphlet. London: Moral Re-Armament, 1959.
Inboden, William. *Religion in American Foreign Policy, 1945–1960: The Soul of Containment*. Cambridge: Cambridge University Press, 2008.
Israel, Martin. *Smouldering Fire: The Work of the Holy Spirit*. London: Mowbray, 1978.
Jaeger, Clara. *Never to Lose My Vision: The Story of Bill Jaeger*. London: Grosvenor Books, 1995.
James, William. *The Varieties of Religious Experience*. Cambridge: Harvard University Press, 1985. First published 1902.
Jarlert, Anders. *The Oxford Group, Group Revivalism, and the Churches in Northern Europe, 1930–1945, with Special Reference to Scandinavia and Germany*. Lund: Lund University Press, 1995.
Johnston, Douglas, and Cynthia Sampson, eds. *Religion: The Missing Dimension of Statecraft*. New York: Oxford University Press, 1994.
Jørgensen, Keld. *Denmark, 1938–55*. Caux: Caux Books, 1955.
Jowett, John Henry. *In the School of Calvary*. London: Clarke, 1910.
Keene, J. Calvin. "The Doctrine of Guidance in the Oxford Group Movement." PhD diss., Yale University, 1937.
Kelly, Thomas. *A Testament of Devotion*. New York: Harper and Brothers, 1941.
Kempis, Thomas À. *The Imitation of Christ*. London: Fontana, 1963.

Kirby, Dianne. "Harry Truman's Religious Legacy." In *Religion and the Cold War*, edited by Dianne Kirby. London: Palgrave Macmillan, 2003.
Kraybill, Ron. "Transition from Rhodesia to Zimbabwe: The Role of Religious Actors." In Johnston and Sampson, *Religion*, 208–57.
Latourette, Kenneth Scott. *World Service: A History of the Foreign Work and World Service of the Young Men's Christian Associations of the United States and Canada.* New York: Association Press, 1957.
Laubach, Frank. *Letters by a Modern Mystic.* London: Lutterworth Press, 1950.
Laun, J. Ferdinand. *Unter Gottes Führung: Zeugnisse religioser Erneuerung moderner Menschen.* Gotha, Germany, 1931.
Lawrence of the Resurrection, Brother. *The Practice of the Presence of God.* London: Allenson, 1930.
Layman with a Notebook. Foreword by L. W. Grensted. *What Is the Oxford Group?* New York: Oxford University Press, 1933.
Lean, Garth. *Frank Buchman: A Life.* London: Constable, 1985.
———. *Good God, It Works: Faith by Experiment.* London: Blandford Press, 1974.
———. *John Wesley, Anglican.* London: Blandford Press, 1964.
Lean, Garth, and Sydney Cook. *The Black and White Book.* London: Blandford Press, 1972.
Lean, Mary, and Elisabeth Peters. *Stories from the Caux School.* Caux: Caux Books, 2009.
Lennox, Cuthbert. *Henry Drummond.* London: Melrose, 1901.
Lester, John, and Pierre Spoerri. *Rediscovering Freedom.* London: Grosvenor Books, 1992.
Livingstone, Richard. *Education for a World Adrift.* Cambridge: Cambridge University Press, 1943.
Lowell, James Russell. *The Complete Poetical Works of James Russell Lowell.* London: Harrap, 1913.
Lunn, Arnold. *Enigma: A Study of Moral Re-Armament.* London: Longmans, 1957.
Lunn, Arnold, and Garth Lean. *The New Morality.* London: Blandford Press, 1964.
Luttwak, Edward. "Franco-German Reconciliation: The Overlooked Role of the Moral Re-Armament Movement." In Johnston and Sampson, *Religion*, 37–63.
MacEwan, Grant. *Tatanga Mani: Walking Buffalo of the Stonies.* Edmonton: Hurtig, 1969.
Macintosh, Douglas Clyde. *Personal Religion.* New York: Scribner's Sons, 1942.
Mackenzie, Archie. *Faith in Diplomacy.* Caux: Caux Books, 2002.
———. Introduction. In Mackenzie and Young, *Worldwide Legacy*, 7–37.
Mackenzie, Archie, and David Young, comps. *The Worldwide Legacy of Frank Buchman.* Caux: Caux Books, 2008.
Major, H. D. A. "A Modern Churchman's Commendation." In Spencer, *Meaning of the Groups*, 121–28.
Marcel, Gabriel. "A Letter of Personal Reassurance." In *Fresh Hope for the World: Moral Re-Armament in Action*, edited by Gabriel Marcel, 1–15. London: Longmans, 1960.
Martin, Morris. *Always a Little Further: Four Lives of a Luckie Felowe.* Tucson: Elm Street Press, 2001.
McComb, Samuel. *A Book of Prayers.* New York: Dodd, Mead, 1912.
McConnachie, John. *The Barthian Theology and the Man of Today.* London: Hodder and Stoughton, 1933.
McGee, Frank. *A Song for the World: The Amazing Story of the Colwell Brothers and Herb Allen: Musical Diplomats.* Santa Barbara: Many Roads, 2007.
McLean, Adam. *Whatever Next. . . .* Yeovil, UK: Linden Hall, 1992.
McLoughlin, William G. *Revivals, Awakenings, and Reform: An Essay on Religion and Social Change in America, 1607–1977.* Chicago: University of Chicago Press, 1978.
Mercadante, Linda A. *Victims and Sinners: Spiritual Roots of Addiction and Recovery.* Louisville: Westminster John Knox Press, 1995.

Meyer, F. B. *The Secret of Guidance*. New York: Fleming H. Revell Company, 1896.
Miller, Richard Lawrence. *Truman: A Rise to Power*. New York: McGraw-Hill, 1986.
Montville, Joseph. "Psychoanalytic Enlightenment and the Greening of Diplomacy." *Journal of the American Psychoanalytic Association* 37, no. 2 (1989): 297–318.
Moody, Dwight L. *Secret Power*. Chicago: Revell, 1881.
Mott, John R. *The Evangelization of the World in This Generation*. New York: Student Volunteer Movement for Foreign Missions, 1900.
———. *The Morning Watch*. Melbourne: Student Movement Press, n.d.
Mottu, Philippe. *Pile and Face: Regard sur Ma Vie*. Caux: Caux Books, 1999.
———. *The Story of Caux*. London: Grosvenor, 1970.
Mowat, Robert C. *The Climax of History*. London: Blandford Press, 1951.
———. *Decline and Renewal: Europe Ancient and Modern*. Oxford: New Cherwell Press, 1991.
———. *The Message of Frank Buchman*. London: Blandford Press, 1951.
———. *Report on Moral Re-Armament*. London: Blandford Press, 1955.
Moxcey, Mary Eliza. *Girlhood and Character*. New York: Abingdon Press, 1916.
Murray, Andrew. *The Secret of Inspiration*. London: Morgan and Scott, 1916.
Murray, Robert H. *Group Movements Through the Ages*. London: Hodder and Stoughton, 1935.
Mussolini, Benito. *Opera Omnia*. Vol. 22. Florence: La Fenice, 1957.
Niebuhr, H. Richard. *Christ and Culture*. New York: Harper and Brothers, 1951.
Niebuhr, Reinhold. *Christianity and Power Politics*. New York: Scribner's Sons, 1940.
———. *Christian Realism and Political Problems*. London: Faber and Faber, 1953.
Nutt, Rick L. *The Whole Gospel for the Whole World: Sherwood Eddy and the American Protestant Mission*. Macon: Mercer University Press, 1997.
Ober, Charles K., and John Mott. *Personal Work: How Organized and How Accomplished*. New York: Association Press, 1892.
Oxford Group. *Rising Tide*. London: Oxford Group, 1937.
Padfield, Peter. *Himmler: Reichsführer-SS*. London: Macmillan, 1990.
Palmer, Richard H. "Moral Re-Armament Drama: Right-Wing Theatre in America." *Theatre Journal* 31 (1979): 172–85.
Panikkar, Raimundo. *The Unknown Christ of Hinduism*. London: Darton, Longman, and Todd, 1981.
Penn-Lewis, Jessie. *The Centrality of the Cross*. Poole, UK: Overcomer Book Room, n.d.
Piguet, Jacqueline. *For the Love of Tomorrow: The Story of Irène Laure*. London: Grosvenor, 1985.
Pius XI, Pope. *Atheistic Communism*. London: Catholic Truth Society, 1937.
Pomerants, Grigorii. *The Spiritual Movement from the West*. Caux: Caux Books, 2004.
Prescott, D. M., ed. *A New Day*. London: Blandford Press, 1957.
Price, Charles, and Ian Randall. *Transforming Keswick*. Carlisle: OM, 2000.
Purdy, Ray Foote. *My Friend, Frank Buchman: A Book of Battle*. London: Initiatives of Change, 2012.
Rahner, Karl. "Anonymous Christians." In *Theological Investigations*. Vol. 6. London: Darton, Longman, and Todd, 1974. Originally published as a broadcast review of Röper, *Die anonymen Christen*, in 1964.
Randall, Ian. "'Arresting People for Christ': Baptists and the Oxford Group in the 1930s." *Baptist Quarterly* 38, no. 1 (1999): 3–18.
———. *"Entire Devotion to God": Wesleyan Holiness and British Overseas Mission in the Early Twentieth Century*. Ilkeston: Moorley's, 1998.
———. *Evangelical Experiences*. Carlisle: Paternoster Press, 1999.

———. "Life-Changing: The Oxford Group as a Movement of Spiritual Renewal." *Christianity and History Newsletter*, no. 16 (1996): 18–41.

———. *Spirituality and Social Change: The Contribution of F. B. Meyer (1847–1929)*. Carlisle: Paternoster Press, 2003.

Raven, Charles. "A Theologian's Appreciation." In Spencer, *Meaning of the Groups*, 9–31.

Roots, John McCook. "An Apostle to Youth." *Atlantic Monthly*, December 1928, 807–17.

Röper, Anita. *Die anonymen Christen*. Mainz, Germany: Matthias-Grünewald Verlag, 1963.

Rose, Cecil. *When Man Listens*. Rev. ed. London: Blandford Press, 1956. First published 1936.

Rudy, David R., and Arthur L. Greil. "Is Alcoholics Anonymous a Religious Organisation? Meditations on Marginality." *Sociological Analysis* 50, no. 1 (1989): 41–51.

Russell, A. J. *For Sinners Only*. London: Hodder and Stoughton, 1932.

Sack, Daniel. "Men Want Something Real: Frank Buchman and Anglo-American College Religion in the 1920s." *Journal of Religious History* 28, no. 3 (2004): 260–75.

———. *Moral Re-Armament: The Reinventions of an American Religious Movement*. New York: Palgrave Macmillan, 2009.

———. "'Reaching the Up-and-Outers': Sam Shoemaker and Modern Evangelicalism." *Anglican and Episcopal History* 64, no. 1 (1995): 37–57.

Schellenberg, Walter. *Invasion 1940*. London: St. Ermin's Press, 2000.

Schöllgen, Werner. "Moral Re-Armament Awakens the Modern Man." In Buchman, *Remaking the World* (1961), 378–82.

Seeley, John. *Ecce Homo: A Survey of the Life and Work of Jesus Christ*. Boston: Roberts Brothers, 1866.

Seldes, George. *Witness to a Century*. New York: Ballantine Books, 1981.

Sentis, Michel. "France and the Expansion of Buchman's Faith." In Mackenzie and Young, *Worldwide Legacy*, 51–64.

———. *L'Avenir Était Au-Delà des Vagues*. Caux: Caux Books, 2012.

Sharlet, Jeff. *The Family: The Secret Fundamentalism at the Heart of American Life*. New York: HarperCollins, 2008.

Sheen, Fulton. *Communism and the Conscience of the West*. Dublin: Browne and Nolan, 1948.

Sherry, Frank H., and Mahlon H. Hellerich. "The Formative Years of Frank N. D. Buchman." *Proceedings of the Lehigh Country Historical Society* 37 (1986): 236–71.

Sherwood, Timothy H. *The Preaching of Archbishop Fulton J. Sheen: The Gospel Meets the Cold War*. Lanham: Rowman and Littlefield, 2010.

Shoemaker, Samuel Moor. *Children of the Second Birth*. New York: Revell, 1927.

Smith, G. D. *Atheistic Communism*. Translation of *Atheistic Communism* by Pope Pius XI. London: Catholic Truth Society, 1964.

Smith, Hannah Pearsall. 1885. *The Christian's Secret of a Happy Life*. London: Nisbet, 1941.

Social and Industrial Council of the Church of England National Assembly. *Moral Re-Armament: A Study of the Movement Prepared by the Social and Industrial Council of the Church Assembly*. London: Church Information Board of the Church Assembly, 1955.

Speer, Robert. *The Marks of a Man*. New York: Revell, 1907.

———. *The Principles of Jesus*. New York: Young Men's Christian Association Press, 1902.

Spencer, Frederick A. M., ed. *The Meaning of the Groups*. Oxford: Methuen, 1934.

Spoerri, Pierre. "Frank Buchman and the Germans." Unpublished manuscript, 2012.

———. *No End of an Adventure*. Caux: Caux Books, 2011.

———. "Reconciliation Comes from Change." In Mackenzie and Young, *Worldwide Legacy*, 302–12.

Spoerri, Theophil. *Dynamic out of Silence*. London: Grosvenor Books, 1976. Originally published as *Dynamik aus der Stille* (Luzerne: Caux Verlag, 1971).

———. "Moral Re-Armament and the Christian Destiny of Europe." In *Report on Moral Re-Armament*, edited by Robert C. Mowat, 3–60. London: Blandford Press, 1955.
Stanley, Brian. *The World Missionary Conference, Edinburgh 1910*. Grand Rapids: Eerdmans, 2009.
Stewart, George. *The Life of Henry B. Wright*. New York: Association Press, 1925.
Stewart, George, and Henry B. Wright. *Personal Evangelism Among Students*. New York: Association Press, 1920.
———. *The Practice of Friendship*. New York: Association Press, 1920.
Stoeffler, F. Ernest. *The Rise of Evangelical Pietism*. Leiden: Brill, 1965.
Stowe, Harriet Beecher. *Uncle Tom's Cabin*. Ware: Wordsworth Classics, 2009.
Streeter, B. H. *The God Who Speaks*. London: Macmillan, 1936.
———. "Professor Barth v. the Oxford Group." *London Quarterly and Holborn Review*, April 1937, 145–49.
Streeter, B. H., and A. J. Appasamy. *The Sadhu*. London: Macmillan, 1921.
Strong, Arthur. *Preview of a New World: How Frank Buchman Helped His Country Move from Isolation to World Responsibility*. Avrika, Sweden, 1994.
Suenens, Léon Joseph. *The Right View of Moral Re-Armament*. London: Burns and Oates, 1954.
Swaim, Loring T. *Arthritis, Medicine, and the Spiritual Laws*. Philadelphia: Chilton, 1962.
Taylor, John V. *The Go-Between God: The Holy Spirit and the Christian Mission*. London: SCM Press, 1972.
Tennyson, Alfred Lord. *Tennyson's Poetry*. 2nd. ed. Selected and edited by Robert W. Hill Jr. New York: Norton, 1999.
Thompson, Vance. *Drink and Be Sober*. New York: Moffat, Yard, 1915.
Thornbrough, Emma Lou, ed. *Booker T. Washington*. Englewood Cliffs, N.J.: Prentice-Hall, 1969.
Thornhill, Alan. *Best of Friends*. Basingstoke: Pickering, 1986.
———. *The Forgotten Factor*. London: Blandford Press, 1954.
———. *The Significance of the Life of Frank Buchman*. London: Moral Re-Armament, 1952.
Thornton-Duesbery, Julian P. *The Open Secret of MRA*. London: Blandford Press, 1964.
———. *Sharing*. Oxford: Oxford Group, 1932.
Tournier, Paul. *The Gift of Feeling*. London: SCM Press, 1981.
———. *A Listening Ear*. Caux: Caux Books, 1998.
Truman, Harry S. *Mr. Citizen*. London: Hutchinson, 1961.
Trumbull, H. Clay. *Individual Work for Individuals*. New York: International Committee of Young Men's Christian Associations, 1901.
Turner, F. M. "Religion." In *The History of the University of Oxford*, edited by Brian Harrison, 293–316. Vol. 8 of *The Twentieth Century*. Oxford: Clarendon Press, 1994.
Twitchell, Kenaston. *Regeneration in the Ruhr*. Princeton: Princeton University Press, ca. 1981.
———. *The Strength of a Nation*. Pamphlet. London: Moral Re-Armament, 1948.
Unknown Christian, An [Richardson, A. E.]. *How to Live the Victorious Life*. London: Marshall Brothers, 1921.
Van Dusen, Henry. "Apostle to the Twentieth Century." *Atlantic Monthly* 154, no 1 (1934): 1–16.
———. "The Oxford Group Movement." *Atlantic Monthly* 154, no. 2 (1934): 240–52.
Vickers, Virginia, comp. *Spin a Good Yarn: The Story of W. Farrar Vickers*. Leeds, UK: MT, 1978.
Victory in Christ: A Report of Princeton Conference, 1916. Philadelphia: Board of Managers of Princeton Conference, 1916.
Waddy, Charis. *The Skills of Discernment*. Caux: Caux Books, 2005. First published 1977, London: Grosvenor Books.

Walter, Howard. *Soul Surgery: Some Thoughts on Incisive Personal Work*. Oxford: Johnson, 1940. First published 1919, Calcutta: Association Press.
Wellman, Francis L. *The Art of Cross-Examination*. New York: Macmillan, 1903.
Wilhelmsen, Jens-J. *Man and Structures*. London: Grosvenor Books, 1977.
Williamson, Geoffrey. *Inside Buchmanism*. London: Watts, 1954.
Williamson, Philip. "Christian Conservatives and the Totalitarian Challenge, 1933–40." *English Historical Review* 115, no. 462 (2000): 607–42.
Wimber, John. *Power Healing*. With Kevin Springer. London: Hodder and Stoughton, San Francisco: Harper and Row, 1986.
Winslow, Jack. *When I Awake*. London: Hodder and Stoughton, 1938.
Winter, Jay. *Dreams of Peace and Freedom: Utopian Moments in the Twentieth Century*. New Haven: Yale University Press, 2006.
Wise, Gordon. *A Great Aim in Life*. Caux: Caux Books, 2006.
W.L.M.C. [William Conner]. *Builder of a Global Force: Some Remarks Noted During Meetings with Frank Buchman at Mackinac Island and Caux During the Late Fifties*. London, 1959.
Wolrige Gordon, Anne. *Peter Howard, Life and Letters*. London: Hodder and Stoughton, 1969.
Wood, John, and Denise Wood. *Have Ocean, Will Travel*. Kennett Square, Pa.: Write Place, 2005.
Wright, Henry B. *The Will of God and a Man's Lifework*. New York: Association Press, 1912. First published 1909 by Young Men's Christian Association Press.
Wuthnow, Robert. *The Restructuring of American Religion*. Princeton: Princeton University Press, 1988.
Yates, Basil Lund. "Dr Frank N. D. Buchman's Contribution to Religious Thought." *Hibbert Journal* 57, no. 1 (1958): 56–63.
You Can Defend America. Washington, D.C.: Judd and Detweiler, n.d., ca. 1941.
Youniss, James. "G. Stanley Hall and His Times: Too Much So, Yet Not Enough." *History of Psychology* 9, no. 3 (2006): 224–35.

INDEX

AA (Alcoholics Anonymous), 30, 134–35
absolute moral standards, 22–28, 152–53, 163
abstinence, 81–82
accountability, 51, 74–77
Acts, 84
Adenauer, Konrad, 47, 112, 118
Agee, Alva, 15
alcohol, 24–25
Alcoholics Anonymous (AA), 30, 134–35
Allen, Geoffrey, 42
American-Japanese Treaty of Mutual Cooperation and Security (1960), 153
Arnold, Thomas, 103
arts, 114–15, 120–21, 141, 143–44
Asia, missionary work in, 16–17. *See also* China; Japan
Austin, Bunny, 166
Austin, Phyllis, 78
Azikiwe, Nnamdi, 110

Baldwin, Stanley, 43, 110
Bardsley, Cuthbert, 71
Barrett, Michael, 48
Barth, Karl, 5, 98
Baynard-Smith, Jim, 52
Beazley, Kim, 152
Bebbington, David, 91
Beecher, Henry, 178 n. 14
Begbie, Harold, 4, 65
Belden, David, 5, 117, 136, 140
Belk, Blanton, 130
Benes, Eduard, 112–13
Bennett, John C., 136
Bethune, Mary McLeod, 149
Bible, 34, 83–84, 115–16
Bibliander, Theodore, 87–88
Birnie, William, 137–38
birth control, 81
Bladeck, Max, 72, 73
Blomberg, Harry, 38
Bockmuehl, Klaus, 85

Bodelschwingh, Friedrich von, 11
Bonhoeffer, Dietrich, 138
Borodin, Michael, 141
Britain, 42, 144, 147
Brown, William, 30–31
Brunner, Emil, 98, 103–4
Buchman, Dan, 9
Buchman, Frank, 35
  approach to politics, 6
  with Bethune, *149*
  birth and early years, 9–10
  with Bladeck and Kurowski, *73*
  controversy surrounding, 2–3
  deteriorating health of, 128–29
  with Gandhi, *88*
  Holy Spirit in philosophy of, 5–6
  influence of, 2–3
  influences on, 4
  at League of Nations lunch, *113*
  at Mackinac conference center, *69*
  ministry of, 1–2
  personality of, 3–4, 67–71, 165–66
  as realist and optimist, 6–7
  with Schuman, *53*
  self-confidence of, 18
  sensitivity of, 65–66
  with Shigemitsu, *121*
  with Streeter, *99*
Buchman, Franklin, 9
Buchman, John, 9
Buchman, Sarah Greenwalt, 9, 37
Buck, Blair, 15
Buckles, Anne, 37
Bushnell, Horace, 27, 32
Butler, Joseph, 22

Cairns, D. S., 41–42, 175 n. 58
Calvary Church, New York, 96–97
campaigns, 75–76
Campbell, Paul, 35, 129
Carmichael, Amy, 56, 75

Catholicism, 95–96
Chambers, Oswald, 21
change, 109, 150–52, 156
character, 4, 24
charisma, 4
charismatic movement, 66
Charrière, François, 96
Chiang Kai-shek, 111
Chiba, Saburo, 112, 153
children, 80
China, 47, 59, 110–11
Christian churches and Christianity, 91–92, 94–102
Churchill, Winston, 139
Church of England, 95
Collis, Robert, 70
"collisions," 67–71
communications, internal, 128
Communion, 96
communism, 100, 110–11, 134, 140–43
community living, 76
conferences
   hospitality and, 111–12
   international, 119–21
   personal work and, 58–60
confession, 29–31
Conner, William, 127, 134
"conscience," 49–50. *See also* guidance
contraceptives, 81
Corderoy, Oliver, 44, 166
creativity, 42–43, 82
criticism, of others, 26
Crucifixion, 11–13
"c's, five," 61
czarism, 135–36

de Gasperi, Alcide, 47
democracy, 133, 145
desegregation, 149–50
details, 111–12
dictators, 136–38, 165
diplomacy, 165
directness, 37, 67–71
discernment, of Buchman, 65–66
discipline, moral, 22–28. *See also* absolute moral standards
divorce, 37, 82
Dohnavur community, 75–76
Driberg, Tom, 6, 116, 123
Drugstore Revolution, 154
Drummond, Henry
   on guidance, 45
   influence of, 18–19, 20, 31, 61
   on mission work, 98
   opposition to, 122–23
   personal work and, 57

Eboué, Eugénie, 69
ecumenical vision, 90–91
Eddy, Sherwood, 15, 16–17, 50, 60–61, 100
Eden, Anthony, 122
Edison, Thomas, 37
education
   of Frank Buchman, 9–10
   theological, 102–3
Edward VIII, 43
El Glaoui, 152
emotion, 31–32
empire, 110
Entwistle, Basil, 119
equality, 150
Escape to Live (Howell), 54
Eucharist, 96
evil, 122–23
eyes, 66

face, 65–66
family, 79–80
fascism, 133, 136, 138
FCCF (First Century Christian Fellowship), 2. *See also* Moral Re-Armament (MRA); Oxford Group
fellowship, 74–77, 109
financing, 124–27
"fingers on the hand" image, 194 n. 112
Finney, Charles, 13, 62
First Century Christian Fellowship (FCCF), 2. *See also* Moral Re-Armament (MRA); Oxford Group
"five c's," 61
flexibility, 108, 128, 159–61
Ford, Henry, 109–10, 114
Forde, Eleanor Napier, 79
forgiveness, 67
France, 118–19
Francis of Assisi, 164
Francke, August Hermann, 10
Frank, Semyon, 196 n. 178
Frankl, Viktor, 161
Freedom, 115, 150
funding, 124–27

Gandhi, Mahatma, 87, *88*
Gandhi, Rajmohan, 65, 89
Gasperi, Alcide de, 47
Germany, 117–19, 136–40

God, surrendering to, 31–32, 93. *See also* Kingdom of God
God Who Speaks, The (Streeter), 54
Great Britain, 42, 144, 147
Greenwalt, Sarah, 9, 37
Grensted, L. W., 51, 104–5
guidance
    accuracy of, 39
    as challenge, 40–41
    checking, 50–51
    creativity and, 42–43
    criticism of, 41–42
    discovery of, 14–15
    Holy Spirit and, 36–37
    inspiration through, 34–38
    international affairs and, 47–48
    leadership and, 51–53
    moral re-armament and, 38–39
    as normal, 39–40
    politics and, 144–47
    practice of, 33–34, 43–47, 49–50, 161–62
    strategy and, 106
    supporters of, 48–49
    unity and, 40
    written works concerning, 53–55
guidance books, 34
Gundersen, Paul, 86

Hall, G. Stanley, 24, 28
Hambro, Carl, 113, 117
Hamilton, Ailsa, 51
Hamilton, Loudon, 63, 64
Hansen, Falk, 74
Harris, Gilbert, 125
Hartford Theological Seminary, 17, 18
healing, 66–67
health, deteriorating, of Buchman, 128–29
helplessness, 124
Henson, Herbert Hensley, 41
Hicks, Roger, 69
Himmler, Heinrich, 137
Hinduism, 87
Hitler, Adolf, 136–39
Holme, Reginald, 76
Holy Spirit
    in Buchman's philosophy, 5–6
    following spiritual experience, 13
    guidance and, 36–37, 41, 162
    intellectualism and, 102
    Jesus Christ and, 85
    leadership and, 51–52
    method and, 83
    moral discipline and, 24
    personalization and, 60
    strategy and, 106
    timing of, 120
homosexuality, 28, 29, 77, 78
honesty, 26
honors, awarded to Buchman, 167 n. 6
Hoshijima, Niro, *121*
hospitality, 111–14
hospiz, 11, 12–13, 32, 127
Hossenfelder, Joachim, 103–4
house parties, 59, 111
Howard, Peter
    on Buchman's personality, 3–4, 69
    collision with, 68
    criticism of, 69–70
    at Mackinac conference center, 69
    on materialism, 134
    MRA leadership and, 130
    theater and, 114, 141, 143–44
Howell, Edward, 54
Ho Ying-chin, 110–11
Hsu Ch'ien, 47
humor, 71
Hunter, T. Willard, 6, 28, 68–69, 98
Hutchinson, Michael, 93, 163
hymns, 13, 27, 74, 85, 107, 162

ideology, 132–33, 143
Ideology and Co-existence, 141–42
impure thoughts, 27–28
Inboden, William, 48
India, 48
individualism, 51
industry, 42, 146–48
inspiration. *See* guidance
intellectualism, 4, 102–5
internal communications, 128
international institutions, 145–46
Islam, 87–88
Italy, 136

Jaeger, William, 52
Japan, 119, 120–21, 152–53, 154
Jarlert, Anders, 6
"Jesus, I My Cross Have Taken" (Lyte), 74
Jesus Christ
    versus Christianity, 91–92
    focus on, 84–85, 162–63
    salvation through, 84
    spirit of, 93–94
Jewish prophets, 84, 151
Jotham Valley, 120–21
journeys, 75–76

Jowett, John Henry, 21

Keene, J. Calvin, 6, 46, 49
Kelly, Thomas, 46
Kerensky, Alexander, 110
Keswick, England, spiritual experience in, 11–14, 93
"Kindle Our Love" (Carmichael), 56
Kingdom of God, 93–94
Kishi, Nobusuke, 153
König, Franz, 95
Kriebel, Oscar, 9
Kurowski, Paul, 73, 90, 184 n. 53

"laboratory," 61
Lake Tahoe retreat, 76
Laubach, Frank, 46
Laure, Irène, 67, 69, 79, 117, 142
Laure, Victor, 69
leadership
    change and, 151–52
    and deteriorating health of Buchman, 128–29
    guidance and, 51–53
    politics and, 135–36
    relationships and, 78–79
    strategy and, 109–11
League of Nations, 113
Lean, Garth
    on Buchman's agenda, 6
    correspondence with, 43–44
    on criticism of Buchman, 71
    on moral re-armament, 38
    on Shoemaker, 96
Lenin, Vladimir, 141
life, 160–61
life-changing. *See* personal work
light, guidance associated with, 37
Lincoln, Abraham, 110, 149
listening, in prayer. *See* guidance
little sins, 25–26
Livingstone, Sir Richard, 152
love
    personal work and, 56
    relationships and, 77–79
luminous thoughts, 36. *See also* guidance
Lunn, Arnold, 82
Luther, Martin, 10
Lutheranism, 159–60
Lyte, Henry Francis, 74

Mackenzie, Archie, 146
Magsaysay, Ramon, 114

Major, H. D. A., 84
Marcel, Gabriel, 54–55, 127, 161, 164
Marie of Romania, Queen, 24
marriage, 10–11, 79, 80–82
Martin, Cecil, 126
Martin, Morris, 29, 75, 128, 164
mass meeting, 108
masturbation, 28
materialism, 134, 143
McCarthyism, 142
McComb, Samuel, 21
medical imagery, 61–62
meditation, 14. *See also* guidance
meetings. *See also* conferences; house parties; mass meeting
    guidance and, 45–46
    personal work and, 58–60
memory, 34
Mercier, Maurice, 89
method, 83, 108
Meyer, F. B., 14–15, 62–63, 83
military service, 148
millennialism, 156
modernism, 102
monarchies, 135
money, 69, 124–27
moral discipline, 22–28, 80–82. *See also* absolute moral standards
morale, 123, 148
moral re-armament, 38, 108
Moral Re-Armament (MRA)
    arts and, 115
    Christian churches and, 95–96
    as church, 96, 164
    communism and, 142–43
    creation of, 2
    funding for, 125–27
    as ideology, 132–34
    Keswick experience and, 93
    military service and, 148
    optimism of, 156–57
    organization of, 128, 129–31
    Oxford Group and, 92
    politics of, 135
    postwar philosophy of, 165
    publicity and, 116
    religious outlook of, 86
    strategy and, 106–8
    theological views of, 6, 84–85, 160–61
Mossadegh, Mohammed, 89
Mott, John R., 57, 90, 157
Mottu, Philippe, 70, 75, 128
Mountbatten, Lord, 122

Mowat, Robert C., 152, 157
MRA (Moral Re-Armament). *See* Moral Re-Armament (MRA)
Murray, Andrew, 20
Murray, R. H., 75
Mussolini, Benito, 136

Na, Tolon, 88-89, *149*
nationalism, 154
nations, 134-35, 143, 153-54
Nazism, 3, 103-4, 137-40
Neguib, Mohammed, 89
Nehru, Pandit, 48
networking, 119-22
New York-World Telegram interview, 137-38
Niebuhr, Reinhold, 6, 138, 157
non-Christian religions, 85-94
normalcy, 39
Nu, U, 114-15

Ober, Charles K., 57
Ogon, Michael, *149*
open-mindedness, 85-94
opposition, 122-24
organization, 127-31
Overbrook hospiz, 11, 127
Oxford Group
  as church, 96, 98
  creation of, 2
  guidance and, 41-42, 46
  Holy Spirit and, 5-6
  Hossenfelder and, 103-4
  influence of, 6-7
  MRA and, 92
  Nazism and, 139-40
  organization of, 128
  politics of, 135
  Quakerism and, 20
  religious outlook of, 86
  story telling and, 63-64
  strategy and, 106-8

paradoxes, 6, 24, 92, 102, 159-60
parties, 59, 111
"Passion for Souls, A" (Carmichael), 56
passivity, 43
Patijn, J. A. E., 113
patriotism, 154
Paxson, Ruth, 78
Penn, William, 144
Penn-Lewis, Jessie, 11-12
Penn State, 14-18

"peripatetic evangelism," 106
persecution, 122-23
personalization
  in personal work, 57-61
  in theater, 114-15
personal work
  analogies and terminology in, 61-62
  charismatic movement and, 66
  directness in, 67-71
  discernment in, 65-66
  expectations in, 72-74
  forgiveness and, 67
  healing and, 66-67
  during interwar period, 64-65
  overview of, 56-57
  personalization in, 57-61
  potential of others in, 71-72
  relationships and, 77-82
  sharing and, 62-64
  teamwork in, 74-77
Person of Christ, The (Grensted), 104-5
physical healing, 66-67
Pickle, Bill, 15, *16*, 25, 36-37
Pickle, Maria, *16*
pietism, 5, 10
"Pioneers" (Whitman), 107
Pius XI, Pope, 38
plays, 114-15, 120-21, 141, 143-44
pleasing others, 78
"point of contact," 60-61
politics
  Buchman's approach to, 6, 134-43
  Buchman's views on, 164-65
  and change in human nature, 150-52
  idealism and, 156-57
  industry and, 146-48
  moral standards and, 152-53
  and national callings, 153-54
  racial harmony and, 148-50
  spiritual inspiration in, 144-46
  unity in, 154-56
  Western values and, 143-44
Pomerants, Grigorii, 160
potential, 71-72
poverty relief, 147
prayer, 33
Princeton Conference, 21
psychological development, 24
Psychological Strategy Board, 143
publicity, 115-17
Purdy, Ray, 37
purity, 26-29, 32, 80-82, 152-53, 163
purpose, finding sense of, 19

Quakerism, 20
quiet times, 33–34. *See also* guidance

racial harmony, 148–50
Radstock, Lord, 109
Rahner, Karl, 94
Randall, Ian, 7, 79–80
Raven, Charles, 43, 105
realism, 6–7, 157
relationships, 77–82
religious terms, 63–64
remarriage, 82
renaissance, 101
responsibility, 77
revival, 100
revolution, 100
Riffe, John, 150
Roots, John, 44, 64, 141
Roots, Logan, 18
Rockefeller, John D., Jr., 128
Rose, Cecil, 54
Russell, A. J., 44
Russian Revolution, 100

Sack, Daniel, 6, 64, 138
sacrifice, 80
Saint Francis of Assisi, 164
Salisbury, Lord, 138
salvation, 84
"salvation, scheme of," 61
"scheme of salvation," 61
Schuman, Robert
    Buchman with, 53
    Caux conference and, 47
    correspondence with, 44
    German-French dialogue and, 118
    on MRA, 98–99
    national defense and, 148
    seeks advice, 52
    strategy and, 124
Schuman Plan (1950), 167 n. 7
scientific analogies, 62
Seldes, George, 137
self, surrender of, 93, 31–32
self-confidence, of Buchman, 18
seminary training, 102–3
sensitivity, of Buchman, 65–66
Sentis, Michel, 69, 96
sexual sin, 27–29, 32. *See also* purity
sharing, 29–31, 62–64
Sheen, Fulton, 155
Shibusawa, Masahide, 119
Shigemitsu, Mamoru, *121*

Shoemaker, Sam, 40, 45, 50–51, 96
shoe shiner, 66–67
Simpson, P. Carnegie, 63
Singh, Sadhu Sundar, 91
sins
    awareness of, 36–37
    confession of, 29–31
    effect of, 172 n. 115
    little, 25–26
    sexual, 26–29, 32
Sioux, 89
Skills of Discernment, The (Waddy), 54
Smith, H. Alexander, 48–49
Smith, Hannah Pearsall, 14
social issues, 32
social justice, 147
social status, 121–22
Söderblom, Nathan, 90–91
Sophie of Greece, Princess, 11
Soul Surgery (Walter), 61
South Africa, 148–49
Sparks, Edwin, 68
speeches, 58, 168 n. 24
Speer, Robert E., 22
Spener, Philipp Jakob, 10
"Spiritual Diagnosis" (Drummond), 179 n. 40
spiritual experience, in Keswick, 11–14, 93
spiritual power, 25–27
Spoerri, Theophil, 5, 80, 106
standards, absolute moral, 22–28, 152–53, 163
Stearly, Garrett, 129
Stoney Indians, 89
story telling, 63–64, 112, 113–14
strategy
    arts and, 114–15
    of developing key individuals, 117–22
    hospitality and, 111–14
    leadership and, 109–11
    money and, 124–27
    OG and MRA and, 106–8
    opposition and, 122–24
    publicity and, 115–17
Streeter, B. H.
    attends Nuremberg rally, 192 n. 38
    Buchman with, 99
    on guidance, 45, 54
    Hansen and, 74
    intellectualism and, 104
    on Oxford Group, 98
    sharing and, 30
Strong, Signe, 46, 67, 71
Sunday, Billy, 38
Sun Yat-sen, 47, 122

supernationalism, 145
surrender, 31–32, 93
Switzerland, 154

Taizé community, 164
teamwork, 74–77
theater, 114–15, 120–21, 141, 143–44
theological beliefs
  on Bible, 83–84
  on intellectualism, 102–5
  liberal elements in, 85–94, 164
  of MRA, 160–61
  regarding Christian churches, 94–102
  regarding Jesus Christ, 84–85, 162–63
theological seminary training, 102–3
Thompson, Vance, 24
Thornhill, Alan, 72, 92, 111, 164
Thornton-Duesbery, Julian P., 4, 29, 98
thoughts, impure, 27–28
timing, 120
Tolon Na, 88–89, 149
totalitarian regimes, 139, 165
Tournier, Paul, 30, 80, 161
"track II" diplomacy, 165
training, 76–77
travels, 75–76
Trösch, Father, 45
Truman, Harry, 147, 156
Trumbull, C. G., 21
Trumbull, H. Clay, 57
Tutz, 34, 60
Twitchell, Kenaston, 81
tyranny, 144

Uncle Tom's Cabin (Stowe), 115
unemployment, 147
United Kingdom, 42, 144, 147
United States, 143–44, 147–50

unity
  in families, 79
  guidance and, 40
  political parties and, 154–56
utopianism, 156

Van Dusen, Henry, 5, 31, 41, 44, 65
Vanishing Island, The, 114–85, 143–44
Vereide, Abram, 43
voice, 65
von Cramon, Anneliese, 137
von der Flüe, Nicholas, 151
Vyshinsky, Andrei, 141

Waddy, Charis, 54
Walter, Howard, 61, 90
"war of ideas," 133
Washington, Booker T., 194 n. 112
Webb-Peploe, Murray, 13, 58
Wesley, John, 21
Western values, 143–44
When I Awake (Winslow), 54
When Man Listens (Rose), 54
will, surrendering, 31–32, 93
Wilson, Woodrow, 156
Wimber, John, 66
Winslow, Jack, 54
women, 78–80
Wood, John, 71, 107
Wood, Lawson, 96
"world front," 132–34
World War I, 64–65
World War II, 65, 67
Wright, Henry, 18–20, 23, 24–25, 51, 57

Yates, Basil, 159
YMCA, 10, 14–16, 18, 90
You Can Defend America, 114

Printed in Great Britain
by Amazon